TENDINGS

TEND-

Nathan Snaza

-INGS

Feminist Esoterisms
and the Abolition of Man

Duke University Press Durham and London 2024

© 2024 Duke University Press
All rights reserved
Printed in the United States of America on acid-free paper ∞
Project Editor: Bird Williams | Designed by Aimee C. Harrison
Typeset in Untitled Serif and Helvetica Neue by
Westchester Publishing Services

Library of Congress Cataloging-in-Publication Data
Names: Snaza, Nathan, author.
Title: Tendings : feminist esoterisms and the abolition of man /
Nathan Snaza.
Description: Durham : Duke University Press, 2024. |
Includes bibliographical references and index.
Identifiers: LCCN 2023036593 (print)
LCCN 2023036594 (ebook)
ISBN 9781478030102 (paperback)
ISBN 9781478025849 (hardcover)
ISBN 9781478059103 (ebook)
Subjects: LCSH: Feminist spirituality. | Feminist theory. |
Feminism and science. | Feminism and literature. | Queer theory. |
Postcolonialism. | Black people—Study and teaching. | Occultism—
Social aspects. | BISAC: SOCIAL SCIENCE / Feminism & Feminist
Theory | BODY, MIND & SPIRIT / General
Classification: LCC HQ1122 . S64 2024 (print)
LCC HQ 1122 (ebook)
DDC 305.42—dc23/eng/20230830
LC record available at https://lccn.loc.gov/2023036593
LC ebook record available at https://lccn.loc.gov/2023036594

Cover art: Ashon Crawley, *i will fear no evil . . . (number 1)*,
2019. Courtesy of the artist.

Contents

Preface. In the Cards

I didn't think much of anything about tarot until sometime around 2016. I'd seen tarot reading represented as "fortune telling" in countless movies and television shows, which always seemed to give it a racialized connotation (via Romani or Creole people), associating it with nomadic social formations in suspicious, if not outright antagonistic, relation to the state. But those representations always simultaneously positioned it as superstition (perhaps even the most exemplary superstition), and usually implied a scam. In the media, tarot hovered somewhere in the vicinity of grift, hoax, nonsense.

Tarot is also a highly gendered practice, and its appearance in cultural texts as nonsense always slides into the mythology of the irrational feminine. The mainstream approach to tarot—in equal measure dismissive and demonizing—allows for a politics of representational countersignification, and tarot seems to have a rather significant presence in various feminisms, with a highly visible presence on social media platforms like Instagram. That is largely where my interest in tarot lies: in contemporary feminist practice, which can also be a practice of anticapitalist, abolitionist, and decolonial worldmaking.

But when I first really began to notice tarot, I wasn't thinking about any of this. I was at a community farmer's market in Richmond, Virginia. I was there with my child, Isadora, who was four, and their mother, Julietta, my best friend. As our queer family wandered the park, dreaming up a week worth's of food from the produce on offer, Isadora found an independence that suited them. They spoke with the farmers (who often gave them a loose berry, or snow pea), or watched musicians (sometimes joining in with spare instruments set out for just such impromptu jams). At some point, I became aware that they had taken to a young person at a rickety card table offering ten-dollar tarot readings. Realizing that Isadora was occupying their time, and potentially making it appear they weren't available to do a reading, we paid them to read for Isadora.

Tarot readings became a common, if irregular, occurrence. Isadora would sit as Natasha pulled cards; usually they would talk without anyone else listening, but once, I sat in. Natasha did a very simple "Three Fates" reading and I was amazed by their ability to explain what they thought the cards meant to a four-year-old. They framed it less in terms of time, and more in terms of things Isadora might be struggling with and aspiring toward. Isadora was completely entranced and appeared to be really thinking through what Natasha was saying. It wasn't in any way a scene of "fortune telling." It was a scene of pedagogy, one that didn't involve a teacher "explaining" something they "knew," but instead involved a complex dance to make sense of a few cards where the reader offers enough of a guide for the querent to construct meaningful sense; *which* cards in which position introduces the necessary aleatory spur to the event, but the event really gathers the whole situation into itself as the reader and querent craft a narrative together. In this moment, I had my first sense that tarot is a practice of modulating attention to the necessarily situated and situational character of all interpretation.[1]

Around the same time, I noticed a curated section of tarot and witchcraft books growing just inside the door, right across from the counter, of Chop Suey Books in Richmond. As someone who reads a lot, I've spent a lot of time in the store since moving to Virginia, and over the years I've come to know the people who work there, following some of them on Instagram. Julie, who curated this particular selection of books, began to devote their Instagram account more and more to tarot, and with a friend, they created a small collective called Practical Witch Supply. The collective offered readings and classes. One of their first nondigital productions was a zine, available at the now-thriving Richmond Zine Fest (held at the Richmond Public Library), called *Anti-Capitalism: Spells and Thoughts*. It offers four spells: "Spells for Turning Anxious Energy/Depression into Righteous Anger," "Spell for Money Healing," "Spell for Protection Against Capitalism," and "Spell for Re-Imagining the American Dream."[2] The spells sometimes suggest gathering with a group "as we are able," but many presume the possibility of a seemingly solitary practice. They work with simple things likely to be at hand: thread, button, flame, breath, something sharp that can cut. What Practical Witch Supply was doing piqued my interest enough that I began to read books that they recommended and took up a fledgling tarot practice.

One of the first books I bought on tarot was Michelle Tea's *Modern Tarot*, a book firmly located in US West Coast queer and feminist punk politics. Tea notes that "we are living in a moment of renewed interest in the mystical. Call it New Age or 'Woo,' call it Witchcraft or the Intuitive Arts or Mind-Body-Spirit; name yourself Bruja or Conjure or Pagan or Priest/ess. The point is, I can't swing a magic wand without hitting someone who's got a crystal in their pocket, or just got their aura read, or is lighting a candle for the new moon" (2017, 6). Tea subtly connects this "renewed interest" to feminist politics (summoning the second-wave mantra, "the personal is the political") and to a kind of attention to materiality and affect that I find enormously resonant with a lot of work in affect theory and feminist new materialisms. Tea writes:

> People are turning to ancestral practices for a sense of enduring longevity, and comfort. To help stay sane and grounded in the midst of so much cultural insanity. To source a different kind of power in hopes of making changes both personal and political. From learning meditation to fighting off a cold with some homemade fire cider; from indigo-dyeing your curtains to strengthening your intuition with the aid of the Tarot, such old world practices are capturing our imaginations and providing us with meaningful ways to impact our world. Tarot offers moments of deep connection during a time when connection is ubiquitous but rarely delves beneath the surface. And in a time where most religion seems irrelevant—dated, boring, antagonistic to peace—the affirming and personal nature of the Tarot offers a spiritual experience that is gentle, individual, and aspirational. (7)

At first, I read all of this with a great deal of embarrassment. Despite an abiding interest in gothic literary texts that engaged with mystical or "supernatural" forces to register the intragenerational violences of capitalist coloniality, my understanding of esoteric and occult knowledges was influenced by the highly dismissive attitude of critical theorists like Theodor Adorno, who scathingly dismisses such knowledge in *The Stars Down to Earth* and, with Max Horkheimer, in *Dialectic of Enlightenment*. My education sutured my thinking to Theory with a capital *T* (mostly "difficult" male, European philosophers), which meant I felt like esoteric texts could be engaged only via critique, only across a distance of skeptical disbelief.

Alexander Chee's story, "The Querent," presented tarot in a way that bypassed my skepticism about "woo-woo" knowledge by tapping into the kinds of interpretation I practice as a literary scholar, even as it short-circuits distinctions between reading and writing, between production and reception. Chee writes:

Much of what I love about literature is also what I love about the Tarot—archetypes at play, hidden forces, secrets brought to light. . . . I felt too much like a character in a novel, buffeted by cruel turns of fate. I wanted to feel powerful in the face of my fate. I wanted to be the main character of this story, and its author. And if I were writing a novel about someone like me, this is exactly what would lead him astray. (2018, 23)

Tarot is the production of story: a patterning of symbols that is simultaneously rule-bound (there are vast traditions of knowledge surrounding tarot interpretation, often drawing from many different religious and esoteric pasts) and completely aleatory. Tarot is a way of storying the world in its ongoing unfolding, a way of sensing tendencies flowing through the present that are virtual, subjunctive, potential. Chee writes, "I learned to offer readings as a portrait of the possibilities of the present" (30). These possibilities adhere in the situation, and tarot is never just about a "reader" (or "querent") and the cards, but about an entire sprawling scene of more-than-human encounter (Snaza 2019b). Tarot is a ceremony for attending to what haunts the edges of what is perceptible, feeling out and articulating what else might be happening.

Chee's story disputes what Tea called the "ancient" or "old world" status of tarot. Arguing that "Tarot is only about one hundred years old" (24), Chee writes:

The conventional history given on most mainstream Tarot study websites says that Tarot began as Triunfo, a card game popular among the nobility in fifteenth-century Italy. It involved neither fortunes nor heresies, though it was informed by esoteric and occult knowledge. It did not become what it is to us now until around the early twentieth century, through the efforts of the Society of Golden Dawn, the group of spiritualists that Crowley and Harris belonged to, who were attempting to codify that esoteric knowledge. They saw their deck as a tool for educating students in everything from Egyptian mythology to astrology to kabbalah. (24)

Tarot, in short, isn't very traditional, and even a rudimentary genealogy of it as a practice reveals that it is, at best, a tangled mess. Its history resonates from within European theology and statecraft turned toward the colonialist project we now gather under the name of modernity, and one of its most important mutations is explicitly linked to a project of unifying distinct esoteric traditions.

But the idea that tarot reading is pedagogical—an educational experience—is profoundly attractive to me, and Mathew Arthur helped me understand how the pedagogical event of tarot reading may be amenable to a decolonizing reorientation precisely because of this messy history. In August of 2019, I was in Lancaster, Pennsylvania, for the first Society for the Study of Affect Summer School (SSASS), where I was coteaching a seminar with Chad Shomura on affect theories of the event. Across the week, Chad and I spent hours with a few dozen others thinking about what work "the event" does in our imaginations of worlds that exceed colonialist orders, that wouldn't be oriented around what Sylvia Wynter (2003) calls Man to describe the heteropatriarchal and colonialist overrepresentation of the human. (These conversations are everywhere felt in this book.)[3]

After the first day's sessions, Mathew and I ended up outside and somehow got to talking about tarot. For the remainder of the week, every time we found ourselves together we'd talk tarot, feminist science studies, the politics of settler engagements with Indigenous knowledge, and spirituality. In the middle of the week, Ann Cvetkovich came to Lancaster to deliver something like a keynote at SSASS. The first part was a talk giving an overview of her earlier work, with particular attention to how she came to affect theory through reading queer archives. She also described current work emerging from her time as a "killjoy" helping visitors process their experiences of visiting Allyson Mitchell and Dierdre Logue's *Inside Killjoy's Kastle* in Toronto and Los Angeles (Cvetkovich 2019).

After the talk, there was an intermission for people to use the washroom, grab a snack, move around and stretch their limbs before the Q&A. After using the washroom myself, I ran into Mathew on my way out, and our enthusiasm about Ann's talk spilled over into more tarot talk. Walking by and hearing me tell Mathew that I was reading Starhawk, Ann joined our conversation. She told me I needed to look at Vicki Noble's *Motherpeace*, a "woman-identified" tarot practice heavily influenced by Starhawk, and she said she had brought a brand-new deck with her, wondering if it would be fun to do the Q&A with the cards: each person who asks a question would draw a card, and it would guide her answer. She told us she had been hesitant, uncertain about how it might be taken, wondering if this was the right space to perform the discussion this way. When we walked back into the conference room a minute later, Ann announced her plan with the cards and passed them around the room to gather everyone's energy. The question I asked was about how to think through the complex affective and political stakes of reading second-wave feminist texts—it was one of my first attempts to articulate, in public, the queries that give rise to this book. Before she answered, I drew the Moon, which "represents the core of the ancient female mysteries" according to Noble's *Motherpeace* ([1983] 1994, 129), even "a call to enter into the darkness" (129). While much of what Ann said that day and the next has shaped how I think about esoterism, it was her willingness in this academic context to practice tarot reading that reshaped my sense of what my project was and where it could go. I felt *Tendings* bloom into existence in that room.

I have come to think of tarot as one specific version of what Cvetkovich calls a "utopia of ordinary habit":

> Although the term *practice*, a repeated action whose meaning lies in the process of performance, might seem more appropriate here, especially because of the connections between daily practice and spiritual practice, the positive and negative connotations of the term *habit* are also relevant. Habit encompasses both the desirable and healthy regularity of practice and the putatively unhealthy compulsions and obsessions of addiction. . . . [H]abit can be a mechanism for building new ways of being in the world because it belongs to the domain of the ordinary, to activities that are not spectacular or unusual but instead arise from everyday life. (2012, 191)

This interest in the ordinary and the everyday guides *Tendings*'s elaboration of esoterisms, where specific ways of being in the world are inseparable from ways of knowing. The ordinary can be an otherwise, an elsewhere.

In *Luz en Lo Oscuro*, Gloria Anzaldúa writes, "When troubled, conocimiento prompts you to take a deep breath, shift your attention away from what's causing pain and fear, and call on a power deeper and freer than that of your ego, such as la naguala y los espíritus, for guidance. Direction may also come from an inner impression, dream, meditation, I Ching, Tarot cards. You use these spiritual tools to deal with various problems, large and small. Power comes from being in touch with your body, soul, and spirit and letting their wisdom guide you" (2015, 151). Anzaldúa's words remind me that my practice of tarot reading is, first and foremost, about attention. As Tea says, "Magic is just what comes about when you concentrate on something in so singular a way, with both purity of heart and an eye for what's possible" (2017, 25). Tarot isn't at all about "fortune telling" but is instead about a specific ritual practice of modulating attention, including attention to the ways we are affected by spirits and materialities that we mostly ignore as part of being post-enlightenment, conscious subjects. It's one practice of inviting the aleatory into our meaning-making and feeling connections between our particular presents and all the other presents, pasts, and futures that virtually, subjunctively haunt us.

INTRODUCTION

Tending Endarkenment Esoterisms

"Now let us shift. . . ."

I want to linger for a moment with this invitation, this hortatory subjunctive. These are the first words in the title of the last chapter in Gloria Anzaldúa's *Luz en Lo Oscuro*: "Now let us shift . . . conocimiento . . . inner work, public acts." She subjunctively summons a plural first person "us" before turning to the second person in key passages. Describing the "bridge" that she associates with coming to consciousness, Anzaldúa writes:

> You stand on tierra sagrada—nature is alive and conscious; the world is ensouled. You lift your head to the sky, the wingspeed of pelicans, the stark green of trees, the wind sighing through their branches. You discern faces in the rocks and allow them to see you. You become reacquainted with a reality called spirit, a presence, a force, power, and energy within and without. Spirit infuses all that exists—organic and inorganic—transcending the categories and concepts that govern your perception of material reality. Spirit speaks through your mouth, listens through your ears, sees through your eyes, touches with your hands. (2015, 137–38)

This second person address, within the context of a plural "we" formed in the wake of the exhortation, individuates the addressee but also holds them in the text's ongoing present tense. This is a ceremony, meditation, prayer—

addressed not to some kind of transcendent deity so much as to *tierra sagrada*. This land—understood as materialities of spirit, or the spiritualities of the material—stretches across all kinds of boundaries and borders that are typically policed in modernist, post-enlightenment ontoepistemologies and their animacy hierarchies.[1] What's more, the speaker—and presumably, then, any listener or reader—is *also* spirit; there is no clear distinction here between knowing subjects and known objects, between people and worlds.[2] We aren't bounded selves—"post-Enlightenment subjects" (da Silva 2007)— so much as participants in the ongoingness of worlds.[3]

Another name for the genre of Anzaldúa's second-person address might be pedagogy: an experienced person or elder leads another (or others) through a modulated, rhythmic course—a curriculum—of encounters with more-than-human environments that stimulate learning. Anzaldúa's is a ceremonial pedagogy of *tierra sagrada*, something adjacent to what Leanne Betasamosake Simpson (2017) has called "land as pedagogy." Writing from "the milieu of Nishnaabewin, not the institution of the school," Simpson says that "within the context of humility and agency, decisions about learning are in essence an agreement between individuals and the spirit world" (155). She notes, "This makes sense because this is the place where our Ancestors reside, where spiritual beings exist, and where the spirits of living plants, animals, and humans interact. To gain access to this knowledge, one has to align oneself within the forces of the implicate order through ceremony, ritual, and the embodiment of the teachings one already carries" (155). Learning and living are not distinct, they are the co-compositional impulses of the biocultural creatures that we are, and these impulses reside less in us as subjects or selves and more in the spiritual-material worlds we participate in. In *Pedagogies of Crossing*, M. Jacqui Alexander focuses on spiritual practices "through which the Sacred becomes a way of embodying the remembering of self, if you will, a self that is neither habitually individuated or unwittingly secularized" (2005, 3). Letting the words of Anzaldúa, Simpson, and Alexander resonate together, we can find the lesson that landed, grounded pedagogies are always specific, nonuniversal, and nonuniversalizable. They can focus our attention on how we participate in tending worlds that turn away from enlightenment world (singular) and its colonialist, homogenizing violence. And they invite us to feel how as spirit, we are always already other than self in any "habitual" sense.

Tendings: Feminist Esoterisms and the Abolition of Man is my attempt, from where I am, to practice something of the attention and care demanded by Anzaldúa's "Now let us shift." It is a book about everyday practices as they participate in the strengthening or dissolution of what Sylvia Wynter calls Man as the overrepresentation of the human (2003). I am interested generally in what decolonial theorists call the pluriverse. Building on the Zapatista call for "a world where many worlds fit" (2018, xvii), Arturo Escobar summarizes his decolonial approach to the pluriverse thus: "*The diversity of the world is infinite*; succinctly . . . the world is made up of multiple worlds, multiple ontologies or reals that are far from being exhausted by the Eurocentric experience or being reducible to it" (68). I understand pluriversal politics as the disruption and dismantling of Man's homongenizing world, and I am especially interested in how that happens at the level of everyday practices.[4] Practices are how we participate in worlding, and the everyday names, for me, a spatiotemporal problematic where *tending* is at stake. This book is a meditation on how we participate in the tending of the colonial world and, potentially, otherwise worlds.[5] I might call this, after Denise Ferreira da Silva, who is echoing R.E.M., "the End of the World as we know it" (2014, 84): world in the singular, a world oriented around Man.

My point of departure for thinking all of this through is a pervasive interest in esoteric or occult knowledge in contemporary feminist and queer cultural production where "the witch," as Kristen Sollée writes in *Witches, Sluts, Feminists*, "is having a moment" (2017, 13). Looking around social media and the curated displays at my favorite bookstores, it's hard not to agree with Sollée; consider the flood of publications like *Queering the Tarot* (Snow 2019) and *Post-Colonial Astrology* (Sparkly Kat 2021); television shows like *The Chilling Adventures of Sabrina* (2018-present), the *Charmed* reboot (2018-present) and *Siempre Bruja* (2019–2020); and the endless streams of Instagram tarot and astrology posts. There are a lot of esoteric vibes in feminist and queer discourse today outside the academy.

Inside, something else seems to be going on, with much of the most exciting feminist and queer theorizing happening in and around fields we call new materialism, science studies, affect theory, and posthumanism.[6] The animating impulses of these currents in contemporary theory all look to call into question certain ideas about what humans are and how they relate to the nonhuman world, and they often (but not, of course, exclusively) articulate their versions of this questioning by turning to work in enlightenment (techno) sciences like biology, physics, chemistry, geology, ecology, and neuroscience.[7]

Let me simply juxtapose two passages. The first is from Jane Bennett's *Vibrant Matter*, one of the most influential books in the "new materialisms," and a book that guides much of my thinking in *Tendings*:

For the vital materialist, however, the starting point of ethics is less the acceptance of the impossibility of "reconcilement" and more the recognition of human participation in a shared, vital materiality. We *are* vital materiality and we are surrounded by it, though we do not always see it that way. The ethical task at hand here is to cultivate the ability to discern nonhuman vitality, to become perceptually open to it. (2010, 14)

The second is a passage from *Dreaming the Dark*, by Starhawk, the primary organizer of the Reclaiming network of covens in the San Francisco area beginning in the 1970s:

Estrangement permeates our society so strongly that to us it seems to *be* consciousness itself. Even the language for other possibilities has disappeared or been deliberately twisted. Yet another form of consciousness is possible. Indeed, it has existed from earliest times, underlies other cultures, and has survived even in the West in hidden streams. This is the consciousness I call *immanence*—the awareness of the world and everything in it as alive, dynamic, interdependent, interacting, and infused with moving energies: a living being, a weaving dance. (9)

Published twenty-eight years before *Vibrant Matter*, the claims are, ultimately, quite similar to Bennett's (even if I want to mark a tendency in her language toward colonial grammars, which I will return to in chapter 2). This similarity leads me to wonder: given that both new materialisms (and other varieties of more-than-humanist feminist theorizing) and esoteric feminisms are similarly concerned with attunement to the more-than-human, how might we think about their very different relationships to the institutionalization of feminist thinking and practice in our moment? Reductively, why is it that esoteric feminisms are proliferating outside of the academy while more-than-humanist theories attuned to post-enlightenment science are thriving inside universities?

At stake in this divergence within contemporary feminist thought is, perhaps most obviously, the matter of what we often think of as spirituality. Anzaldúa reminds us that "academics disqualify spirituality except as anthropological studies done by outsiders, and spirituality is a turn-off for those exposed to so-called New Agers' use of flaky language and Pollyanna-like sentiments disconnected from the grounded realities of people's lives and struggles" (2015, 39). New materialisms, by articulating their claims about vital matter and nonhuman agency within the coordinates of post-enlightenment secular(ist) science, upset some important presumptions about the human and its relations to the world, but also continue to tend (in the sense of granting attention to and caring for) the specific grammars and logics of that science, which I follow Denise Ferreira da Silva and Sylvia Wynter in seeing as *colonial* logics because of presumptions about liberal selves as knowing agents and the orientation of truth claims toward objective universality. And this raises for me some questions about scholarly feminist field imaginaries.

In 2008, two years before Bennett's *Vibrant Matter* was published, Sara Ahmed was already wondering about what kinds of narrative fantasy generation and policing were required to found what was coming to be called the "new materialism." In particular, she pressures the adjective "new" and the work that does, or refuses to do, in grounding the present feminist moment in claims about feminism's past(s). Thinking through the "politics of attention" that sustain (I would say tend) field imaginaries, Ahmed avers that, as a matter of ethics, "we should avoid establishing a new terrain by clearing the ground of what has come before us" (36). Ahmed's particular interest in "Imaginary Prohibitions" is the role of scientific knowledges and attention to "matter" in feminist theory, where the provocation of new materialisms to "tak[e] heed of developments in the natural sciences" (Coole and Frost 2010, 3) has to actively (if not necessarily consciously) disavow all the ways that has been happening within feminist history in order to "clear the ground" on which the adjective "new" can be enunciated.[8]

Tendings is also concerned with the role of science in feminist theorizing, and with the questions this concern raises about how fields work, but my specific interests are different from Ahmed's in two ways. First, I want to ask not about how a history of scientifically oriented feminism gets forgotten by the current scientifically oriented feminism, but about why *scientifically oriented feminisms* are a presumptive field attachment. That is, I wonder what role "science" (or, as science studies would prefer, sciences or scientific practices) plays in how "feminist theory" works as a matter of tending, which is ultimately what I think a "discipline" or "field" is: a pattern in the ongoingness of worlds. I wonder how attachment to science articulates feminism through what I will call, after Anzaldúa but also work in science studies itself, a politics of disqualification whereby spiritual, esoteric, or nonrational (according to enlightenment standards) knowledges have to be disavowed, ignored, or discredited.[9] Second, I want to ask about the ways that attachments to "science" also enclose feminist theory in homogenizing colonialist grammars of enlightenment at the levels of the (knowing, "self-determined") subject and the emplotment of history. As Jayna Brown puts it, "a trust in Western scientific knowledge must be interrogated, and the 'we' of new materialist thinking situated historically. . . . Materialist studies need to attend to the ways in which systems of inequality are embedded in our understandings of that materiality and the processes by which scholars theorize it" (2021, 124). This question of a first-person plural—the kind of socialities that endure in/as worlds—and its subjunctive articulation guides *Tendings*'s interest in esoterisms as, perhaps, the possibility of a "we" that refuses the homogenizing aims of universality and inclusiveness. That is, I wonder if a "scientific" we—a we that is produced through grammars of universality and its globally homogenized subject—is also a colonialist we. Modulating this "we" from an indicative presumption to a subjunctive, future-oriented dream of the end of the world (singular) requires that we don't reify science, but that we assume that it too is *storytelling*.

"Science and story are not discrete," says Katherine McKittrick, riffing on Wynter, "rather, we know, read, create, and feel science and story simultaneously" (2021, 9). What we have come to call "science"—even in feminist theory that is critically committed to thinking through science's intersectional politics in complex ways—is part of how worlds are storied around Man into world. McKittrick states, "Although science is a knowledge system that socially produces what it means to be biologically human, it is also the epistemological grounds through which racial and sexual essentialism is registered and lived" (131). This isn't about being opposed to the kinds of careful attention to more-than-human material worlds that happen in and around various practices marked as "science." It's about how those practices—what I call tendings—are articulated through colonial grammars, what Brown calls "the epistemological grounds" of Man. There are sciences that (attempt to) turn away from enlightenment, colonialist science. Sandra Harding talks about "sciences from below," especially feminist and postcolonial sciences. Leroy Little Bear (2001) theorizes a distinction between a decolonial "native science" and "Western science" (arguing in favor of specific modes of collaboration). Britt Rusert tracks "fugitive sciences" linked to abolitionist politics in the nineteenth and early twentieth centuries. Donna Haraway's "Situated Knowledges" makes very clear that each of these would have to turn on "the standpoints of the subjugated" (1991, 191), where knowledge is articulated through careful (response-able) attention to the specific political relations shaping encounters that generate claims without denying "the critical and interpretive core of all knowledge" (191). There are, potentially, subjunctively esoteric "scientific" tendings, but in improvisationally tending other grammars of worlding, they may become quite unrecognizable as "science."

I have been wondering if some of this investment in science is about the knowledge economies of the university today, and specifically about what Robyn Wiegman calls feminist and queer field imaginaries. Given how the institutionalization of fields of minority knowledge—women's studies, gender studies, ethnic studies—has always been uneasy and disputed (as, for example, when they were recently called "grievance studies"), the fields are always engaged in agonistic contact with university homogenization and capture (Wiegman 2012; Ferguson 2012). These fields ("our" fields?) always risk running afoul of logics of disqualification precisely because they deviate from enlightenment grammars of knowing (with a presumption of disinterested, nonpolitically motivated knowledge production), so one way to (perhaps less than generously) read the investment in scientific knowledges is as a way of grounding their "political" claims on supposedly settled ontological grounds. And this is no less the case when the explicit aim of the feminist theorizing is to rethink "ontology" as queer becoming by turning to work, for example, in biology or physics (thinking about this is part of what motivates my interest in grammar, as I will explain below).[10]

One hunch I've had is that for most of us feminist and queer thinkers interested in new materialisms, affect theory, posthumanisms, more-than-human ecologies, and so on (mostly trained, as we are, in the social sciences and humanities), part of our interest has to do with how these can feel like esoteric knowledges. How many of us can really follow the finer points of Barad or Stengers's engagements with physics, or Haraway's engagements with biology? Those texts are exciting to me, at least, because they tune into and make palpable worlds that feel very different from mine, more-than-human relationalities that feel hyperspecific (sometimes in single laboratories, for instance). It's not just about knowing different things, but about knowing differently, knowing otherwise. So maybe all these "new" turns in feminist thinking *could be*, at least subjunctively, esoteric orientations, if they could be storied differently, oriented not toward enlightenment universality but toward endarkenment pluriversality.[11] This would mean, among other things, giving up on grounding claims—about politics or the human or anything else—in a presumption that there exists one world. The book's project, then, is articulating a feminist and queer tending of the more-than-human that draws from work (and worlds) disqualified by enlightenment science and work that understands enlightenment logic as a matter of colonial tending.

Turning Away from the Light: Esoterism and Endarkenment

The tensions between a secularist, scientifically oriented feminist and queer thinking of more-than-human worlds and an avowedly spiritual, esoterically oriented feminism lead me to two questions that guide this book.[12] First, what happens to how we think about worlds—and ourselves as participants in those worlds—if we give up on presuming post-enlightenment rationality and its disqualification of spiritual knowledges? And second, how does an orientation toward the political articulation of a pluriverse—a world where many worlds fit (Escobar 2018)—affirm the necessity of *many* knowledges (and the socialities that are co-compositional with them) flourishing without being subjected to the kinds of epistemological and biopolitical violences that mark coloniality? Asking these questions, I have found myself consistently pulled away from the enlightenment grammars of a universal, homogeneous world and toward what I call esoterisms: bounded fields of more-than-human affective relationality that endure precisely through the ongoing attention to and care for their material, energetic, spiritual conditions of persistence. To compose this concept, I explore the current feminist and queer turn to the esoteric (tarot, magic, witchcraft, astrology) to pressure a kind of secularist investment in enlightenment science and rationality, but I also feel out how these occult-adjacent practices still largely operate with the conceptual grammars of enlightenment rationality. To articulate that orientation, and the potentialities for otherwise orientations that always eventually recur, I organize the book around a tension between enlightenment and endarkenment as tendencies of worlding.

What I'm calling esoterism in this book is distinct from what that means in the indicative archives of history and anthropology. I'll offer a first sketch of this difference using the definition offered in Antoine Faivre's canonical *Access to Western Esotericism* (1994; but originally published in French between 1976 and 1979). Faivre's book lays out a vast archive of what he calls "Western esotericisms," a distinct tradition that, for him, lurks on the borders of Christianity, especially as it draws from "Eastern" traditions, most importantly Hindu (but also Egyptian and Sumerian) traditions. In an effort to clarify what both "Western" and "esotericism" mean, Faivre lays out six elements, the first four of which are "fundamental":

1. Symbolic and real correspondences ("as above so below")
2. Belief in a "living nature"

3. The interrelation of imagination and practices of mediation (via symbols, rituals, etc.)
4. Experiences of transformation (including initiation and alchemy)
5. Insistence upon concordance (the search for a single, universal knowledge)
6. Transmission by initiation (1994, 10–15)

While Faivre is writing without much engagement with the explicitly feminist esoterisms of his moment (especially goddess religions), these elements don't require any reconfiguration at the abstract level to fit feminist and queer witchcraft projects. What's perhaps more striking is that they fit the "new materialisms" as well, and this project initially emerged from thinking about that confluence. New materialist theories and these esotericisms would, despite their shared commitment to concordance, fall into dispute about how to understand it. That is, a new materialist valorization of scientific rationality (in the form of verifiability according to strict controls) disqualifies most of the esotericist knowledges because they are too "particular," too based in a nonuniversal (read: nonscientific) rationalities. Rather than take a side, what I want to do in *Tendings* is to think about knowledging *without* presuming or aspiring to concordance.

Rejecting concordance turns out to have ripple effects across how I think about the other five elements too. For instance, while I will also affirm pedagogies of initiation, I worry about the ways that Faivre—based on his particular archive—thinks about initiation (and therefore all the semiotic and knowledge practices adumbrated in elements 1–4) through a logic of hierarchized homogenization. To whit, he defines the esoteric dialectically against the exoteric by referring to "what is reserved for an elite versus what is addressed to all" (33). My concept of esoterism foregrounds, much more than any specific beliefs about knowledge, a highly processual understanding of esoterisms as practices operating in tension with the exoteric, but with a crucial difference from Faivre. When the "empirical" esoterisms studied by Faivre are secret, elite societies that seek power in the wider field, they remain entirely within what I will call the homogenizing colonial grid of the singular world (they presume a universal sociality but with highly restricted access to knowledge practices tied to control). Some of these esotericisms have tended toward statal homogenization, toward imperialism, toward (cis)masculinist violence.[13] For me, the *exoteric* names that presumptive totalizing frame (world, singular), and a refusal of reference to it as the (only) field of intelligibility is precisely what is at stake in what I'm calling "esoterisms." Esoterisms, in my sense, would reject any possibility of elitism, vanguardism, or representational concentration of power-knowledge. My use of "esoterisms" is processual in that it does not name specific phenomena that can be empirically known, but instead is meant to draw our attention to the tending of worlds in which more-than-human socialities and knowledge practices would be co-compositional.

It is worth saying directly at this point that while *Tendings* proposes that we take (more) seriously and make (or keep) space for esoteric, nonscientific, spiritual knowledges both in our feminist, queer, decolonial, and abolitionist projects and in our spaces of pluriversal gathering (such as a university), this is not, in and of itself, a necessary break with homogenizing and disqualifying logics of enlightenment humanism. In fact, just as my thinking about new materialisms is always in conversation with decolonial, abolitionist, and queer of color critiques of the field, I will attend to the ways that feminist and queer esoterisms sometimes similarly tend to(ward) coloniality. Thus, by rejecting concordance—and the ontological presumption of a single world—I am weaving a conception of esoterism that might gather practices explicitly marked as "esoteric" and practices marked as "science" as well as modes of knowledging that have little resonance with either of those labels.

To amplify this difference between the empirical concept of esotericism laid out by Faivre, and esoterisms as speculative, subjunctive worldings (as I theorize them in this book), I cannot simply insert the adjective "new," for all the reasons Ahmed articulates in her critique of the "new materialisms." Rather, across this book, I map my elaborations of tending—as the attentive and careful participation in the endurance of worlds—by orienting my analysis around two main concepts: esoterism and endarkenment. Endarkenment names a kind of heuristic orientation: an adjectival (indeed, deictic) marker of the directionalities (outside of Euclidian geometric space) that turn away from enlightenment, which is to say, from Man. Enlightenment, too, names a tendency, or an orientation of tending in the polyvalent sense: an ongoing durability or endurance that is ontogenetically a matter of how attention and care are practiced. Specifically, by "enlightenment," I do not mean a discrete historical moment in the philosophical and political career or Europe, although it also cannot be detached from those geopolitical and historical coordinates. What I mean may be similar to Foucault's reading of enlightenment as an *ethos*, but unlike him, I see this orientation as one that can be refused.[14]

My basic sense of what enlightenment tending entails begins with Kant's famous essay "What Is Enlightenment?" in seeing it as the "free," reasoned, public debate about matters of importance where that discussion allows a powerful state to use its force to enact policy; this represents the maturing of "mankind" because people recognize enlightenment law as *just* to the extent that it is rational. Collective reason—asymptotically universal in ambition (and highly restricted in practice)—props up sovereign, biopolitical power.[15] This power's apogee appears in the kinds of large-scale state-planning projects James C. Scott analyzes in *Seeing Like a State*, where rational and centralized state power seeks an absolute homogenization, destroying worlds in order to generate a world of transparent legibility. This homogenization is necessarily linked with what I call, following Anzaldúa, Latour, and Stengers, a politics of disqualification. Scott writes: "The imperial pretense of scientific modernism admits knowledge only if it arrives through the aperture that the experimental method has constructed for its admission" ([1998] 2020, 305). What counts as reason, as "public" discourse in the statal sense, is a question of homogenizing, colonialist grammars. Enlightenment is the orientation of biopolitical state power toward a single world of universal intelligibility and planning, where the violences of extraction, expropriation, accumulation, and dispossession attend the distribution of non-Man knowledges and socialities (always mutually co-compositional) *within* that grid.[16] Enlightenment is the fever dream of world in the singular, structured by "light's violent, surveilling reach" (Cervenak 2021, 63).

Endarkenment is the opposite; or rather, I'm using it to feel how a wide array of practices deviate and tend otherwise worlds. If we imagine Man as a single, central point of light organizing enlightenment space, then darkness abides and withdraws in every direction beyond any kind of (grammatical) mapping. My use of the word "endarkenment" is indebted to Ashon Crawley's call for "endarkened logics of otherwise sociality" (2017, 209) and to *On Spiritual Strivings*, in which Cynthia Dillard draws on Black women's experience to theorize "an endarkenment feminism [that] seeks to resist and transform [racist and sexist] social arrangements . . . , seeking political and social change on behalf of the communities we represent as the purpose for research, versus solely the development of universal laws or theories for human behavior" (2006, 27). Dillard's formulation underscores how "endarkenment feminisms" are committed to situated knowledges and standpoint epistemologies, spiritual practices, and communitarian ethics expressed in everyday relations as care and vulnerability.[17] Dillard writes: "To know something is to have a living relationship with it, influencing and being influenced by it, responding to and being responsible for it" (20). Taking living and knowing as co-compositional in the tending of worlds can be constellated with Zoe Todd's argument that "Indigenous thinking must be seen not just as a well of ideas to draw from but a body of thinking that is *living and practiced by peoples with whom we all share reciprocal duties as citizens of shared territories (be they physical or the ephemeral)*" (2016, 17).

Because I understand coloniality to be a vast and immanently organizing "event" that takes manifold evental forms such as franchise and settler colonization, slavery and its afterlives, extractivist capitalism, and nation states articulated through governmentalities of the subject, endarkenment orientations turn away from liberal subjects (of knowledge, of state participation) and away from homogenizing grammars of temporality (that is, from "history"). I fully acknowledge that the very project of writing an academic book on this (or really any other) "critical" question implicates me in precisely these governmentalities.[18] This noninnocent participation is precisely what the book sets out to theorize: tending is not something that happens "outside" of the colonial field it would disrupt, which is why the question of orientation becomes so crucial: it's not about our positionality as such, as if politics follow from the sheer fact of self-location, but how we attune to what makes *this* positionality possible, what this modality of being (as verb) that "I" am brings into contact and cares for.

To turn away from Man's light is not to turn in any single direction, and I try to think through these other worlds (plural) as much as possible from what Julietta Singh (2018) calls dehumanist perspectives by thinking relationally with the dehumanized, the dysselected, *les damnés*. This means attending to the "dark materialisms" of what Tavia Nyong'o calls Afro-fabulation (2019, 47), where the everyday is "the texture out of which the eventfulness of fabulation arises" (5).[19] It is also to feel what José Esteban Muñoz calls "the brownness of the world" (2020, 118), and Audre Lorde calls "what is dark and ancient and divine within" each of us (2007, 69).[20] As Paule Marshall wrote in "Reena," "We live surrounded by white images, and white in this world is synonymous with the good, light, beauty, success, so that, despite ourselves sometimes, we run after that whiteness and deny our darkness" ([1970] 2005, 27). Darkness animates (and is animated by) non-Man worlds, but I think of darkness in its paraontological distinction from the people racialized as "dark," and I emphatically do not mean to conflate darkness with Blackness, or Indigeneity, or Brownness. Endarkenment thinks of racialization as a matter of evental tending, not identities: identities are features of sub-jects.[21] Endarkenment worlds are about intimate and erotic participation, not the identitarian capture of being, becoming, worlding.[22] This is a matter of what J. Kameron Carter calls "that dark knowing that exceeds theo-political constraint" (2020, 171). Beyond enlightenment (empiricist) fetishization of light and vision, there are vast realms of perceptual, sensorial, spiritual, affective relationality.

Knowledge practices involve sustained relational responsibilities, and these demand ongoing care. Knowledge is always contextual, always emer-gent from specific socio-material-semiotic webs, and the political question is about how entities—which are, in fact, nothing more than expressions or ongoing effects of events—*participate* in the ontogenesis of worlds. This is where many of the risks of appropriation, mistranslation, erasure, and other colonialist forms of encounter reside. Audra Simpson's (2014) work on the Indigenous politics of refusal, especially around anthropological work that extracts and accumulates knowledge from Indigenous groups, addresses this problem in a different context, as does Kim TallBear's (2013) work on genetic technoscience as a problem for Indigenous belonging and sovereignty. Not everything can or should be made available to outsiders, and indeed, one significant axiom of my approach in this book is that I must learn to respon-sibly think with concepts and practices that I *do not own*, cannot master, am not able to reduce to property.[23] I am explicitly not trying to "do" Black studies or Indigenous studies in this book, but rather attending to the ways my feminist and queer thinking, writing, and teaching participate in the (more-than-human) pluriversal politics of abolition and decolonization.[24] I follow Wynter in feeling the absolute necessity of a collective dismantling (or dissipation) of Man. But esoterisms, as bounded socialities that seek to flourish as worlds—through tending—have evental borders, and I am also trying to tend (toward) an ethics of affirming refusal, affirming the flourishing of worlds that do not include everyone, that do not include me. Mario Blaser and Marisol de la Cadena write, "Encounters (everyday or extraordinary) across partially connected (and also heterogeneous) worlds may be sustained by conversations that draw from domains in which not all participants in the encounter participate" (2018, 9). For this reason, much of the book tends to my particular situation as a white settler feminist and queer reader, lis-tener, and teacher as I move through the pedagogical sites of farmers' markets, academic conferences, bookstores, musical performance spaces, and class-rooms. The question for me is what it means to affirm worlds that aren't mine not by participating "in" them but rather by (at)tending to how my everyday practices enable or disenable those other worlds' persistence.

Tending Feminist, Queer, Decolonial, and Abolitionist Worlds

Tending, for me, is a capacious, polyvalent term—less a technical or philosophical concept than an irreducibly polysemous index of what I call the evental ontogenesis of worlding.[25] Worlds are composed in and through events, where a vast array of intra-active actants—"humans" and nonhumans on multiple spatiotemporal scales of intimate dispersion—are made by worlds in the same gesture as they make worlds.[26] Worlding can baffle the grammars of enlightenment rationality, agency, and temporality we are habituated to think and feel the world through; or, more simply, enlightenment, colonial grammar is the homogenizing *capture* of otherwise worldings. Endarkenment is the word I'm using to tune into socialities that escape, refuse, or disrupt that capture, tending non-Man, not (completely) colonized worlds. Worlding is not a (merely) human matter. For Anna Tsing, "we are surrounded by many world-making projects, human and not human. World-making projects emerge from practical activities of making lives" (Tsing 2015, 21–22). What Tsing here calls "practices" marks the milieu I'm trying to think in with what I call "tending." Starting from more-than-human ontogenic worlding, I want to think about tending in a cluster of four (maybe five[27]) semidistinct, interdependent ways: as inertial but evental ongoingness, as care, as attention, and as anticipation. Even when I use tending in ways that seem (based on context cues) to amplify specific meanings, they all resonate.

The first sense of tending comes from process philosophy, where what's at stake is, as Deleuze and Guattari say, "a world created in the process of its tendency" (1983, 322). In his book on Alfred North Whitehead, Didier Debaise notes that "the sole aim, the sole goal of any 'society,'" "is to maintain its historic route, the movement of its inheritance, the taking up, the transmission of the acts of feeling that compose it" (Debaise 2017, 73). Societies endure in and as affective transmission. Their hanging together *as* societies is a matter of the tendency to hold particular patterns across their evental ontogenesis. Tending names the ways that societies—which include small ones like a water molecules and vast phenomena like coloniality—are oriented in their becoming toward endurance, a conglomeration of felt semistability. The colonial world tends to endure in its unlimited drive toward mastery (Singh 2018). But this world is always shifting in specific material (often violent) encounters with otherwise worlding, always troubled by an "immanent outside" (Massumi 2019) that animates it, but which it has to enclose to maintain its historical tendencies.[28] This grammar of capture tends (toward) the homogenizing plotting of selves and stories.

Stories participate in the ontogenesis of worlds; they are the material-semiotic patterning that circulates within, across, through a world. I get this claim from Sylvia Wynter, whose concept of "the sociogenic principle" (2001) reconfigures Fanon's (1967) "sociogeny" via a turn to cybernetics in order to think about how different praxes or performances of the human—as a *genre* of living—take place as the entangled becoming of story and life, mythos and bios. Different genres of the human are sustained through the circulation and autopoietic materialization of stories. Different stories or practices of storytelling are co-compositional with different genres of the human, where specific, historical forms of being the entities that we "are" are inseparable from "descriptive statements" (2003, 264) about what it is "to *be*, and therefore what it is *like to be*, human" (Wynter 2001, 31). In the post-1492 moment (Wynter 1995), "*storytellers storytellingly invent themselves as being purely biological*" (Wynter and McKittrick 2015, 11) in relation to a "biocentric descriptive statement" (2003, 264), and Man uses the global violence of what Alexander Weheliye (2014) has called "racializing assemblages" to over-represent "itself as if it were the human itself" (Wynter 2003, 260). While Wynter sometimes sees this bios-mythos "hybridity" as a particularly human matter, I want to follow Jayna Brown's move "from Wynter's call for a new genre of the human to new genres of *existence*, entirely different modes of material being and becoming" (2021, 9). Storytelling might then name the patterning of all worlds, including those we now think of as pertaining to "humans" as participants.[29]

Thinking through this participation—and its complex hierarchies, asymmetries, and ethico-erotic frictions—is what the second sense of tending amplifies: tending as care, as cultivation, in specific practices of holding material worlds together through immanent participation.[30] Such participation is always necessarily specific and situated, a matter of haptics, an erotic biopolitics of touch. In Maria Puig de la Bellacasa's more-than-humanist remix of feminist care ethics and standpoint epistemologies, "standpoints manifest visions that have *become* possible by collective ways of learning to care for some issues more than others—rather than by following a normative ideal. . . . [S]tandpoints, even when they develop normative tendencies, are not fixed or essentialist, they depend on material configurations and on our participation in (re)making them" (2017, 59). This (re)making refers to the ways that worlds endure as worlds through care practices. What we tend, what we care for, is inseparable from how more-than-human worlds (Whitehead's "societies") endure.

I want to highlight Puig de la Bellacasa's word "manifest," which moves toward esoteric discourses of magic, as a way of approaching the third resonance of tending, via lexical proximity: what Ahmed calls "the politics of attention" (2008) or what Tsing calls "arts of noticing" (2015). I am interested in modes of attention—where that word refuses to be enclosed within conscious thought and even within the kinds of perception we associate with "living things" as presumed in biological discourse—as the material feeling that the tendencies of worlds to endure (and come into situational contact) works *through us*, thereby opening up the possibility of affectively sensing the evental ontogenesis of worlding and *tending* in some directions rather than others. When worlds collide with other worlds (as they do at every moment), the encounters among all the tendencies involved in those worlds generate specific margins for improvisation, and I'm trying to think about how we feel or attune to those margins, how we learn to play them (Massumi 2014).[31]

One way to think about the imbrication of attention and care at the affective level is to evoke here, anticipating a slightly slower engagement in chapter 4, Lauren Olamina's poem on the first page of Octavia Butler's *Parable of the Sower*: "All that you touch / You Change. / All that you Change / Changes you" (O. Butler [1993] 2000, 3). These lines propose the evental ontogenesis of the world (as Change) but also the complex modalities of participation—animated by *touch*, not by enlightenment vision or rational or empiricist epistemologies—that keep worlds going.[32] The word "all" suggests a nonuniversal expansiveness; this is an "all" not of rational abstraction or conceptual (or juridical or carceral) universalization, but an affirmation of the entirety of haptic contact. "All that you *touch*" is not everything, but some things, a messy multiplicity of them. Worlds "are" situational touch across intimately distributed scales of time and space, and they are sustained by affective semiosis—the patterning or "meaning" that I find in Wynter's conception of storytelling—which is also inseparable from practices, including everyday ones, from a whole erotics of care. Tending is a matter of what Audre Lorde calls "the necessity of reassessing the quality of all the aspects of our lives and of our work, and of how we move toward and through them" (2007, 55). Tending is about how we move through and sustain worlds in our participation.

Lorde also helps me hear how tending as attention and care always summons attending in my fourth sense: as waiting, as anticipation, as a feeling for the "not yet" that Muñoz felt in queerness (2010,1). It invites us to cultivate what Bennett calls "a certain anticipatory readiness . . . a perceptual style open to the appearance of thing-power" (2010, 5). Anticipation need not reach toward the new, but it can take shape as the desire for temporal endurance. Elizabeth Povinelli, thinking with Indigenous people around Anson Bay in Australia, reminds us that "in these situations, to be the same, to be durative, may be as emancipatory as to be transitive" (2011, 130). This tension between a proleptic hope signaled by the "not yet" and a politics of endurance is, in the evental ontology I am trying to think with in this book, one that is not to be worked out in abstraction, where critical calculation enables the construction and elaboration of ever-more-inclusive theories of the world's vast horrors, but rather in lived praxis, in the everyday, other-than-fully-conscious realm of living as participation in worlds as they collide (Massumi 2014). In events, the temporal logics of enlightenment causality and progress aren't the ontologically *given* coordinates of worlding so much as enduring tendencies that require, for their durativity, the tending of participants; these grammars are orienting in the sense that they prime events for particular, "probabilistic" outcomes but those outcomes are always in virtual contact with different potential worlds, potential endurances, potential becomings. Turning myself toward what Weheliye, riffing on Wynter, calls "the abolition of Man" (2014, 4), I am trying to feel out how in this complex assemblage of tending we can tap in the virtual, subjunctive potentialities for otherwise worlds that always attend *this world* and its crushing coloniality. And I'm trying to feel out how this abolition, this decolonization, can guide our everyday practices. As Leanne Simpson writes, "If we want to create a different future, we need to live in a different present, so that present can fully marinate, influence, and create different futures" (2017, 20). Esoterisms (can) tend these different futures, these endarkenment worlds after or beyond Man's homogenizing world.

Tending the Grammatical

Much of my attention in this book turns toward the grammatical: to the structuring logics of boundary maintenance spanning multiple modalities of worlding, to the basic iterative structures articulated in stories that hold worlds together. I mean grammar in the everyday sense of the patterning of sentences, but also, following Hortense Spillers and Saidiya Hartman, in the expanded sense of architectures of the thinkable and doable within a particular cosmological or metaphysical field.[33] One way to think with Spillers and Hartman is in a tension between descriptive, and pre- or proscriptive approaches to grammar.

Rules attempt to govern the ongoingness of worlds in their tendings, and a whole range of things—including criminality, delinquency, fugitivity, refusal, failure, aberration, and errancy—disrupt those rules.[34] Pre- and proscriptive grammar tell you what is "correct," and in the inherited grammars of Man's world, this often amounts to an enclosure of the potentiality of worlding within specific parameters of "parts of speech" and the standardization of language (and thinking) toward state legibilities. But there are other(wise) grammars—or anagrammatical energies[35]—where different patternings (can) happen. We might attune to the potentialities hovering around broken rules, "bad" grammar, inappropriate semiosis because those are indices not of nonsense, but an entirely different, subjunctive, field of potential worlds that move according to different grammaticalities.

As a matter of how worlds are patterned, grammar is a site where worlding encounters its semiotic conditions, for worlds are always co-compositional with storytelling and the ways stories emplot things like "subjects" and "actions." Stories distribute agency and its absence (or diminishment), and they pattern events (for instance as "causality" or "chronology"). Stories sociogenically shape the tending of biocultural human creatures, overrepresenting Man precisely because the stories are *immanently* material, co-compositional with worlds in their ongoingness (Wynter 2001). In the post-1492 moment, this requires tuning in to how coloniality—in its differential biopolitical and heteropatriarchal modes as franchise and settler colonialism, the transatlantic slave trade and its afterlives, extractivist capitalism, secularist science, and nation state governmentalities—shapes semiosis through modulating its epistemic, grammatical fielding.

My interest in endarkenment tending is, in part, a way to move away from the critical logics underwriting this framing of structural or grammatical "antagonism" (logics that operate within the colonial, homogenizing grammar of Man) toward improvisational grammaticalities that enact, as orienting tendencies, worlds that wouldn't be structured by the universalizing grammars that make it seem like affiliation is an either-or choice.[36] It's not about critical decision so much as affective participation, how we (adjacently) tend the dismantling of the world that encloses our questions about what might be possible.[37]

My attention in this book is sometimes on nouns and their (colonial) declension into subjects and objects—distributed differentially through (de) humanizing assemblages and their animacy hierarchies—but also to the grammar of verbs, particularly around tense as the structuration of temporality (a site of struggle around homogenization and dispersal[38]), and shifts in verbal mood. There are four verbal moods in English. The imperative gives commands, and except as a problem to be improvisationally disrupted when possible (as I discuss in chapter 4), I have no particular interest in it.[39] The interrogative asks questions, and I'm attentive—especially in chapters 1 and 4—to how the force of the interrogative can unsettle worlds and/or summon them. The indicative mood describes states of affairs, facts, empirical reality; when it appears, it is meant to delimit and define reality, truth, things that are solid and indubitable (or, at least, to cover over such things with untruths, dissimulations, deceptions). This mood, too, is one I seek to disrupt as much as I can (whatever the grammar of my individual sentences).

This brings me to the fourth, subjunctive mood, which makes no such claims, instead shifting into the realm of counterfactual, the possible. For Wai Chee Dimock, the subjunctive's "allegiance is to a ghostly region, a kind of syntactic underground, hovering just below the threshold of actualization, casting its shadow on the known world, turning sharp bright lines into a dense thicket, at once insubstantial and impenetrable, a vectorial field not yet hardened or pruned. A still-undecided past and a still-hypothetical future are housed by this syntactic form: counterfactual, not often accredited, but available all the same as virtual sites, thinkable versions of the world" (2009, 243). The word "virtual" here comes close to, or can be read proximally to, that word's use in the conceptual web of Deleuzian thought[40]—indeed, Dimock's gloss on the subjunctive here offers a surprisingly accurate, if manifestly gothic, riff on the virtual as a modality of what might have been and may yet be.

It's not that I'm uninterested in what is, but what I want to think through and learn to feel in this book takes shape elsewhere: in this "ghostly region." Dimock remains an excellent guide here: "If works of fiction are always subjunctive to some extent, dwellers in some counterfactual universe, literary scholarship can also afford to go some length in that direction. Indeed, taking our cue from the texts we study, our methods can be part empirical and part conjectural, starting out with some hard facts, but stretching these into airy vehicles, tentative on purpose, carriers for ghostly trajectories half-formed, half-glimpsed, and half-intuited" (244). My abiding concern is that colonial grammars operate through homogenizing logics that presume the indicative mood; they speak in facts (which can be proven and disproven), they articulate history as the causal or semicausal accumulation of such facts, and they ground the struggle for future worlds in their linear emplotment of history.[41] In "Venus in Two Acts," Hartman asks: "Is it possible to exceed or negotiate the constitutive limits of the archive? By advancing a series of speculative arguments and exploiting the capacities of the subjunctive (a grammatical mood that expresses doubts, wishes, and possibilities), in fashioning a narrative, which is based upon archival research, and by that I mean a critical reading of the archive that mimes the figurative dimensions of history, I intended both to tell an impossible story and to amplify the impossibility of its telling" (2008, 11). My interest in the subjunctive is about trying to feel out (both in and through the texts I engage at length) other possibilities for processually enacting, in praxes of more-than-human tending, different kinds of worlds than Man's asymptotically homogeneous world.

I am guided here by Dimock and Hartman, and also by Maryse Condé's subjunctive recreation of Tituba, which I explore in chapter 1, "'What Is a Witch?': *Tituba*'s Subjunctive Challenge." I closely read Condé's *I, Tituba, Black Witch of Salem* as a frustrating fiction oriented—at the level of its enunciation as the "re-creation" of spare historical "fact" and at the level of the narration and its decolonial, poethical grammars (da Silva 2014)—toward the refusal of the indicative mood, or rather, toward helping readers feel out the coloniality of that mood. Whenever Tituba, as narrator, encounters the question "What is a witch?," she answers by problematizing the utterance, situating it in a context of heteropatriarchal coloniality's violent encounters with the knowledges and worlds she tends and inherits from Mama Yaya. Condé's novel shifts from the indicative to the subjunctive and in doing so offers a theory of endarkenment esoterisms that isn't legible in its representation per se (we do not see an endarkenment esoterism depicted in any "clear" way) but in its rhetorics, narrative emplotments, vertiginous anachronies, and metadiegetic moves. Condé's novel foregrounds how "the witch" as a discursive field is delimited in the colonial context, marking confrontations between enlightenment's homogenizing world and the knowledge practices and worlds (the esoterisms) that Man disqualifies and subjects to violence. In the process, the novel unfurls a richly erotic (and potentially queer) attention to how worlds collide in violent and traumatic ways, but also in ways that generate pleasures, desires, and more-than-human (which includes spiritual) relationalities.

What I learn from Tituba, as character and text, is method of reading deictically and subjunctively that I carry through the following three chapters, which work something like a spiral, accumulating concepts additively as I track how tending works in three specific sites of pedagogy: (feminist) bookstores, underground music performance spaces, and the university. In my previous book, *Animate Literacies*, I theorized the "literacy situation," in which "a whole host of actants and agents animate literacy in scenes of pre- or aconscious collision and affective contact. . . . The situation is where intrahuman politics of race, class, gender, sexuality, and geography shape the conditions of emergence for literacy events that animate subjects and the political relations with which they are entangled" (Snaza 2019b, 4). Tituba helps me explore how "events" of conscious meaning making, such as applying the name "witch," always emerge in colonial situation, where there is always more going on than any participant can rationally know. Reading "through" witchcraft to the subjunctive tendencies that haunt that concept, the book theorizes across distinct if not entirely or always separate sites of pedagogy that I encounter as I move through my worlds, paying attention to pedagogical encounters (ceremonies) where those subjunctive possibilities can be *felt*.

In contrast to how Tituba as narrator and Condé as writer refuse the indicative logics that would stabilize "witchcraft" as a material-semiotic field, in chapter 2, "Feeling Subjunctive Worlds: Reading Second-Wave Feminist and Gay Liberationist Histories of Witchcraft," my focus is on second-wave feminist and post-Stonewall gay liberationist histories of witchcraft. These are texts that often appear on displays of feminist esoteric books in bookstores I frequent, and they would seem to inform a vast amount of the current explosion of feminist and queer writing on witchcraft and other esoteric practices. By taking up Tituba's subjunctive modulation of the indicative, I read Barbara Ehrenreich and Deirdre English's *Witches, Midwives, and Nurses*, Arthur Evans's *Witchcraft and the Gay Counterculture*, and Starhawk's *Dreaming the Dark*—texts that I see as articulating the general field in which the contemporary "reclaiming" of feminist and queer esoteric practices happens—to feel out their tendencies toward enlightenment logic. Attentive to moments where their indicative logics break down, by seeing them as "doing history badly" (Freeman 2019), I attempt to modulate their indicative claims toward the subjunctive. While the goddess feminism in these texts was famously used as an essentialist foil against which a "contaminated" or "cyborg" feminism could be articulated (Haraway 1991), this chapter is invested in thinking about what happens if we instead read these texts as a tangled, messy, problematic archive. This archive allows me to do two things at once: chart a set of topoi or keywords around which my understanding of esoterisms take shape (these include care, erotics, a more-than-human perception that is at least open to spiritual participation, and education as initiation to a bounded sociality), and think in detail about how homogenizing grammars try but also fail to enclose the subjunctive potentiality of esoterisms within the indicative, colonialist formation "witchcraft." When we participate in contemporary feminist and queer esoterisms—like witchcraft, tarot, astrology, and so forth—there are thus crucial questions to be asked about how certain kinds of participation tend coloniality more than they disrupt it.

I amplify the question of participation in "Man's Ruin: Hearing Divide and Dissolve," the third chapter, where I explore how we attune to and tend our participation in coloniality and its potential disruption, and I do this by asking how we might come to *hear* settler colonization as a spatiotemporal problematic. Extending and shifting from chapter 2's engagement with how esoterisms appear in my situation as a feminist, queer reader and social media consumer, this chapter finds me thinking about the "everyday" rituals of attending underground metal shows (and musical performance more generally), playing vinyl records, and walking around wearing earbuds linked to streaming services as pedagogical events, indeed as decolonial pedagogies of subjunctive space. Hearing Divide and Dissolve—an Indigenous and Black duo who play slow, instrumental doom metal that blurs into free jazz—I think about performance as a field in which tending is modulated and practiced. Divide and Dissolve's music—which is always co-composed in, with, through particular spaces because the sonic itself is irreducibly spatiotemporal— allows us to hear the sound of endarkenment worlds that circulate, subjunctively, throughout the colonial capture of homogenization. And they do this, as Dylan Robinson's *Hungry Listening* (2020) helps me consider, by refusing the kinds of settler ("hungry") listening that presumptively make the whole world available to liberal subjects expressing their (free) taste. That is, Divide and Dissolve's music affectively poses the question of participation in (settler) coloniality, and works to summon into the event of performance the *feeling* of otherwise, endarkenment worlds.

Chapter 4, "Ceremony: Participation and Endarkenment Study," brings all of these concerns with tending into an extended meditation on the everyday politics of endarkenment in the university and its colonial ecologies of accumulation, dispossession, and affective suture to Man. In many ways the crescendo of this project, the chapter explores what it means to (at)tend the educational undergrowth (Snaza and Singh 2021) of the university as a colonialist assemblage articulated around the production of post-enlightenment subjects of science and history (da Silva 2007), around Man (Wynter 2003). The chapter elaborates Sylvia Wynter's "ceremony" (at once concept and praxis) as a question of education as worlding—where knowledge is cocompositional with a sociality—and the ethics or politics of pedagogical encounters adhere in improvising toward endarkenment, a problematic I call, after Erin Manning, "event-care." The chapter locates these concerns in three relationally evental happenings: a sign appears outside the building I work in detailing entanglements between its namesake—the first president of the university—and the transatlantic slave trade; I study Christina Sharpe's *In the Wake* in that building, as the sign and Sharpe's book push us to think of our class itself, our study (Harney and Moten 2013), as (erotic) participation in the wake; and Alexis Pauline Gumbs performs on campus at a celebration to mark the anniversary of a feminist organization, conjuring endarkenment ceremony in a situation presumptively organized through Man's grammars. I draw out Gumbs's ceremonial poetics by engaging her trilogy of Black feminist study, *Spill*, *M. Archive*, and *Dub*.

These three events, nested within other events situated at different scales, allow me to think through the vibratory, improvisational potentiality of the everyday, of practices that tend endarkenment worlds. The everyday is where the violence of coloniality takes place, where the wake of slavery, (settler) colonialist violence, and extraction are embedded so as to almost disappear to Man's perception, relegated at best to an increasingly irrelevant "past" or simply naturalized as the way nature—or the economy—works (Hartman 1997; Wynter 2003; Murphy 2017; Coulthard 2014). Dwelling with Sharpe's account of the evental ontologenesis of worlds, I argue that the colonial world is not a fact, not a structure that awaits dismantling (Wolfe 2006), where this dismantling can only follow upon the elaboration of a universal critical frame that could orchestrate a global "we" against coloniality. Rather, the colonial world is but one possible pattern in the ongoing ontogenesis of worlds, a pattern that holds thanks to how, for many of the Earth's inhabitants, our everyday practices tend this world whether we attune to it or not. At every single moment, we engage in practices that either uphold or disrupt (and often both) the world of Man. In the post-1492 moment, we all participate in this, but participation is highly uneven—it can be humiliating, punishing, or violating; it can also be immensely pleasurable, "rewarding." What I try to practice in this book is a deictic attunement, attending to how these questions arise for me in my own everyday worlding.

The everyday, and its erotics of participation, is also therefore a site of uncertainty and possibility where tending is *at stake*. Erin Manning invites us to think our evental participation as "opening . . . the everyday to degrees and shades of experience that resist formation long enough to allow us to see the potential of worlds in the making" (2016, 15). What she calls "degrees and shades" points toward that "ghostly region" (Dimock) of the subjunctive, and also toward endarkenment: worlds beyond Man's colonialist homogenization of the human, worlds that tend different "genres of existence" (Brown 2021). Education here becomes a site of multiscalar collision of worlds, where evental participation tends some worlds rather than others, tends some kinds of (non)self more than others. If enlightenment ceremony conjures subjects (on the colonial grid of Man's homogenized world), endarkenment ceremony suspends selves except insofar as we can come to feel ourselves *as* participation, as patterns (specific but not stable, durative but processually open) in the worlding of worlds. And it helps us feel our affective participation in a collective, distributed, heterogeneous, pluriversal dream of the end of the world as we know it, which is to say the dream of the endlessly pluriversal improvisation of being.

ONE

"WHAT IS A WITCH?"

Tituba's Subjunctive Challenge

> In the face of such gaps, we need willfully
> speculative and creative accounts of
> black women's engagement with and
> challenges to racial science.
> —Britt Rusert, *Fugitive Science*

Maryse Condé's *I, Tituba, Black Witch of Salem* [*Moi, Tituba, sorcière... Noire de Salem*] ([1986] 1992) is a novel based on scant but extant historical references to Tituba, the single woman of color (possibly "Indian," possibly a slave of Afro-Caribbean descent) in the Salem Witch Trials (1692–1693).[1] A great deal is known about the white Congregationalist minister in Salem Village who enslaved her, Samuel Parris; the preachers, like Cotton Mather, whose writings played a key role in the hunt and trials; and many of the women (and at least one man) accused and executed as a result. Most of what is known about Tituba, however, is sketchy at best, more rumor than empirical fact. Tituba is thus paradoxically one of the most marginalized figures of the Salem Witch Trials even as she—and her affirmative answer (later recanted) to the charge of witchcraft, which sparked elaborate if vague descriptions of pacts with the devil—is central to the emplotment we inherit (Glover 2021, 42).

The kernel of known facts, beyond what is preserved of her incredible testimony, includes this, from *Salem Witchcraft Papers*: "Tituba, an Indian woman brought before us" (Boyer and Nissenbaum 1977, 286). Condé (re)creates Tituba, a Caribbean woman conceived during a rape on a slave ship whose presence in Salem is due to marrying an enslaved man named "John Indian," and her novel's enfleshed take on historical paucity weaves together the transatlantic slave trade, settler colonization of North America, and patriarchal violence in nuanced ways. Building on Sylvia Wynter's (2003) claim that in colonial modernity, a specific (imperialist, white, heteropatriarchal) version of the human—Man—violently "overrepresents" itself as if it were the *only* way of being human, I am attentive to how claims about what "is" (what is real, what is true) work to settle scenes of possibility into hardened, indicative facts. I will argue that Condé's novel tries to unsettle such indicative claims by foregrounding the subjunctive mood where counterfactuals (what could be, might be, may be) hold open potential and possibility. In this chapter, I read, Condé's novel as theory that turns to history in dubious or disputed ways, but which does so in the service of forwarding an understanding of "witchcraft" as a discursive concept that appears in *colonial* situations. Condé's novel thus enacts the challenge to racial science that Britt Rusert notes in the epigraph. Rusert advocates responding to the "gaps" that surround Black women's subjectivities and sexualities in the archive by opening up imaginative space for knowledges that aren't "science" but aren't disqualified as nonknowledge. In shifting from the indicative to the subjunctive, *Tituba* challenges us to feel otherwise worlds that might have been as they call us toward futures that might yet be (Crawley 2017).[2] I want to follow Katherine McKittrick here: "If we are committed to relationality and interhuman dialogue, if we are committed to academic practices that disobey disciplines, then the song, the groove, the poem, the novel, the painting, the sculpture must be relational to theory and practice" (2021, 52). Condé's novel is subjunctive theory, and importantly this works both at the level of the novel's enunciation and at the level of what I would call, after Denise Ferreira da Silva, its poethics in that Tituba's narration "carries the necessary tools for dismantling the existing strategies for knowing, and opening the way for another figuring of existence without the grips of the tools of scientific reason" (2014, 82).

My reading follows but ultimately diverges from Kaiama Glover's interpretation of Tituba (and *I, Tituba...*) as refusing a certain expected commitment to community in Afro-feminist Caribbean discourse. The aim of her reading is "to draw particular attention ... to Tituba's resolute, erotic self-love as subtly critiquing the communalist and implicitly Puritan underside of even the most adamantly subversive 20th-century Caribbean discourses—including that of Afro-feminism itself" (2012, 184). For Glover, the field attachments of Afro-feminism orient readers to find feminist collectives in the texts they read. But for Glover, "Tituba in fact expresses a narcissistic defiance of the very concept of community on which such perspectives are premised" (181–82). This may be most legible at the schematic level of the plot: Tituba, after an apprenticeship to Mama Yaya in Barbados, marries John Indian, an enslaved man about to leave for Massachusetts, so joining him is, in effect, a consensual entry into slavery. Her time in the colony, which overlaps with existing historical record, ends with her entering into slavery *again*, this time legally bound to a Jewish merchant, Benjamin Cohen D'Azevedo, who eventually frees her and helps her return to Barbados. There, she takes up with Christopher, the leader of a band of maroons planning a revolt, but Tituba is hesitant to participate.

In Kadji Amin's (2017) terms, we might say that Glover is attentive to how *I, Tituba* is a deidealized object, one that doesn't bear the promises that our radical theories of anticolonial politics demand. The novel's depiction of feminist endarkenment esoterisms is dispersed across the text, and because this esoterism eludes humanist grammars, Tituba's politics can feel genuinely disappointing when read through neat questions about how her actions conform to our field imaginaries in the early twenty-first century. But by tracking its exploration of endarkenment esoterism, I also try to feel out how, beyond anthropocentric understandings of feminist collectives, Tituba suggests a more-than-human, dehumanist sociality, one where care relationships link entities (including spirits, nonhuman animals, and plants) across many borders that typically limn humanist political thought. Tituba shifts our awareness, as Gloria Anzaldúa would say; "If reality is only a description of a particular world, when a shift in awareness happens we must create a new description of what's perceived—in other words, create a new reality" (2015, 45). This chapter traces how *I, Tituba* subjunctively (re)creates (a) reality, refusing indicative colonial logics in favor of subjunctive logics of decolonial and abolitionist esoteric tending.

In Tituba's impossible, extratemporal narrative voice, the novel engages directly with the historical archive and its ongoing interpretation by (racist) historiographers. On her way to prison in Ipswitch during the Salem Witch Trials, Tituba feels a "future injustice that seemed more cruel than even death itself" (110): being forgotten. She thinks:

It seemed that I was gradually being forgotten. I felt that I would be mentioned only in passing in these Salem witchcraft trials about which so much would be written later, trials that would arouse the curiosity and pity of generations to come as the greatest testimony of a superstitious and barbaric age. There would be mention here and there of "a slave originating from the West Indies and probably practicing 'hoodoo.'" There would be no mention of my age or my personality. I would be ignored. As early as the end of the seventeenth centuries, petitions would be circulated, judgments made, rehabilitating the victims, restoring their honor, and returning their property to their descendants. I would never be included! Tituba would be condemned forever! There would never, ever, be a careful, sensitive biography recreating my life and its suffering. (110)

Not for the last time, the novel here ironically declares the historical impossibility of its very existence, since this last sentence is probably as good a summary as anyone could construct of *I, Tituba, Black Witch of Salem*. And the sentence also gestures at the novel's refusal of a clean distinction between history and fiction: biography is re-creation. The details of Tituba's life in the historical archive are so sketchy that the editors of *The Witchcraft Sourcebook* can write, introducing a transcript of her testimony that appears, almost verbatim, in Condé's novel: "Tituba remained in prison during the entire episode and might very well have been executed at the end of the trials, but she was released in the general pardon by the governor" (Levack 2015, 285). That is, while some of her testimony survives, and scholars generally agree that she was pardoned, it's not possible to reconstruct the judgment against her ("might very well have" is hardly a locution signaling established empirical fact; even "would have been" might suggest a stronger empirical claim).[3] In her "Historical Note" appended to the novel, Condé attributes the relative paucity of "facts" around Tituba (compared to the white Puritans) to racism:

> Around 1693 Tituba, our heroine, was sold for the price of her prison fees and the cost of her chains and shackles. To whom? Such is the intentional or unintentional racism of the historians that we shall never know. According to Anne Perry, a black American novelist who also became passionately interested in our heroine, Tituba was bought by a weaver and spent the rest of her days in Boston.
>
> A vague tradition says Tituba was sold to a slave dealer, who took her back to Barbados.
>
> I myself have given her an ending of my own choosing. (183)

As Angela Y. Davis, in her foreword to the first English translation of Condé's novel, writes, "As an African-American feminist, I offer my profound gratitude to Maryse Condé for having pursued and developed her vision of Tituba, Caribbean woman of African descent. Should a Native American Tituba be recreated, in scholarly or fictional terms, this would be true to the spirit of Condé's Tituba and her revenge. For in the final analysis, Tituba's revenge consists in reminding us all that the doors to our suppressed cultural histories are still ajar. . . . And sometimes there is magic behind those doors, sparkling clues about possibilities ahead" (xi). The words "sometimes" and "ajar" remind us that we have to be careful *how* we approach and think about "our" suppressed histories, staying attentive to the violences of homogenization and indicative thinking and tending the possibilities for other worldings that haunt us subjunctively.

Discourse in the Contact Zone

Throughout the novel, Tituba continually poses the question "What is a witch?" and then, instead of answering in the indicative, refers it to the conditions of the concept's enunciation: Who says "witch"? In what context? With what material supports for their discourse? My aim in this chapter is to draw out how Tituba herself teaches us that the answer is not a denotative, indicative statement but instead the patient unfurling of conditions of discourse appearing in what Stephan Palmié has called "Atlantic modernity": "What I take this concept to refer to is, in part, a set of structural linkages that, since the early sixteenth century, transformed the Atlantic Ocean into an integrated geohistorical unit: an expanding theater of human interaction defined by a vast and intricate web of political and economic relations objectively implicating actors and collectivities on three continents in each other's histories" (2002, 15). "The witch" is a part of the discursive construction and elaboration of Atlantic modernity, one that does—in different ways and at different times—a great deal of cultural work to reinforce enlightenment tendings by generating its constitutive outsides. Uttered indicatively, "the witch" participates in enlightenment modes of homogenization, but in Tituba's narration, its sense switches modes, referring instead to a collision of relational knowledge practices where colonial tending is *at stake*.

Local esoterisms that become "witchcraft" through homogenization tend "to be tied up with moral systems" that "have to be understood in [cultural-historical] context" (Moore and Sanders 2001, 4). "Witchcraft" is almost always a linguistic translation of a local vernacular term, a deictic practice bound with local cosmologies and more-than-human relations. The contributors to *Sorcery in the Black Atlantic*, a volume gathering a range of recent anthropological research, explore specific practices that are sometimes, even often (but seldom always), folded into a concept like witchcraft: *feitiçaraia*, fetishism, sorcery, Candomblé, brujería, magic, and so forth. Not only are of these potentially distinct systems of belief and practice, but they are also tied in complex and contradictory ways to valuation: "white" versus "black" magic, for instance (or, popularly, the *Wizard of Oz*'s Good Witch versus Wicked Witch). Witchcrafts proliferate and evolve, and this happens in very specific conditions, but the indicative account of these practices still generally participates in conceptual homogenization, where the term "witchcraft" (or "sorcery" in the Francophone and Lusophone contexts) conceptually flattens practices that are "disqualified" by enlightenment rationality.[4]

All the linguistic and conceptual complexity attends a very simple fact that emerges across *Sorcery in the Black Atlantic* and much of the anthropology that is adjacent to it. Rather than witchcraft being the name for premodern or sometimes Indigenous knowledges that are superseded by rational, enlightenment, scientific thought, it is a specific discursive space opened within the colonial contact zone. That is, it is a word that appears when imperialist enlightenment projects encounter knowledge practices that constitute alternatives—alternatives that are forced to change due to colonial violence. Witchcraft, then, is not "outside" of modernity, it is a particle around which Atlantic modernity stabilizes, and tries to expand, its borders. João José Reis writes, drawing on the work of Rachel Harding, that "Candomblé was not simply a slave religion, which is one primary reason why it is somewhat complicated to discuss it in terms of slave resistance. Candomblé would rather seem to be a set of beliefs and practices that implied resistance by different groups and individuals to predominantly Western values, in particular Catholic conventional doctrine, as well as medical and other allegedly scientific procedures" (2011, 57). Generalizing toward the reading I am about to give of Condé's novel, I want to suggest that witchcraft signals a confrontation, though highly unequal in force, between colonialist expansion and the knowledge practices associated with genres of being human—and indeed more than-than-human "genres of existence" (Brown 2021)—that colonialism disqualifies by homogenizing them into "witchcraft." "Witchcraft" and its cognates only appear where autochthonic or vernacular knowledges (especially those associated with women or care practices, or both) encounter colonialist force (as with Mama Yaya's knowledge in *Tituba*). Neither "Indigenous" nor "colonial," witchcraft is a concept that arises in confrontation between different tendings in colonial contact zones. The specifics of the colonial situation (and they were and are manifold) determine how "witch" as an appellation sticks in peculiar ways to people (mostly women), things, practices, phenomena.[5] Condé's novel draws our attention away from a focus on this homogenizing concept toward how Tituba attends to and tends otherwise worlds, endarkenment esoterisms, that accompany enlightenment tendings as (at least) virtual or subjunctive possibilities.

"What Is a Witch?"

This question appears on page 17 of the English translation of *I, Tituba, Black Witch of Salem*, and is raised often, directly or indirectly, throughout the novel. Near the end of the book, when Tituba is involved with Christopher, a maroon on Barbados organizing a slave revolt, he asks her, "Are you a witch?" In response Tituba sighs and says, "Everyone gives that word a different meaning. Everyone believes he can fashion a witch to his way of thinking so that she will satisfy his ambitions, dreams, and desires . . ." (146). While Christopher doesn't have the "patience" "to stay here listening to you philosophize," what I want to do in this chapter is linger with how, in the novel, the word "witch" becomes a refrain that allows Condé to insist on the inseparability of her esoteric practices and political projects animated by decolonial, feminist, abolitionist, and even queer desires. Thinking this inseparability through, then, may be called "philosophizing."

In its first iteration, the question appears in relation to a quip by Tituba's lover—an enslaved man named John Indian—who says "What are you doing, little witch?" Tituba thinks: "He was joking, but it made me think. What is a witch? I noticed that when he said the word, it was marked with disapproval. Why should that be? Why? Isn't the ability to communicate with the invisible world, to keep constant links with the dead, to care for others and heal, a superior gift of nature that inspires respect, admiration, and gratitude?" (17). Tituba registers the difficulty, if not impossibility, of separating claims about what things are (or that they exist) and judgments about value. In order to think through subjunctive understandings of what the "witch" *might* be, Tituba enlists the interrogative mood to pry apart what seems inseparable. This interrogative approach is most explosive in the barest sentence here ("Why?") which is, grammatically, nothing but that interrogative force.

Summoned here, this force makes legible how any indicative statement ("a witch is . . .") is one of many possible ways of indicating something about a world. In settling that potential into seemingly ontological claims, indicative statements mask the extent to which they arise *within* and as *part of* struggles over the existence of worlds. Condé underscores how ontology, conceptual language, and judgment are intra-active with another question, a question crucially in the subjunctive mood: "Consequently, shouldn't the witch (if that's what the person who has this gift is to be called) be cherished and revered rather than feared?" (17). When we use human language to talk about things (always, but pointedly in cases where these things have an ontologically uncertain status) our relation to them is constitutively shaped by the conceptual labor of words and the ways value judgments prime our perception of the world.

The paragraph ends with Tituba reflecting on her love for the man who just and in jest called her "little witch." She reflects: "I recalled my mother's lament: 'Why can't women do without men?' Yes why?" (17). There is something about the ontological-linguistic-evaluative cluster appearing around the word "witch" that leads Tituba quickly back to her own familial history and to another sentence amplifying the interrogative force, this time elongated only by a word ("yes"), serving to join Tituba, through affirmation, to a prior interrogative utterance. Mother and daughter here speak, as it were, together, and citational or iterative practice creates a kind of collective speech across an "unreal" expanse of time. The force of the mother's question—which calls into question how sexuality and patriarchy have been linked—resounds into the present, where Tituba joins in with her own amplifying voice. And the paragraph's structure loops this (hetero)sexual question in with the prior questions about what a witch and her value are. That is, the question "What is a witch?" is brought into a circuit with the question of why women "can't do" without men.

Except, of course, they can. The novel doesn't do more than gesture in this direction, but a crucial pair of questions is sounded after Tituba, imprisoned in Salem, shares a cell with Hester Prynne from Nathaniel Hawthorne's *The Scarlet Letter*. The two women commiserate by sharing their experiences of patriarchal violence, although adultery (with a minister) and witchcraft constitute different crimes against the patriarchal Christian state. Just before Tituba is released from prison following the Massachusetts governor's general pardon of those accused of witchcraft (119), and just after Tituba hears of Hester's suicide by hanging, we read the following, which hovers somewhere between memory, fantasy, and haunting:

That night Hester lay down beside me, as she did sometimes. I laid my head on the quiet water lily of her cheek and held her tight. Surprisingly, a feeling of pleasure slowly flooded over me. Can you feel pleasure from hugging a body similar to your own? For me, pleasure had always been in the shape of another body whose hollows fitted my curves and whose swellings nestled in the tender flatlands of my flesh. Was Hester showing me another kind of bodily pleasure? (122)

Separated by a sentence that signals the kind of standpoint epistemology that we find called for in feminist theory after at least the Combahee River Collective Statement, two interrogative sentences suggest a kind of answer to Tituba's mother's question. While we might underscore how sex here determines the shape of a body more than race, queer erotics—where "bodily pleasure" need not solely take the forms we are taught to recognize in "sexuality"—signal a possible, subjunctive line of flight away from the patriarchal state's carceral and dispossessive hold on feminine pleasures, bodies, and knowledges. This line of flight, or what Omise'eke Tinsley (2010) has called "thiefing sugar," isn't represented in the novel's plot, which finds Tituba continually subjected to statal violence, almost all of it the result of Tituba's proximity to the state caused by her sexual desire for men. But readerly attention can be turned away from the plot so that these questions' impact is not muted through disavowal or disinterest. Tituba's pleasure, at the very least, holds open the potential—stumbled upon not conceptually but by her body's affective apparatus—to recognize how heteropatriarchy in effect overwrites the whole of pleasure with a meager field of heterosexual pleasures. This recognition similarly drives Audre Lorde's "The Uses of the Erotic," where Lorde distinguishes between the "sensation without feeling" of pornography (1984, 54) and the erotic as "a resource within each of us that lies in a deeply female and spiritual plane, firmly rooted in the power of our unexpressed or unrecognized feeling" (53). Unlike the bounded, paltry field of "pornographic" sexuality, the erotic's "deepest and nonrational knowledge" (53) extends throughout an entire haptic field, one immanent to (feminist) living; "When I speak of the erotic, then, I speak of it as an assertion of the lifeforce of women; of that creative energy empowered, the knowledge and use of which we are now reclaiming in our language, our history, our dancing, our loving, our work, our lives" (55). Lorde's examples of "erotically satisfying experiences" include "dancing, building a bookcase, writing a poem, examining an idea" (56–57). Shimmering beyond the edges of the sexual, the erotic names the ("female") haptic pleasures that give rise to joy as an affective part of the becoming of worlds.

Apprenticeship as Esoteric Education

I want to track back to the opening pages of the novel. Only nine pages after the "little witch" jest, the word "witch" appears again in a way that causes Tituba to query its meaning and its performative force. Here, John Indian's master, Susanna Endicott, asks Tituba, "Weren't you brought up by a certain Nago witch called Mama Yaya?" The force of this question, or more specifically the word "witch" in it, causes Tituba to stammer: "'Witch,' I stammered. 'Witch? She took care of people and cured them.'" What Tituba learns through apprenticeship from Mama Yaya doesn't fit, to her, the valences of the word "witch."

Before getting to a conversation on the next page where Tituba and John Indian discuss what this word means to Susanna Endicott, I want to back up to the very beginning of the novel where Tituba details what she learns from Mama Yaya. After Tituba's mother is hanged for the crime of taking up a cutlass against her master as he is about to rape her (8), Tituba is taken in by "an old woman"; the woman is "not an Ashante like my mother and Yao, but a Nago from the coast, whose name, Yetunde, had been creolized into Mama Yaya" (9). After a paragraph detailing being given a "bath of foul-smelling roots" and "a portion of her own concoction" to drink when she's first taken in, Tituba offers three anaphoric paragraphs that sketch the esoteric curriculum that guides her apprenticeship:

> Mama Yaya taught me about herbs. Those for inducing sleep. Those for healing wounds and ulcers. Those for loosening the tongues of thieves. Those that calm epileptics and plunge them into blissful rest. Those that put words of hope on the lips of the angry, the desperate, the suicidal.
>
> Mama Yaya taught me to listen to the wind rising and to measure its force as it swirled above the cabins it had the power to crush.
>
> Mama Yaya taught me the sea, the mountains, and the hills. She taught me that everything lives, has a soul, and breathes. That everything must be respected. That man is not the master riding through his kingdom on horseback. (9)

The first four words repeat across the paragraphs, and the grammar immediately thereafter suggests an increasingly diminished distance between

Tituba and what are only badly (if grammatically) called the "objects" of her study: "about herbs" to "to listen" to no preposition at all, with "the sea, the mountains, and the hills" being direct objects. The grammatical diminution may suggest an inverse *increase* in importance from knowledge "about" entities like herbs, to specific attentive or perceptive practices, to knowledge of place and the vitality of things.

Although Tituba's apprenticeship to a diasporic Yoruban woman in Barbados differs in many ways from the Indigenous Nishnaabeg context in which Leeanne Betasamosake Simpson writes, I think we could conceptualize Mama Yaya's teaching as an iteration of what Simpson calls "land as pedagogy." For Simpson, "Indigenous education is not Indigenous or education from within our intellectual practices unless it comes through the land, unless it occurs in an Indigenous context using Indigenous processes" (2017, 154). Condé's novel frames Indigenous and other land-based knowledges as subjunctive kin, and this helps me to underscore the difference between schooling as a (settler) state practice and education that is contextual, apprenticed, deictic, and land based. Furthermore, it highlights the ways that abstract ontological postulates ("everything is alive"), while perhaps correct, are only apprehended in specific milieux. Simpson argues that "this is the place where our Ancestors reside, where spiritual beings exist, and where the spirits of living plants, animals, and humans interact. To gain access to this knowledge, one has to align oneself within with the forces of the implicate order through ceremony, ritual, and the embodiment of the teachings one already carries" (155). As we shall see later, when Tituba is taken from Barbados to Massachusetts, she will have to reconfigure her practices because there are different plants, different animals, different relations. It is not the same land, which is understood as a "*system of reciprocal relations and obligations*" more than as a group of objects or entities (Coulthard 2014, 13). In other words, her education does not, unlike what contemporary schooling ostensibly aims for, prepare her for abstract citizenship and employability, but instead amplifies the deictic potential of tending. She is brought into intimate attentive contact with a singular place, its rhythms and relations. Her "powers" require such intimacy, and they gather around the specific kind of tending that Tituba practices in specific places or situations.

Even while Tituba's esoteric education is rooted in the deictic specificity of Barbados, what Mama Yaya teaches her also resonates with Jane Bennett's call for modes of perception attentive to the vitality of things. While Tituba is taught that "everything is alive," many of us who have been through statal schools plugged into enlightenment rationality have been taught that matter is inert and nonvital. For Bennett, this is a crucial part of how we have arrived at a global mode of production that has ushered us into the Sixth Great Extinction and the associated phenomena gathered under names like Anthropocene, Capitalocene, Plantationocene, Cthulucene, or Eurocene.[6] She writes:

> Why advocate the vitality of matter? Because my hunch is that the image of dead or thoroughly instrumentalized matter feeds human hubris and our earth-destroying fantasies of conquest and consumption. It does so by preventing us from detecting (seeing, hearing, smelling, tasting, feeling) a fuller range of the nonhuman powers circulating around and within human bodies. These material powers, which can aid or destroy, enrich or disable, ennoble or degrade us, in any case call for our attentiveness, or even "respect." (ix)

Bennett is clearly speaking to contemporary late-capitalist subjects whose educations have insisted on a seriously sanitized vision of Newtonian matter and causality (Newton was, after all, interested in magic and alchemy!), and so her project requires that she "advocate" a position that was always virtually possible but not actualized. In other words, she proposes a subjunctive reimagining of education that might actually inculcate in us this range of practices for "detecting" nonhuman power.[7] Unlike those of us who attended post-enlightenment schools, Tituba gets this education the first time around and doesn't need, say, university courses in materialist philosophy to thus attune to the world.

If Mama Yaya's pedagogy is rather unlike the contemporary institutionalization of statal schooling, her caring and curing practices are similarly out of synch with contemporary medical business. In fact, Mama Yaya (and later Tituba) fits very closely the feminist interpretation of the European witch hunts that Barbara Ehrenreich and Deidre English offer in their 1973 pamphlet, *Witches, Midwives, and Nurses: A History of Women Healers*. The first paragraph of their pamphlet reads:

> Women have always been healers. They were the unlicensed doctors and anatomists of Western history. They were abortionists, nurses, counselors. They were pharmacists, cultivating healing herbs and exchanging secrets of their uses. They were midwives, traveling from home to home and village to village. For centuries women were doctors without degrees, barred from books and lectures, learning from each other, and passing on experience

from neighbor to neighbor and mother to daughter. They were called "wise women" by the people, witches or charlatans by the authorities. Medicine is part of our heritage as women, our history, our birthright. (25)

For Ehrenreich and English, as for Silvia Federici's later biopolitical account, the attack on traditional feminine caring and curing practice was a necessary precondition for the consolidation of state power and the corollary development of masculinist medical power concretized in institutions like the hospital, clinic, and university. While this passage tends toward homogenization (even essentialization) and is overly invested in a politics of selves that might be managed through inclusion, their account allows us to notice that Mama Yaya and Tituba's powers aren't an aberration: they are rather a continuation of prestate (or parastate) organizations of knowledge, practice, and education.

Federici's *Caliban and the Witch* offers a more directly Marxist and biopolitical take on the attack on traditional healers. Her interest is in the phenomenon Marx (1990) calls "primitive accumulation" or the dispossession of people from life-sustaining commons, which Marx believed constituted the necessary precondition for the emergence of capitalism. Federici understands the witch hunts in Europe from the sixteenth and seventeenth centuries as a major part of that accumulative dispossession, but she also sees in the state and capital war on women a modality of political maneuver that extends into the present: primitive accumulation turns out not to be "primitive" at all, but an ongoing dispossession (a point Indigenous scholars like Glen Sean Coulthard also make). Federici writes:

Reading the "transition" [from feudalism to capitalism] from the viewpoint of the anti-feudal struggle of the Middle Ages also helps us to reconstruct the social dynamics that lay in the background of the English Enclosures and the conquest of the Americas, and above all unearth some of the reasons why in the 16th and 17th centuries the extermination of the "witches" and the extension of state control over *every aspect of reproduction*, became the cornerstone of primitive accumulation. (2004, 22)

Federici's claim here, partly indexed in the quotation marks around "witches," is that the devaluation of traditional modalities of healing was inextricably linked to both the dismantling of precapitalist organizations of social, economic, and physical space *and* the colonization of the Americas by Western European countries. (*Caliban* doesn't do quite enough with the latter, reserving only a short chapter for it, but her recent book *Re-Enchanting the World* gives much more attention to the politics of accumulation outside of Europe.) I want to modulate Federici's account to foreground how the resignification of healing as "witchcraft" is a part of the colonialist overrepresentation of the human by Man. This politics takes place at the level of discourse for sure (linked to what Sylvia Wynter calls "sociogeny") but it is first and foremost a question of materiality, relations, and institutions. Healers like Mama Yaya stand apart from Man, practicing not just different genres of the human, but what Jayna Brown calls "new genres of *existence*, entirely different modes of material being and becoming" (2021, 9).

This all leads me back to Susanna Endicott and Tituba's conversation with John Indian about what Endicott thinks the word "witch" means. John Indian speaks "frantically": "Not a year ago Governor Dutton had two slaves who had been accused of dealing with Satan burned in the square at Bridgetown. For whites that's what being a witch means . . . !" (27). Here, the valuation of traditional healing bifurcates and is linked to the modern, Man-centric project of (state) racialization: whites interpret traditional care as "dealing with Satan." Tituba replies, "Dealing with Satan! . . . Before setting foot inside this house I didn't know who Satan was!" (27). For Tituba, the appellation "witch" when understood to mean a compact with Satan functions like a catachresis: an ab-use of a word. While historians have attempted to un-pack some rather nuanced differences among the clergy and citizens of New England when it comes to differing kinds of magic (practical magic, white magic, countermagic, etc.), noting that there could be a wide gulf between the official legal definition of witchcraft as dealing with Satan and the un-derstandings circulating among the populace who made accusations, the fact is that the state's conflation of Satanism and witchcraft (due to the almost total control Congregationalists had on Massachusetts law) meant that any practices of healing not sanctioned by the state would lead to being accused of Satanic dealings, in effect branding the accused enemies of church and state. Put differently, the state overrepresents traditional healing *as* "dealings with Satan" in such a way that being caught doing this healing removes the accused from the orbit of Man, consigning the accused to less-than-human status. This is the colonial homogenization of worlds into world through the disqualification of non-Man genres of existence.

Less-than-human status, of course, was already forced upon Tituba and her fellow Barbadians by slavery and its gratuitous violence. Very early in the novel, when her mother is still alive, Tituba travels to Bridgetown in Barbados and finds a carnival where the slaves "came in from all corners of the island to try and forget they were no longer human beings" (16). The dehumanizing machinations of the colonial project (including racial slavery) were such that Tituba states, "My color was indicative of my close connections with Satan" (65; see also 77) among the white New England colonists. It is on this point that the novel stages a dispersed but forceful articulation of the politics of global coloniality authorizing settler colonization and genocide, the transatlantic slave trade, and new forms of patriarchal violence. The most succinct articulation of the link between settler colonization and slavery occurs when Tituba and John Indian have been brought to Boston where Samuel Parris awaits an assignment as a minister (which eventually he finds in Salem). Lacking employment, and having spent "the little savings he had brought back from his incursion into the world of trade in Barbados," Parris hires out John Indian to a local tavern called the Black Horse. It is here that John makes contacts with people from around the world. Chapter 7 begins with a conversation between John and Tituba, where she eventually uses the information he relays to query why white Puritan colonists feel so threated by "Satan" everywhere. The passage is worth quoting at length:

> He told me that the slave trade was being intensified. Thousands of people were being snatched from Africa. I learned that we were not the only ones the whites were reducing to slavery; they were also enslaving the Indians, the original inhabitants of both America and our beloved Barbados.
>
> I listened in amazement and revulsion. "There are two Indians working at the Black Horse. If you could see how they are treated. They told me how they were being deprived on their land, how the white man destroyed their herds and gave them 'fire water,' which sends a man to his grave in next to no time. Ah, white folks!"
>
> These stories puzzled me and I tried to understand. "Perhaps it's because they have done so much harm to their fellow beings, to some because their skin is black, to others because their skin is red, that they have such a strong feeling of being damned?" (47)

While Tituba's question attempting to "understand" the relations between anti-Black and anti-Indigenous modulations of coloniality (the devastating globalization of whiteness) is not as nuanced in its attentions to divergent histories as we may need, I think this passage offers a few important insights. In the present moment, there is a lot of energy being devoted to articulating a critical perspective that can adequately link Indigenous and Black struggle, a project that has to address widely discrepant relations to state power, law, sovereignty, racialization, and land. Two of the most compelling recent books to undertake this—Tiffany Lethabo King's (2019) *The Black Shoals* and Mark Rifkin's (2019) *Fictions of Land and Flesh*—do it by thinking through the distinct metaphorics through which struggles are figured (land and water and land and flesh, respectively). What Tituba offers is a way of looking back to how, no matter how much these struggles diverge in the present, anti-Black and anti-Indigenous assemblages emerged from *the same* material ecology of states, churches, law, knowledge production, and technologies tuned to conquest.[8]

Further, John Indian's "Ah, white folks!" followed by Tituba's speculations about why "they" experience such powerful affects (tied to belief in damnation), signals that whatever the crucial distinctions between settler violence and the violence of the slave trade, both ultimately have a common cause: white folks. Tituba's phrase "their fellow beings" posits a common humanity ("fellow") that is crucially not affirmed by white folks who would see both the Indians and slaves not as "fellow beings" but as less-than-humans to be eradicated or treated as property. This common experience of colonial dehumanization positions Tituba to feel closer to the Indigenous inhabitants of the area than to the whites among whom she lives: "The Indians? I was less frightened by those 'savages' than I was of the civilized beings I lived with who hanged old women from trees" (50). The distinction here may be precisely the one Wynter makes between Man (tied to whiteness) and its not-quite-human constitutive outsides, including those who may be exposed to what Afro-pessimists like Jared Sexton and Frank Wilderson, III, call gratuitous or ontological violence.[9] The experiences of different groups dehumanized by Man do not need to be coincident or even homologous: their affiliation appears in having a common source for their miseries in Man. Intersectional analysis of differential violence produced by colonialist, enlightenment tendings (aggregate transhistorical endurances of dispossession, elimination, and extraction) can allow for careful solidarities among socialities with distinct modes of knowing, doing, being. Rather than seeing such solidarities as contingent upon articulating broadly agreed-upon critical frames for conceptualizing that differential experience, my sense is that solidarities arise in scenes of material, more-than-human contact where questions of meaning and responsibility necessarily arise as entities are (re)oriented in worlds around what Maria Puig de la Bellacasa calls "matters of care" (2017).

Temporality, Intersectionality, and the Tending of Worlds

The colonial-racial problematics of post-enlightenment Man intersect with—which is to say, continue and reconfigure—older patriarchal forms of violence.[10] And no doubt owing to the particular conversations happening in global feminisms in the 1970s and 1980s, *I, Tituba* offers what our present vocabulary would call an intersectional analysis of slavery, (settler) colonialism, and heteropatriarchy. But it does so in a way that can be discomfiting. Let me return to Kaiama Glover's reading, sketched above. She notes that Condé's 1979 *La parole des femmes* was crucial to the organization of a coherent Caribbean feminist literary tradition in relation to a largely masculine Negritude.[11] Glover writes: "Not only was Condé instrumental in recognizing the contributions of Caribbean women writers to global literature at a time when few readers were paying attention, but she also analyzed the specific ways in which women's literature had been dismissed with the region itself. No one has been more thorough and succinct than Condé in outlining the tendency of Caribbean literary canons to oblige allegiance to a masculinist status quo and, more broadly, to a representative 'we'" (2021, 17). Glover's final locution helps to frame her specific reading of *I, Tituba* as what I'm calling, after Amin (2017), a deidealized object. Glover writes that, "by refusing to surrender to the vision others have of her, and insisting on her own regard as the sole frame within which she ultimately understands and loves herself, Tituba subtly upends long-standing conventions of both colonial and postcolonial feminine self-telling" (44). Most importantly, Tituba's "self-love" adheres in her willingness to be enslaved *twice* in the novel (66), and in that she "strategically affirms neither Black nor white sisterhood with any degree of reliability" (59). Tituba's protointersectional analysis was, and no doubt remains, sometimes "problematic," especially when considered through the vicissitudes of contemporary thought. What interests me here, though, is how that analysis operates through narrative—or, better, poethical—gestures that disinvest in the indicative mode toward which critique tends. I want to follow Tituba as she constructs a perhaps dissatisfying critical account of how race and gender intersect in colonial ecologies, but one that emerges in a felt, affective scene of sociality that ontologically precedes and exceeds the bounds of rational critical thought. Solidarity is nothing if not a shift in how one attends to (in the sense of granting attention) the ways that one's daily habits either facilitate the ongoingness of a colonial homogenizing world—its tending or endurance—or instead processually enact otherwise modes of being, other genres of existence (this enactment can only ever be partly conscious).

I begin with a crucial early passage in which Tituba reflects on how difficult it was for her to leave the solitude of her shack on the edge of the village to live with John Indian among his master and other white folks. This passage is directly concerned with one of Condé's most troubling acts of "self-love" as Glover puts it, and it directly considers how gender cuts through racialization. White men in particular are the predominant source of violence: "My mother had been raped by a white man. She had been hanged because of a white man. I had seen his tongue quiver out of his mouth, his penis turgid and violet. My adoptive father had committed suicide because of a white man. Despite all that, I was considering living among white men again, in their midst, under their domination" (19). Here, sex, gender, race, and violence are entangled in a knot whose untangling may be possible at a certain level of abstraction, but only at the risk of a significant reduction in feeling the accumulative force of their mutual amplification.

These intersectional questions structure one of the most self-consciously postmodern scenes in the novel: when Tituba meets Hester Prynne in a Salem jail. I've already noted how the scene ends with the potentiality of queer erotic pleasure coursing through Tituba's affective system as she imagines possible futures not as tightly bounded by Man. Having Tituba—whose story is a fiction, but one woven starting from scant but empirically verifiable historical records—meet Hester introduces a kind of vertiginous affect, at once foregrounding the imaginative and even speculative nonreality of Tituba as a character (a kind of *Verfremdungseffekt*), and simultaneously pulling Hester out of one of the most famous and widely read nineteenth-century US novels and into the "real" present. That is, this scene works to unravel distinctions among historical times and the boundary between the "historical" and "fictional," revealing both to be modalities of reading that presume different relations between words and worlds (and often, as Joan Scott [1992] notes, working out their methods in dialectical tension). At stake is a shift in thinking away from the indicative and toward subjunctive potentialities.

The scene opens with the two characters sharing their names, which immediately leads to a recognition of patronymic politics. In a gesture of both racialized cultural presumption and subjunctive desire for different possibilities, Hester expresses her disappointment that Tituba "accepted the name a man gave" her, and then "muses": "I was hoping . . . that at least some societies were an exception to this law. Yours for example" (96). This leads

Tituba to "muse" as well, foregrounding the dispossessive violence of the slave trade which sunders people from land, from language, from cultures, from traditions: "Perhaps in Africa where we come from it was like that. But we know nothing about Africa any more and it no longer has any meaning for us" (96). What's so striking about this, as a way into the conversation, is that by negating Africa as a source of "any meaning," Tituba's language cannot help but introduce the meaning of Africa (in the subjunctive) into the frame and links that to the historical and political machinations of coloniality that *never stop dispossessing* the enslaved. We are here not "after" the moment of theft and enslavement, but, as Christina Sharpe (2016) puts it, in its wake.

Immediately following the contagious "musing," Hester asks Tituba, "Why were they calling you a witch?" (96), which leads Tituba to again reflect on how that word's particular modulation of ontological postulation and affect-laden valuation are tied to specific forms of (colonial) social life. She says, "Why in *this* society does one give the function of a witch an evil connotation? The witch, if we must use this word, rights wrongs, helps, consoles, heals . . ." (96, ellipsis in original). Tituba here clearly separates the word "witch" (she will say a bit later, "Here I was again, up against that epithet" [135]), from the *function* of a witch. She also separates both the function and the word from "connotation" as something given. This pithy meditation on the complexities of signification could be read, in one way, as a symptom of the novel's postmodernity, whereby a mise en abyme is set up to affectively disorient readers not only at this moment, but at every moment they encounter words, both while reading the novel and in any other context. But more than a shift to some kind of semiotic free play, this passage attunes to a political and historical, which is to say *colonial*, grammar governing significatory operations, thus revealing the extent to which postmodern affirmations of play largely remain(ed) within coloniality.

Condé's ellipsis trailing after Tituba's list of practices attributable to "the witch" sets up an unexpected reaction from Hester: "She interrupted me with a burst of laughter. 'Then you haven't read Cotton Mather!'" (96). Cotton Mather's sermons played a crucial role in the events in Salem, and yet, unlike the novel's presentation of Tituba's testimony before the court (104–106), which is taken nearly verbatim from historical records,[12] Condé introduces Mather's ideas by having Hester do a mocking impression: "She puffed herself up and solemnly declared: 'Witches do strange and evil things. They cannot perform true miracles; these can only be accomplished by the visible saints and emissaries of the Lord'" (96). When Tituba says, "Who is this Cotton

Mather," Hester "did not answer." For the novel, then, Mather—a preacher, like his father Increase (the president of Harvard College at the time of the trials), whose surviving sermons are the basis of much of the historical work trying to understand the theological conditions of possibility for the "witch hunt" in Salem—is important as a historical quilting point, but is refused any direct, nonsardonic citation. It is as if the ideas of Mather—a matrix of Puritan gravity, colonial ambition, patriarchal rage, and pedantic border policing—are simply not worth serious engagement, even as this refusal to cite also speaks to its force in shaping the discursive field of "witchcraft" (the novel's silence is a response to its omnipresence). Here the novel suggests that critique—the patient, attentive grappling with oppressive ideas in order to undermine them through rational exegesis and problem-posing—always risks propping up the power and persuasiveness of the thought it would ostensibly undermine. If thought is an economy of attention, critique's *material existence* as attention paradoxically cares for the conditions it purports to disrupt. Rather than engage in dialectical antagonisms, we might instead turn away, wandering off in queer, feminist, decolonial, and abolitionist directions.

Across the next few pages, Hester coaches Tituba to "give names, give names!" (100) when she is interrogated during the trial, which leads to a reflection on patriarchal structures that cut across race: Hester says, "Life is too kind to men, whatever their color." This prompts Tituba as narrator to articulate something she doesn't say aloud: "something deep inside me told me she was telling the truth. The color of John Indian's skin had not caused him half the trouble mine had caused me. Some of the ladies, however Puritan they might be, had not denied themselves the pleasure of flirting with him" (101). Here again, we see a direct presentation of the intersecting operations of race, gender, and sexuality where (white) Puritan women, Black men, and Black women can all be differentially dehumanized relative to white men in ways that both conjoin their experiences and struggles and generate *relative* proximities to Man such that violence is not smoothly distributed, but uneven, asymmetrical, and contradictory.

This is followed by a more general statement about what happens between Tituba and Hester in the cell: "When we were not rehearsing our testimony, Hester and I talked about ourselves." This phrase *could* mean something like the sharing of experiences, and indeed, the entire description of their conversations could well be read as a kind of consciousness raising exercise. Within that context, the paragraph abruptly shifts to a singular utterance by Hester that again *could* be read as an indication of the novel's postmodernity: "I'd like to write a book, but alas, women don't write books! Only men bore us with their prose. I make an exception for certain poets. Have you read Milton, Tituba? Oh, I forgot you don't know how to read. *Paradise Lost*, Tituba, a marvel of its kind. . . . Yes, I'd like to write a book where I'd describe a model society governed and run by women! We would give names to our children, we would raise them alone . . ." (101). Beyond the obvious irony at play with "women don't write books!" here, I find Hester's slippage from poetry to speculative political theory important.[13] This shift, for Hester, most immediately serves to make the books less "boring" but it also underscores, yet again, the political force of language: books can become subjunctive spurs for emergent worlds. We might read Hester's two particular interventions as somewhat insignificant shifts enabled by a world "governed and run by women," but I'd like to see the two details offered as somewhat synecdochic. That is, a disruption of patrilineal descent quickly blurs into an entirely different, nonmasculinist modality of thinking history, tradition, and inheritance; it intervenes precisely in the field of the subjunctive, seeking to reconfigure the *virtual* conditions from which possible worlds are generated. And second, "raising" children "alone" shifts the political focus away from a Marxist, capitalist, and usually masculinist obsession with production to the field of what Marxist feminists call "reproductive labor" or, more simply, "care." These, then, are not policy proscriptions aimed at the reshaping of a mode of production or the state form so much as the seizing of the matrix of relations—historical and reproductive—*from which* all social (and economic, cultural) formations emerge. It is a matter of tending worlds in their ongoingness, turning away from enlightenment homogenization toward a pluriverse of endarkenment socialities.

Hester's proleptic sketch of a book project leads Tituba to note, about children, that "we couldn't make them alone," to which Hester replies, "Alas, no. . . . Those abominable brutes would have to share in a fleeting moment" (101). I would note three things about this locution. First, "brutes" functions to dehumanize the men who, in the current colonial-patriarchal order are positioned closest to the sources of dehumanizing violence. While this may well be a pragmatic reversal of a political binary opposition, it hardly displaces the binary or jams the assemblages of (de)humanization. Second, and in a different register, Hester's subjunctive "would" alights from that indicative utterance into a less certain, subjunctive mood effectively placing the status of "those abominable brutes" in question. This questioning leads Hester to foreground *time*: "a fleeing moment." It is this third thing that spurs Tituba to respond, "Not too short of a moment. . . . I like to take my time" (101). Tituba thus claims her sexual desire and refuses an imaginary future where that desire is not (at)tended.

It is at this moment that the novel offers one of its most important exchanges. Immediately after Tituba asserts her sexual desire, we read:

> She ended up laughing and drew me close to her.
> "You're too fond of love, Tituba! I'll never make a feminist out of you!"
> "A feminist. What's that?"
> She hugged me in her arms and showered me with kisses. "Be quiet. I'll explain later."
> Later? Would there be a later? (101)

The ironic anachronism of "feminist" being uttered in the 1690s but with its explanation deferred until "later" foregrounds how for Condé, as for Nietzsche and Foucault, what matters is history of the present. Something like accuracy is jettisoned in favor of a disjointed, nonlinear, *queer* temporality in which words, affects, desires, and political struggles don't stay where they "should." The novel signals a desire that in its now (the early 1980s) language might be able to explicitly articulate what Hester and Tituba were unable to in the 1690s. The anachronism makes explicit that the exchange is, in fact, an instance of *feminist* consciousness raising that reaches toward what would be come to be called intersectional analysis. And it does this by positioning *us* readers as inhabiting precisely the "later" time that the novel attends in the sense of waiting for.

I, Tituba offers protointersectional attention to how power and history shape the present and the ways that different people are able to differently attune to how that history saturates the present not just as a set of material conditions and habits orienting action in certain directions (that is, as colonial tending), but also as virtual, subjunctive possibilities that *may* be tapped into. While the homogenizing violence of the post-enlightenment world touches all of us and its tendencies shape the conditions of our (un)livability, we do not participate in its maintenance or disruption and dismantling in the same ways, nor can we. This is why tending is necessarily and radically situated: one has to feel—often beyond anything that could be called conscious or rational thought—how the colonial world endures through our everyday lives (material, juridical, intellectual, spiritual, sexual) so that otherwise manners of being, tending away from colonialist light, endure and thrive. In the face of a colonialist world that asymptotically pursues total mastery through horrific violence (Singh 2018), the question we must ask is how we are implicated in its tending through how we participate in the tending of worlds. Referring to how white readers and viewers such as themself engage scenes of anti-Black violence, Syd Zolf calls for us "to look . . . not as voyeurs or spectators but as participants in an ongoing disaster" (2021, 12). Participation in the disaster that is Man can be differentiated across a range of positions within critical frames: settler, arrivant, native (Byrd 2011, xxx); or persons, nonpersons, and some (women and children) who could participate in personhood only by participating in patriarchy (Perry 2018, 23). Rather than abstractly formulate rules for engagement and plans for constructing worlds from critical blueprints, I want to foreground how Tituba thinks less with conceptual frames than through feelings, less with identitarian understandings of freedom—or even, ultimately, *individual* understandings of it—than as a particular expression of what Mel Chen (2023) calls the emergent agitation of differential being.

Conclusion: Erotic Autonomy and Endarkenment Nonselves

Glover notes that what is most fundamental to Condé's Tituba is "her assertion of herself as a loving, decidedly non-procreatively erotic being" (2021, 62), one whose "erotic self-regard" "disrupts models of communal solidarity" put forth by Caribbean feminist writers (58). I'd like to end by thinking about this as a question of what M. Jacqui Alexander has called "erotic autonomy," which for her names freedom from the heteropatriarchal capture of female sexuality.[14] In her famous 1997 essay, "Erotic Autonomy as a Politics of Decolonization," she analyzes this capture through legal changes in domestic violence policy and the criminalization of same-sex desire, both of which take place in the context of global capital's recolonization of the Bahamas after the official end of colonization. Autonomy, for Alexander, is linked to anticolonial desire for "self-determination" (2005, 54), which is why "women's sexual agency and erotic autonomy have always been troublesome for the state" (22). In this sense, Tituba most certainly foregrounds her erotic autonomy more than any legible communal politics.

What interests me is what happens when the distinction Alexander makes between "sexual agency" and "erotic autonomy" is amplified by recalling Audre Lorde's expansive (more-than-sexual) sense of the erotic. That is, I think Glover's reading holds when focused on how Tituba's sexual desires for male partners are given more credence than her commitment to progressive feminist, anti-racist, or anticolonial abstractions or categories. But I want to attune more toward a claim Tinsley makes near the end of *Thiefing Sugar*: "This expansive eroticism gives voice to the complex ways in which radical black feminism is not something *out there* but *in here*, a set of praxes and ways of knowing woven into Afro-Caribbean women's daily interactions with themselves and others" (2010, 204). Calling this "a different kind of erotic autonomy" (20), Tinsley turns to Wynter in a claim she makes about erotic autonomy in the writing of Mayotte Capécia:

> The she-devil's alluring heterosexuality is a strategically fabricated illusion that veils what Sylvia Wynter, in her groundbreaking "Beyond Miranda's Meanings" names "demonic ground"—"an alternative sexual-erotic model of desire" in which the Caribbean woman's eroticism refuses to be fixed on one "appropriate" object but instead circulates endlessly as Capécia's Cambeille [River], creating a black feminist subject who threatens to reveal desires as numerous and dangerous as snakes on a Gorgon's head. (154)

Might these "numerous and dangerous" desires not exceed those that are legible within human sexuality and instead unfurl along vast pathways of more-than-human relationality?

I read Tituba not as refusing the communal so much as refusing an understanding of the communal that begins with an abstraction presuming identitarian belonging that she doesn't *feel*. What are the worlds she tends in the company of plants, nonhuman animals, and sprits like Mama Yaya if not socialities that she cares for? One way to conceptualize this company is with Aisha Beliso-De Jesús's concept of "copresences," developed in a reading of Santería.[15] "Copresences," she writes,

> are sensed through chills, shivers, tingles, premonitions, and possessions in and through different transnational Santería bodies and spaces. They are active spiritual and religious subjectivities intimately tied to practitioners' forms of movement, travel, and sensual bodily registers. Dead African slaves, Yoruba diaspora oricha, and other racialized entities form part in a reconfiguration of practitioners' body-worlds. (2015, 7)

If we read Tituba as participating in worlding with entities that might be thought of as "natural" as well as copresences, we might also shift a conceptualization of Tituba's will, her willfulness, from a self as subject toward a distributed world: worlds, in their tendings, will persistence. To the extent that Tituba is willful in her navigation of a colonialist world, her will is an expression of—and a participation in—a world's willing. Judith Butler suggests something similar in *Precarious Life* when she writes, "if we think moral authority is about finding one's will and standing by it, stamping one's name upon one's will, it may be that we miss the very mode by which moral demands are relayed. That is, we miss the situation of being addressed, the demand that comes from elsewhere, sometimes a nameless elsewhere, by which our obligations are articulated and pressed upon us" (2004, 130).

Tituba's political orientation is toward such a "nameless elsewhere," socialities that exceed humanist and anthropocentric frames. The worlds she tends are those that resist and disrupt coloniality and heteropatriarchy, but not necessarily in the ways identitarian modes of critique expect or require. Tituba's world does not include any of us, nor does it articulate itself in our terms. There is no invitation to join her world. The novel, instead, poethically demands that readers think about their own deictic situations and the ways their lives continue and disrupt colonial tendings (where one mode of colonial continuance is to *presume* one is always invited). For this demand, which is also a refusal, an indicative understanding of witchcraft is beside the point. What's needed is the feeling that other worlds are already happening, that we are already an expression of them (in contact with colonial tendings), that we aren't selves in the post-enlightenment mode of the "transparent," "self-determined self" (da Silva 2007). In relation to a post-enlightenment "transparent" self, positioned in and against a "universal nomos" (47), da Silva calls for "displacing transparency" (xviii). We might turn away from this universal nomos toward pluriversal nomoi, where the stability of ordered worlds is agentially located not in a bounded "self" but in an entire sociality. Socialities, not "selves," are autonomous. This is why, immediately after referring to Tituba in "Seeing Things," Fred Moten can write that "the poetics of the open field, especially when performed in the padlocked cell, was always tied to the social practice of riot, of generative differentiation and expropriative disruption as the non-selves' self-defense" (2017, 187). Tituba, participating in tending a(n always-shifting) world, lets us (at)tend to what J. Kameron Carter calls "a condition of being dispossessed of a self, which is a condition of possession anterior to property, anterior to propertied self-possession, indeed, anterior to self" (2020, 166).

Following Carter, and Moten following Tituba, we may not, in fact, really be selves at all except insofar as they are semistable conglomerations of matter, a patterning of worlds in their differential becoming. Imani Perry writes that "choices, interpretations, actions of 'witches' are always contingent on something beyond the dominant structure and order—something vital; something intellectual and sensual at once; something emotional and affective" (2018, 175). Since, as she notes, Tituba's story points us toward "the architecture of nonpersonhood" (28), we can say that the endarkenment nonself would not be a matter of identity or a subject so much as a matter of how we erotically sense and participate in more-than-human genres of existence as semistable, porously bounded entities. It's a matter of how we consciously and other-than-consciously feel our way through and tend worlds that subjunctively take shape away from the light that regulates a homogenizing Man-centric world.

TWO

FEELING SUBJUNCTIVE WORLDS

Reading Second-Wave Feminist and
Gay Liberationist Histories of Witchcraft

> The point, then, is not wholly or even
> mostly about the designated (by self
> or other) witch. It is about recuperating
> the energy signified by the witch, restoring
> it to our social and political imaginary.
> —Imani Perry, *Vexy Thing*

By 2018, I was no longer surprised when I'd walk into a bookstore—let's say Bluestockings' iconic though now defunct Allen Street location in New York City, or Chop Suey Books in Richmond, Virginia, where I live—and find a section devoted to feminist witchcraft, tarot, and esoteric practice. At Bluestockings, a sign reading "Hex the Patriarchy" sat above books like Silvia Federici's *Caliban and the Witch*, Barbara Ehrenreich and Deidre English's *Witches, Midwives, and Nurses*, and Kristen Sollée's *Witches, Sluts, Feminists*. Such displays are how I came across Ariel Gore's *We Were Witches*, and her newer book *Hexing the Patriarchy*, as well as Michelle Tea's *Modern Tarot*. And every time I come back to browse, I find the selection growing.

Fig 2.1. A "Hex the Patriarchy!" book display at Bluestockings' iconic but now defunct Allen Street location, New York City, June 1, 2019. Photograph by the author.

Sollée's introduction to *Witches, Sluts, Feminists* may put the attraction most succinctly: "Like many millennial women, I see a reclamation of female power in the witch, slut, and feminist identities. Each of these contested words conjure [*sic*] and counter a tortuous history of misogyny, and each in its own way can be emblematic of women overcoming oppression" (2017, 7). Looking back to self-consciously feminist covens like the Women's International Terrorist Conspiracy from Hell (W.I.T.C.H.), founded in New York in 1968,[1] and the Reclaiming covens in San Francisco orbiting Starhawk, contemporary feminist cultural production claims words like "witch" precisely because they are, as Sollée suggests, "contested": they function as terms used to police supposedly irrational claims—as when the forty-fifth US president suggested that any investigations into his potentially illegal actions were "witch hunts"—but they are also available for affirmative resignification.

In this chapter, I am concerned with the stakes of this reclamation and resignification, and specifically with the ways that feminist turns to witchcraft sometimes articulate this reclamation in homogenizing terms, where resignification takes place without unsettling colonial grammars of self and temporality. I am at the same time interested in what these histories tap into and make available for thinking and feeling that exceeds the capture enacted by the concept of "witchcraft"—what Imani Perry calls, in this chapter's epigraph, the "energy signified by the witch" (2018, 175). Building on my reading of Maryse Condé's *I, Tituba, Black Witch of Salem* in chapter 1, I understand the concept of "witchcraft" to be emergent in colonial contact zones where the homogenizing force of Man's overrepresentational project encounters non-Man knowledges and socialities, the irreducible ensemble of which I call "esoterisms."[2] Feminist and queer attempts to resignify "the witch" can and do enact forms of attention and care that tend coloniality. Taking up the turn to New Age and esoteric knowledge in contemporary discourses of trans care, Hil Malatino writes: "Every time a white, trans person charges their crystals during a full moon, moves through an asana, does a tarot reading for themselves or a friend, appeals to the stars for relationship advice, or considers traveling to the desert for a peyote retreat, we become further embedded in this long history of romanticization, piecemeal appropriation, and exoticizing commodification that has consistently resulted in the production of [what Arun Saldana calls] white viscosity" (2022, 188–89). My reading is similarly concerned with the way these practices can tend coloniality, but I also try to feel out what happens if it's not "every time." I wonder what would be required for feminist, queer, and trans esoteric practices to *not* tend (toward) coloniality, to not be oriented toward white viscosity but instead, away from Man's light. I want to do this by attending to the subjunctive field that accompanies that "witchcraft" in its moment of reclaiming (a feeling that in the colonial contact zone, things can always go otherwise). Following Tituba, my reading practice is constantly unsettling indicative claims about "witchcraft" by amplifying the subjunctive potentiality that exceeds and haunts that concept's "agential cut."[3]

The homogenizing logics of feminist witchcraft projects are precisely what's at stake in the last paragraph of Donna Haraway's "Cyborg Manifesto," which famously ends, "Though both are bound in the spiral dance, I would rather be a cyborg than a goddess" (1991, 181). Specifically naming investments in "universal, totalizing theory" and "anti-science metaphysics," Haraway positions goddess feminisms as the dialectical other against which cyborg feminisms are legible, where the latter are committed to "permanently partial identities" and "contradictory standpoints" (154). It's worth noting, here, that the phrase "spiral dance" appears on two pages in the essay—in fact on both pages I have just cited (the appearance on 154 also includes a note explaining "the spiral dance"); in neither instance is Starhawk named despite this concept coming from her writings and activist coven-building.[4] These uncredited citations and dialectical distanciations suggest an anxious affect I want to play with and amplify in this chapter, forwarding the possibility that these esoteric feminisms, including goddess religions, might be every bit as partial and contradictory as the cyborg feminisms Haraway envisions in opposition to them. More than simply reversing Haraway's preference, I wonder here, and in *Tendings* more broadly, what happens if we don't oppose the spiritual to the scientific per se (they have a stranger bond), but instead attune ourselves to what Haraway herself describes very well: "the skillful task of reconstituting the boundaries of daily life, in partial connection with others, in communication with all of our parts" (1991). I'm trying to feel out what feminist histories of witchcraft, precisely because they are messy and contradictory, make available to us in our tendings.

This chapter is an elaboration of my claim in the introduction that Antoine Faivre's six elements of "Western esotericism" could be reconfigured in new materialist terms. While I have no interest in doing that schematically, the chapter addresses, with differing kinds of attention, the presumption of correspondences (including scalar entanglements), belief in living nature, the importance of mediation (in symbols or rituals), experiences of transformation, a search for concordance, and an investment in initiation. I will not be systematic, but this chapter explores what it would mean to affirm many axioms of a new materialist orientation by largely drawing on an archive of feminist and gay witchcraft projects that would be disqualified (in whole or in part) by the more techno-scientifically oriented feminisms. As I noted in the introduction, it is on the matter of concordance (what I call homogenization) that new materialist and feminist witchcraft projects differ from each other, and the topic on which I differ from both projects the most. While I hope my approach might, among other things, make more space for spiritual and other non"scientific" knowledges in contemporary feminist and queer discourse (in modalities other than inclusion), I want to make it very clear that I don't see a drift in orientation from techno-scientific investments to more esoteric ones as necessarily disrupting coloniality even if I call for that drift. Indeed, goddess and scientific feminisms struggle to think through decoloniality and abolition in strikingly similar ways. While critique undoubtedly motivates my engagement with these texts' homogenizing tendencies, the practice of subjunctive reading that I learned from *Tituba* in chapter 1 helps me turn, at those moments, toward speculation on what endarkenment esoterisms that reject concordance might be.

Subjunctive Reading

Feminist and gay reclamation projects construct histories of their activist identities stretching back to the burned witches in early modern Europe, and often further back to pre–Bronze Age goddess religions. Such histories are capacious enough to draw in a range of figures not conventionally associated with witchcraft.[5] For example, Sollée's chapter "Political Witch: Rebellion and Revolution" includes Elizabeth Cady Stanton, Susan B. Anthony, Sojourner Truth, and Victoria Woodhull as "witches." These texts create, in a distributed way, a specific ontoepistemological field that delimits the discursive regime they call "witchcraft." Sollée's impulse here—to include within "witchcraft" an enormous variety of socialities, projects, and historical moments—derives, in a fairly obvious way, from the 1970s and 1980s histories of witchcraft I read in this chapter: Barbara Ehrenreich and Deirdre English's *Witches, Midwives, and Nurses* (1973), Arthur Evans's *Witchcraft and the Gay Counterculture* (1978), and Starhawk's *Dreaming the Dark* (1982). Read together, these books delineate distinct, but affiliated, concepts of witchcraft that animate and are animated by specific social movements: the Women's Health Movement of the 1960s and 1970s, the post-Stonewall gay liberation movement, and second-wave feminist allegiances with anarchism and ecology. These three texts are para-academic histories, incorporating (some) academic conventions (including citational practices), but also explicitly addressing nonacademic audiences with political arguments. The books eschew the disinterested, positivistic "addition" to a progressive stockpile of knowledge, borrowing from academic work (largely in anthropology and history) in order to construct concepts and narratives responsible to different constituencies than disciplined academics, but they also largely assume the colonialist grammars that underwrite post-enlightenment history, especially in terms of their presumption of a specifically post-enlightenment "transparent" self (da Silva, 2007) and their assumption that present struggles should be grounded in indicative claims about the past.

In Kadji Amin's terms, I offer up these feminist and gay liberationist histories of witchcraft as deidealized objects, ones that might be, as Amin conceptualizes it, "disturbing." This approach will require me to figure out how to read the indicative (or the asymptotically indicative) toward the subjunctive (modulating history into genealogy).[6] Amin cautions against queer theory's commitment to this destabilization as a temporary moment in the pursuit of more hopeful future; he hopes to make room in queer theory for "a new range of objects to materialize before the critical and theoretical gaze" (31). Amin is interested in objects that disturb the field imaginary of queer theory and its political attachments. And while what I offer in this chapter will not be the kind of patient analysis of a field's current discourse that Amin and Wiegman, among others, have done, I do hope it is a provocation to think about the ways feminist and queer theory are sometimes emplotted within enlightenment and colonialist grammars which structure debates about intersectionality, the state, and temporality.

I take *Witches, Midwives, and Nurses, Witchcraft and the Gay Counterculture*, and *Dreaming the Dark* to be both what Elizabeth Freeman calls "doing history badly" (2019, 103) and "erotohistoriography" (2010). In these texts, we see a historiography that *tends* toward the indicative but ultimately *fails* even as it makes the past's subjunctive saturation of the present *felt*.[7] These texts help me to conceptualize a queer erotics of the more-than-human world as an ethics of resisting state capture (requiring forms of educational relations that don't take place in schools[8]), by making available the *felt*, subjunctive— virtual—potentiality of such resistance across queer temporalities.[9] This feeling is muted by the texts' indicative tendencies, but they are not entirely unavailable precisely because they fail. These contradictions allow me to follow Tituba in trying to read *through* "witchcraft" to the "energies" attending that concept in these books, energies that animate endarkenment esoterisms, or the co-composition of knowledge practices and more-than-human socialities tending away from Man.

Most obviously, these books' failure adheres in their citational and rhetorical inclination toward sweeping, indicative claims about the past. These claims are often indirectly, but sometimes very directly, supported by citing the work of Margaret Murray, the British Egyptologist whose work after World War I proposed, against a dominant framing of witch trials as an expression of cultural hysteria or irrationality, that the trial evidence reveals the *empirical* existence of large networks of women practicing vestigial goddess religions. Murray's work—which inspires the feminist and gay liberationist texts I engage here as well as an enormous amount of cultural production around "witchcraft" in the twentieth century—was subjected to a scathing "frontal attack" by historians beginning in the late 1960s (Gaskill 2010, 25).[10] While this attack came entirely from within the indicative, homogenizing logics of academic historiography, my critique is somewhat adjacent to theirs in that we agree Murray's uncertain, subjunctive archive is (inappropriately) indicativized by her (and in incredibly homogenizing gestures that flatten differences among socialities), presenting speculation about a widespread network of goddess religion practitioners as historical fact. The difference is that historians object to her indicativized statements based on insufficient evidence and scholarly rigor, and I am trying to think dis-oriented from in- dicativization as a logic. (Put in Faivre's terms, historians think Murray is not invested enough in concordance; I think we shouldn't be invested in it at all.) Much of the late twentieth-century witchcraft discourse relies upon work that most professional historians dispute or reject. This pulls these indicative "nonfiction" histories toward the subjunctive, toward fiction, toward a kind of speculative plotting of other worlds.

Before turning to the texts, I want to directly sketch some of the stakes of my engagement with feminist witchcraft projects by turning to *White Magic* (2021), where Elissa Washuta, a member of the Cowlitz tribe, thinks through her relationship as an Indigenous feminist to the titular white magic, under- stood as a racializing formation. She writes of an internet scandal:

> Not long ago, the witches got upset on the internet. Sephora was going to sell as "starter witch kit"—tarot cards, sage, rose quartz, perfume—and the witches thought it was wrong for the makeup store to peddle spiritual tools alongside pore refiners. As a Native woman and an occult enthusiast, I had an opinion. I had an opinion about a Macklemore video interview in which a non-Native astrologer teaches him to burn white sage, a tradi- tional medicine for California Native peoples; in the wild, it's threatened by non-Native overharvesting. I had an opinion when I saw an Instagram promoted post featuring a pentagram dream catcher beside the text of a "Good Luck Spell" and tagged #witch #wicca, and anything close. (4)

This passage does a few important things. First, it signals a general femi- nist discomfort with the commoditization of witchcraft, a discomfort that appears around a sense that such corporate promotion appropriates, inappropriately, witchy signifiers and materials. But Washuta then stages her discomfort with *that* discomfort, underscoring indirectly how much that feminist critique disavows its own appropriative logics. These logics are not, for Washuta, simply questions of "cultural appropriation"; they also directly concern the material relations that sustain worlds. Non-Native (white or settler) witchcraft's appropriation of white sage is relationally implicated in, or even responsible for, the dismantling of Indigenous socialities. The word "overharvesting" signals—in a linguistic resonance with Wynter's use of "overrepresentation"—the violence of homogenization and its intimate ties to extractivist capitalism. In presuming that everything is available to them for use, colonialist witchcrafts, even feminist ones, participate in the material politics of elimination, which is to say they actively contribute to the *disruption* of enduring Indigenous socialities. White magic here is settler magic, colonialist magic: these esoteric practices tend the colonial world, which is to say participate in its ongoingness as historical force. The problem isn't simply the corporate use of witchcraft, but the ways that "witchcraft" is always caught up in appropriative, homogenizing logics, even, or perhaps *especially*, when witches strive to "include" other esoteric practices or protect "their" witchcraft from corporate fetishism. As Washuta forcibly puts it, "I just want a version of the occult that isn't built on plunder, but I suspect that if we could excise the stolen pieces, there would be nothing left" (5).

In 1979, Audre Lorde wrote a public letter to Mary Daly after the publication of the radical feminist *Gyn/Ecology: The Metaethics of Radical Feminism*. Lorde begins by referring to a spate of murders of Black women at the time, before expressing a kind of regret that an in-person meeting between her and Daly hadn't taken place, and offering Daly some well wishes for the success of the book. This is followed, relatively quickly, by Lorde describing a kind of affective turn accompanying her reading of the book:

> When I started reading *Gyn/Ecology*, I was truly excited by the vision behind your words and nodded my head as you spoke in your First Passage of myth and mystification. Your words on the nature and function of the Goddess, as well as the ways in which her face has been obscured, agreed with what I myself have discovered in my searches through African myth/legend/religion for the true nature of old female power.
>
> So I wondered, why doesn't Mary deal with Afrekete as an example? Why are her goddess images only white, western european, judeo-christian?

Where was Afrekete, Yemanje, Oyo, and Mawulisa? Where were the warriror goddesses of Vodun, the Dahomeian Amazons and warrior-women of Dan? Well, I thought, Mary has made a conscious decision to narrow her scope and to deal only with the ecology of western european women. (2007, 67)

While the examples listed by Lorde would seem to suggest the problem is a lack of inclusion and exclusion, one of the aims of this chapter is to think through how homogenizing, indicative accounts of witchcraft would still enact colonial violence if they did engage such figures as Lorde notes. That is, Lorde notes that Daly homogenizes "women" into a category in a way that doesn't think differ-ence within that category (the difference generated precisely by homogeniza-tion), let alone move toward thinking outside of the dominant grammatical categories of enlightenment logic (70). One effect of this is that the knowledges and socialities of Black women enter Daly's frame only to lend authority to claims about victimization (Daly quotes Lorde "to introduce your chapter on African genital mutilation," when "my words which you used were no more, nor less, illustrative of any of this chapter than "Poetry is Not a Luxury" or my other poems might have been of many other parts of *Gyn/Ecology*" [68]). No matter how you frame it, inclusion, not just the lack of it, is colonialist.

Between Washuta and Lorde, I am trying to feel out how the mirrored problems of cultural appropriation and a lack of inclusion both make sense as problems within a specific grammar of world, one that I follow Wynter in seeing as dominant in the post-1492 moment. That is, I specifically think the problem adheres in how such histories as Daly's and the kinds of practices Washuta worries over are the results of a presumption of a specific kind of self at work in "occult" practices and in "feminist" politics. Denise Ferreira da Silva (2007) has called this the transparent, self-determined self that organizes colonial grammars of history and politics. Wynter calls it Man. Specifically, this self is liberal: bounded, individual, self-same, volitional, and rational. This self exists autonomously "in" a world (or in *the* world) and so in these feminist accounts of witchcraft what we often find is magic understood as a modality of helping a liberal self assert its will in mastering some part of the world (Singh 2018).

But I want to amplify feminist witchcraft's ambivalent relationship to this notion of self by attending to Starhawk's definition of magic as "*the art of changing consciousness at will*" (1982, 13). This definition, of course, fits within a tradition of feminist "consciousness-raising" that decades of feminists of color and queer feminists (and others) have pointed out could be modulated toward the articulation of cisgender white feminism as the presumptive subject of the feminist project even as it holds decolonial and abolitionist potential. The issue, here, is precisely how we locate the "will" that is grammatically appended to change via the preposition "at." While this formulation might be read as presuming precisely the transparent self da Silva sees as the subject of coloniality, we might instead read this will as arriving from elsewhere, from outside the self. More specifically, this will might be read as the affective force of a world, or worlds, which arrives to the encounter in the form, or pattern, of its (more-than-human) participants. Magic might be the agentic modulation of consciousness, but the agencies involved come from far beyond anything that might be a "self."

If selves are the durable but dissipative patterns created by distributed, more-than-human, and spiritual agencies, then we might need to imagine genders and sexualities not as properties of bodies but as more-than-human patterning in worlds or situations.[11] Ultimately, I think this has tremendous bearing on conversations about the reception of 1970s or "second-wave" texts in our present moment, where we have to ask "what historical feminisms *do* in the present when we remember, study, or otherwise enliven them" (McKinney 2020, 25). To begin to stage this question, we might look no further than goddess religions' notorious understanding of the feminine. Starhawk writes, "The importance of the Goddess symbol for women cannot be overstressed" (1999, 34), going on to argue males need the goddess, too, "because women give birth to males, *and* nurture them at the breast, and in our culture are primarily responsible for their care as children" (34). It feels overdetermined in my present moment to read sentences like this as the expression of essentialism at both the biological and cultural levels. Whether anchored in biology or in cultural practice, recent feminist, queer, and trans work has posited that biologized binary sex difference is always already a racializing, colonialist move.[12] At the same time, as A. J. Lewis has argued, with reference to an archive that includes Starhawk, "inasmuch as these writings appealed to the mystical, cosmic, or geological feminine powers as animating forces, today, they may evoke unsophisticated reifications of essentialism. And yet far from dematerializing or supplanting the complexity of the subject, these practices fomented an intensely deterritorialized and permeable self" (n.d., 7). As I read these texts subjunctively, I am trying to feel out precisely this knotty mess, where tendencies to presume and prop up enlightenment selves and histories are entangled with tendencies toward endarkenment temporalities and causalities, where more-than-human modes of sociality might even inform what Lewis calls feminist witchcraft's conceptualization of "self-loss" (13) *as* feminist agentic capacity.

Knowledge, Care, and the Problem of the Self: *Witches, Midwives, and Nurses*

Barbara Ehrenreich and Dierdre English's pamphlet situates its arguments in a frame that, anticipating Michel Foucault's famous definition a few years later, is resolutely biopolitical: "Political and economic monopolization of medicine meant control over its institutional organizations, its theory and practice, its profits and prestige. And the stakes are even higher today, when total control of medicine means potential power to determine who will live and who will die, who is fertile and who is sterile, who is 'mad' and who is sane" (2010, 28). Ehrenreich and English thus situate care, especially medical care, and attention to biopolitical state power as foci that accompany the question of witchcraft; this is, for me, the most important contribution of their work for my thinking about esoterism. As I work to draw out some of the contours of this linking of care and attention to state power—a field of struggle I want to designate as the erotic biopolitics of tending—I don't downplay three things about the pamphlet that strike me as tending toward colonial grammars. The first is their indicative—which is to say homogenizing—attention to history. I want to raise this concern by asking about what presumptively links their first two chapters on the history of early modern witches and the founding of the American Medical Association in the antebellum United States a century or two later. My second concern hovers around the word "monopolization" in the quote above. Theirs would potentially be a version of the claim I make in this book about the political necessity of rejecting homogenization toward a proliferation of worlds and more-than-human socialities, but the pamphlet suggests that their concern is less with a monopolization of erotic biopolitics per se than a critique of how that field has been monopolized by men and patriarchy. In other words, they lean in toward a politics of inclusion that would (significantly) reconfigure the homogenized field, but not disrupt its unifying grammars. And finally, I want to attend to how their work presumes, and then retroactively maps onto early modern witches, a specifically empirical, enlightenment self as willful, knowing subject, both of knowledge production and political governmentality.

"The women's health movement of today," write Ehrenreich and English, "has ancient roots in the medieval covens, and its opponents have as their ancestors those who ruthlessly forced the elimination of witches" (33). The present is here indicatively linked to the past—an ontological postulate attending the simple past verb "has"—in such a way that the present is an outgrowth of these "ancient roots." The past emerges as a site that not only grounds, through indicative truth claims, the correctness of their present political aims, but those aims are simultaneously rendered traditional, "ancient." The witches, as an indicative instance of what we might call feminist empirical science, become necessary primarily for the way they lend a patina of tradition to the women's health movement.

The pamphlet turns to witch hunts to offer an account of how at a moment of fundamental reconfiguration of the economies of Europe, institutions of patriarchal authority—church and state—sought ways of attacking, disqualifying, and criminalizing traditional forms of feminine knowledge.[13] For Ehrenreich and English, the witch hunts must be understood as specifically *masculinist* violence: "Three central accusations emerge repeatedly in the history of witchcraft throughout northern Europe: First, witches are accused of every conceivable sexual crime against men. Quite simply, they are 'accused' of female sexuality. Second, they are accused of being organized. Third, they are accused of having magical powers effecting health—of harming, but also of healing. They were often charged specifically with possessing medical and obstetric skills" (39). On Ehrenreich and English's reading, this patriarchal attack on women's knowledge was motivated, paradoxically, by governing institutions' fear of empiricism. For the men in charge of such institutions, "the witch was an empiricist: she relied on her senses rather than on faith or doctrine, she believed in trial and error, and cause and effect" (48). Here, witches are interpreted as forerunners of enlightenment, secular science, in contrast to the church which "was deeply anti-empirical" (48). The pamphlet thus sets up a reversal of popular history which tends to see the state as the site of rationality and witchcraft as superstitious unreason, and the authors' valorization of witches works precisely by mobilizing readers' presumed commitments to empirical rationality. In a move that prefigures many contemporary more-than-human materialisms, we are asked to think seriously about how witches understood matter and care precisely because they were *more scientific* than the contemporary "medical" knowledges circulating in official institutions of governance. But this same move is where the presumption of the post-enlightenment self is most at play, for we are asked to think of feminist witchcraft as the knowledge production of liberal, knowing selves who can use that knowledge to masterfully intervene in the world's becoming.

The account of the statal war on witchcraft is presumptively linked, across a chapter break, to a question Ehrenreich and English answer in detail in chapter 2: "How did one particular set of healers, who happened to be male, white, and middle class, manage to oust all the competing folk healers, midwives, and other practitioners who dominated the American medical scene in the early 1800s?" (62).[14] Their account focuses on a shift from lay-practitioners (often women, Indigenous people, or former slaves, but also including those who would come to be called "snake oil salesmen") toward a narrowly educated and credentialed profession. A crucial moment in this history was the founding of the American Medical Association (AMA) in 1848. This organization consolidated male power over and against traditional female knowledges and practices, working to ensure that hospitals hired "qualified" male doctors. The demand for credentials certifying competency led to the founding of the first US medical school at Johns Hopkins in 1893. By the turn of the century, the Carnegie Foundation was pouring millions of dollars into medical schools, provided that schools met certain criteria. As Ehrenreich and English put it, "The conditions were clear: conform to the Johns Hopkins model or close" (82). Abraham Flexner, the staff member of the Carnegie Foundation who inspected medical schools, pushed, in 1910, for the closure of many medical schools, including six out of the eight existing Black medical schools. Thanks to the work of this new, foundation-supported credentialing model, "medicine had become a white, male, middle-class profession" (84).

The emergence of the "white, male, middle-class profession" undoubtedly happens through disqualifying and dismantling midwifery and other care practices, but given the trajectory of the book, one wonders what this has to do with the witch hunts explored in chapter 1; what intervenes in the hundred or so years elided by the chapter break (and the accompanying narrowing of focus from European and North American framing to a US-specific one) that requires a repetition of the old struggle between "opponents"? I raise this question not to attempt an answer, but to mark how much the pamphlet presumes readers will fill in based on their indicative assertion of the factual connection between the two moments. Ehrenreich and English note that around 1910, half of all US births were delivered by midwives and "most were blacks or working class immigrants" (85). Their interest here is the capture of maieutics from women as part of the expansion of hospitalization, which had the effect of both shifting authority to men (or, better: Man), and of capturing birth within institutions fueled by capitalist expropriation and accumulation. Giving birth would, from this moment until the expansion of feminist self-care politics driven by consciousness-raising and a politiciza-tion of medical care,[15] be an occasion overseen by men that generates profits for doctors, hospitals, and insurance companies. Thus, in the conclusion to the pamphlet, Ehrenreich and English write: "Our enemy is not just 'men' or their individual male chauvinism: it is the whole class system which en-abled male, upper-class healers to win out and which forced us into subser-vience. Institutional sexism is sustained by a class system which supports male power" (100).

Whiteness, named in the pamphlet's analysis of the AMA's founding, is absent from this *theoretical* claim about what the "enemy" is, which tends toward an analysis of patriarchy delinked from coloniality and thus incapable of or disinterested in asking questions about the grammars of personhood that link those fields (Perry 2018). In the space opened up by this elision, I see questions about how the gendered politics of health care intersect with racial biocapitalism, since, as Alys Eve Weinbaum argues, "it behooves us to recognize that we cannot fully comprehend biocapitalism unless we examine its relationship to slavery as a way of knowing and being in the world" (2019, 14). This means that we need to shift our understanding of how race, class, sex, gender, and sexuality relate, not seeing race in terms of addition to critical approaches foregrounding class or gender, but instead beginning from the insight that "not only gender but also the physiological category of sex are variegations of race and effects of racial biopower" (Schuller 2017, 18). This queer of color insight shifts the analytical parameters of attention to the poli-tics of reproductive labor and care, refusing to begin with the supposition of binary gender and a whole host of assumptions about nature and biology that sometimes attend that binarism.[16] And in the same gesture, such an analysis refuses the structural whiteness—the colonial grammar—that subtends and enables "biological" concepts of binary sex and gender difference. As C. Riley Snorton has argued, "the emphasis on civility between physicians evinces, at least in part, the manner with which the AMA conceptualized the role of medical practice as a form of civilizing work not incompatible with slavery's regime of sovereign biopower" (2017, 28). Taking this seriously would open up a more complex way to consider how Ehrenreich and English's history of witchcraft as feminist (health) care could be subjunctively elaborated in more explicitly abolitionist and decolonial directions through a reconfig-ured attention to differential (de)humanization.[17] The witch consigned to burn was not seen as inhuman or less-than-human in the same way that the chattel slave or the vanishing Native[18] were, but we might hear Zakiayyah

Iman Jackson's claim that "gender, maternity, and sexuality are central to the autopoiesis of racialized animalization that philosophers, theoreticians, and historians of race hope to displace" (2020, 5). Health care—including healing and midwifery—is a field of racial biopower and needs to be theorized as such. What Ehrenreich and English call "witchcraft" is one of that field's discursive patterns.

Witches, Midwives, and Nurses ambivalently rejects *and* tends (toward) enlightenment rationality. Their critique of a "class system which supports male power" invites readers to recognize how that system has been inappropriately configured by the power dynamics of gender instead of the empirical rationality which would better guide it. They write, "it was not science that enabled men to win out: the critical battles took place long before the development of modern scientific technology" (28). "Witchcraft" for them is "a more human, empirical approach to healing" (27) than what is offered by statal-patriarchal medicine. A feminist politics of care, for them, offers the possibility of a better, more empirical, more rational approach to reproductive labor. "Witchcraft" and "science" come close to being synonymous, or, more specifically, both turn out to be actual expressions of the same virtual, subjunctive field that modulates practices of knowing: "Her magic was the science of her time" (48). As masculinist, statal medicine emerges, it articulates knowing in the most masterful possible way (in large part because of its colonialist imbrications, although they don't note this). While the Women's Health Movement had aims that assumed the possibility of women's inclusion within existing medical institutions and reform from inside (thus setting the conditions for what Michelle Murphy has called "protocol feminism"[19]), Ehrenreich and English don't just suggest a reversal of control in gendered institutions (from a men's science to a women's science), they also suggest the need for a genealogical account of the emergence of nursing and medicine as concepts (which are material configurations of worlding). Witchcraft, in contrast, is more committed to intimacy, vulnerability, and care. Their witchcraft may be, then, a euphemism for feminist science.

While I think there are ways situated scientific practices might be modulated toward esoterisms, I want to underscore how anchoring care politics in the post-enlightenment subject tends (toward) coloniality. Da Silva writes: "When rewriting reason as the secular regulative force acting on every existing thing, the framers of science transform nature into the holdings of a power that acts solely as law, that is, as universal *nomos*" (2007, 47). This amplifies two things about Ehrenreich and English's conception of witchcraft as feminist science: it codes witchcraft, by being empirical, as a protosecularist project detached from spirituality. Concomitantly, it imagines the nonhuman world as governed by natural law that is managed by knowing, self-determined subjects, which is to say, mastered (Singh 2018). Empiricism, in this sense, tends to think worlding through detached vision instead of intimacy and touch, even if it is committed to the a posteriori. (Knowledges are always materially erotic participation in worlds, even if their discourses disavow this.) Da Silva argues: "Not only is the knowing subject now interested in what it gathers with the senses, in experience, that is, the confused and contingent happenings of the world of things; it conceives of these events as the manifold particular effects of general causes, the laws of nature, the forced deployed by the rational (divine) will" (47). The evental becoming of worlds is reduced by empiricism to a set of effects of general, knowable laws in a world (singular) that can be controlled (in scalable ways[20]) by the post-enlightenment subject. Which is to say, empiricism is oriented in and toward a homogeneous, Man-centric world.

Erotics and Abolition: *Witchcraft and the Gay Counterculture*

If *Witches, Midwives, and Nurses* turns to the history of witchcraft to authorize a feminist politics of care and reproductive labor for the Women's Health Movement, *Witchcraft and the Gay Counterculture* is driven by a more general "revolutionary" political praxis tied to queer desire. This project is most clearly articulated at the end of the book, when Evans offers an explanation of why liberal reformism and socialist takeover of industry fail as revolutionary projects: "Whenever any socialist society deliberately undertakes to industrialize itself, it immediately comes under tremendous pressure toward state capitalism" (143). Instead of either reforming or seizing control of state institutions, "We look toward the passing away of the state, the church, the university, the large corporation, the prison, the mental hospital, and all other institutions that rob people of the meaning of life. . . . There is no reason in the nature of things why these practices and institutions should be part of human experience" (150). This queer, anarchist vision pitched toward "stop[ping] the patriarchy" (148) is grounded in an account of human life outside of institutional capture, and Evans turns to witchcraft for historical evidence that such politics are available to animate present and future struggles for the abolition of statal institutions. The book thus seems split between, on one hand, the desire to imagine erotic worlds outside of institutional capture and the homogenizations we associate with statal violence, and, on the other, a tendency to think with indicative claims about history that homogenize the past into the ground of the present. One corollary of this is that Evans also tends to imagine freedom in individual terms, thinking of subjects (including the gay subject) within the grammars of post-enlightenment world. To put a finer point on it, Evans's queer anarchism is one that might exist within the world as a universalizing field, not one that disintegrates world into esoteric worlds beyond colonial capture.

The account Evans offers largely takes as its point of departure the stat-ist, Christian, imperial war against this field of queerly erotic ethics. He cites Samuel Angus who claims that once the Greco-Roman, Christian state began to take form, "copulation itself became a sin. . . . Matter was looked upon as evil or as the seat of the evil principle" (cited in Evans, 52). This denigration of sexuality and, indeed, of matter itself was part of a larger imperial project of stamping out older, pre-Christian worldviews and religions, especially the polytheistic ones. According to Evans, "Followers of the old religion lived rural lives in direct dependence on nature and felt a sense of community with all plant and animal life" (88). Unlike later imperial formations that set learning apart from this sociality, "both ancient pagans and later witches were learned people, possessing a vast storehouse of knowledge about herbs, plants, animals, signs of the weather, astronomy, and medicine. This knowledge, along with their myths and poetry, was transmitted by word of mouth from one generation to the next. Learning was thus a matter of close personal dialogue" (89).

This account, while undoubtedly romanticized, is crucial because it en-courages us to think about how forms of education relate to forms of life. Pedagogical contact and experiences of learning *can* be immanent in the social field, part of the ongoing, intra-active becoming of the world. Evans thus allows us to conceive of education in terms of tending in a capacious sense that gestures toward the endurance of social formations (which are al-ways more-than-human), modulation of attention as an ontoepistemological matter, and haptic, erotic care practices. The move to abstract learning from sociality in institutions like schools and universities is not only a way of creat-ing conditions for a homogenized yet highly stratified world, it also mutilates knowledge by sundering it from the endurance and flourishing of specific ways of (more-than-human) life.[21] In Evans's account, these ways of life are structured by (queer) sensuality: "Living in this way, early rural pagans and later medieval witches viewed their sensuality as the key to who they were as people, and not as some kind of low-level crud to be scraped off their souls.

Their very survival depended on being in touch with their bodies and knowing how to communicate with plants and animals. As a result, theirs was an enchanted world, the world of natural feelings" (95).

This "enchanted world" is, of course, precisely what contemporary feminist and new materialist thinkers like Silvia Federici (2019) and Jane Bennett (2001) would like to reclaim. For Bennett, this is about "an Epicurean picture of the world as a lively and endless flow of molecular events, where matter is animate without necessarily being animated by divine will or intent" (2001, 14). They tend to think of this "re-enchantment" in terms of epistemological projects, political theories, and reproductive labor, and while Evans is clearly thinking in the same general direction, his focus on specifically "gay" counterculture leads him to a critique of reproductive logics: "The industrial system has reduced sex to a productive activity, just as it reduces all functions to productive activities. Under industrialism, the purpose of sex has become purely economic: to breed consumers, workers, and soldiers for their proper roles in industrial and military hierarchies. Sexual relations have been reduced to productive relations. The basic unit of people-production is the monogamous heterosexual family" (132).[22] Evans's critique of marriage here resonates with Marxist-Feminist analysis, although without their sustained attention to matters of reproductive labor, even as it attends to what Adrienne Rich soon called, in 1980, "compulsory heterosexuality."

But the phrase "industrial system" doesn't seem to account for how some precapitalist societies also reined in sexual relations through family and kinship assemblages. Gaye Rubin's 1975 "The Traffic in Women" offers a more nuanced take, noting that "if sexism is a byproduct of capitalism's relentless appetite for profit, then sexism would wither away in the advent of a successful socialist revolution" (2012b, 33). Rubin's survey of work in anthropology, psychoanalysis, and political economy makes her far less sanguine about this conditional politics than Evans seems to be, since (as other Marxist-Feminists have also noted) male supremacist social formations precede capitalist ones and function at least semi-independently. While Evans is not wrong about the ways sexual relations are policed (Rubin's "Thinking Sex" from 1982 (2012a) still stands as one of the most crucial texts on this problem), his emphasis on "the industrial system" gives too much priority to a narrowly Marxist frame here, especially when one of *Witchcraft and the Gay Counterculture*'s larger projects is thinking about the present by constructing a history stretching back to matriarchal social formations that predate heteropatriarchal ones.[23] Evans (inconsistently) reduces the gender, sexual, and racial dynamics of kinship biopolitics to the problems of class-based, capitalist mode of industrial production.[24] Beyond this conceptual waffling creating some problems for his chronology and causalities, it creates uncertainty about what exactly Evans means by abolition as the proper goal of "gay counterculture" politics. Is the target the industrial system? Christianity? The state? Patriarchy? Some confluence of all of those? Rather than critique Evans's uncertainty, I want to subjunctively amplify it, proposing that, without being able to articulate it on his presumptive grid of colonial historicity, Evans's text makes available the *feeling* that feminist and queer tending might ultimately involve nothing less than the abolition of Man.

In *The Undercommons*, Stefano Harney and Fred Moten propose, via Ruth Wilson Gimore and Frantz Fanon, just such a conception of abolition as the scrambling and rearticulation of the homogenizing grammar of singular world. They write:

Ruth Wilson Gilmore: "Racism is the state-sanctioned and/or extralegal production and exploitation of group differentiated vulnerability to premature (social, civil and/or corporeal) death." What is the difference between this and slavery? What is, so to speak, the object of abolition? Not so much the abolition of prisons but of a society that could have prisons, that could have slavery, that could have the wage, and therefore not abolition as the elimination of anything but abolition as the founding of a new society. (2013, 42)

At the nexus of Harney and Moten's subjunctive abolitionism—where prison, slavery, and the wage intersect—we find Man, the post-enlightenment self that can only be articulated within a homogenized, colonial world (da Silva 2007; Hartman 1997; Wynter 2003).

For Evans, "witchcraft" names the scattered fragments of prestatal practices that have endured through centuries of patriarchy and colonialism; to articulate this claim, he has to be affected by something exceeding indicative understandings of "witchcraft," a subjunctive excess I am calling esoterism. The book makes available less a thick description of an indicative nonstatal society that could function as a model for guiding social administration, and more a feeling that ways of living entirely otherwise might be possible. To act toward abolition, we need not have an empirically available prestatal social "fact" as authorization, but we cannot do without the erotic feeling of its possibility, which is tied, for Evans, to a feeling of more-than-human sociality that he calls the "enchanted" world.

While Evans is deeply invested in offering a communist, more-than-human, erotic, and spiritual conception of social life, he continues to situate the human and its "culture" as existing within a natural surround—what da Silva calls "the universal *nomos*": he calls for the "creation of a post-Industrial communist nature-society where Gay culture can flourish free from repression and exploitation" (151). Despite the proximity here to a thinking of what Latour and Haraway would call "nature-cultures," the grammar of Evans's claim situates "Gay culture" as happening *in* a wider context associated with nature. This imagines a very different relationality between human subjects and nature (one that foregrounds erotic biopolitics), but it doesn't think about purportedly human selves as *expressions* or *effects* of that wider more-than-human sociality.

Erotics, Immanence, and Processual Worlding: *Dreaming the Dark*

For Starhawk, constructing an indicative history of witchcraft and magical practice matters because it anchors the ongoing worldbuilding project of the Reclaiming covens in and around San Francisco. She is thus highly attentive to how social formations institutionalize (or formalize) educational practices geared toward particular worldviews and ontoepistemologies. While Ehrenreich and English's project (which Starhawk affirmatively cites) was largely one of feminist reform of medical institutions and practice, and Evans's thrust was more anarchist in its refusal to imagine futures structured around existing statal institutions, Starhawk is most concerned with cultivating alternative forms of social and spiritual relationality. Unlike the other two texts I've considered here, Starhawk's book is not simply a critique of the existing world that calls for feminist repair, nor is it a manifesto that dreams of queer, anarchist politics. It is, instead, one statement in a now decades-long project of emergent coven-building, centered in San Francisco, California. Starhawk is interested in a project of collective worldmaking that is ongoing, pragmatic, and attuned to the complex realities of people coming to the Reclaiming covens with different "conditions of arrival."[25] In important ways, Starhawk's processual worldbuilding relies on rituals—anticipating many of the questions I raise in chapter 4, "Ceremony"—that link knowledging and the endurance (the tending) of a bounded sociality (the coven). In this sense, Starhawk comes closest of all the books in this chapter to articulating what I am calling esoterisms as the co-composition of knowledge practices and more-than-human sociality. But attending to that requires that I also feel out the ways her project simultaneously participates in the tending of homogenizing coloniality. This is most legible, again, in the ways her indicative account of history presumptively grounds Reclaiming witchcraft as "traditional" and in the ways her sustained attention to the problematics of sex and gender obscure the force of colonial grammars authorizing sex difference *as* part of racial biopower. This latter clicks into focus in her 1999 preface to the twentieth anniversary edition of *The Spiral Dance*, where she directly addresses the problem of inclusion.

The Spiral Dance (1979) offers an overview of the history of witchcraft that is almost identical to the one offered by Evans, which is in turn an elaboration of Murray's project. Alongside this history are chapters that develop, in a sometimes tense relationship with Gerald Gardner's development of Wicca starting in the 1950s,[26] a theological and philosophical—that is, a *spiritual*—account of goddess religion. Most of the book is kind of grimoire of rites and rituals, some solitary but many requiring communal, collective performance. *Dreaming the Dark* (1982) expands on the theological and philosophical elaboration, and adds many chapters in the second half of the book explicitly about the group governance processes of Reclaiming covens in and around San Francisco. Starhawk writes that "witchcraft can be seen as a religion of ecology" ([1979] 1999, 35), and this is immediately apparent in the covens' participation in antinuclear and other forms of social activism in the 1970s and 1980s. In the twentieth anniversary introduction to *The Spiral Dance*, Starhawk writes, "In spite of fears by some political feminists that interest in the Goddess would divert energy from political work, Pagans and Witches have accrued a proud record of involvement in feminist issues, gay liberation, and antinuclear, antiwar, and environmental campaigns" (1999, 7).[27] I want to think about how her philosophico-theological outline of Reclaiming witchcraft as a version of traditional goddess religion dramatizes the complexity that attends "witchcraft" as a concept that only appears where coloniality encounters esoterisms, and offers us, subjunctively, a kind of "spiritual activism" (Anzaldúa 2015, 19) that might animate what I think of as endarkenment tending.

The key terms governing Starhawk's account are "estrangement" and "immanence." For her, "Estrangement is the culmination of a long historical process. Its roots lie in the Bronze-Age shift from matrifocal, earth-centered cultures whose religions centered on the Goddess and Gods embodied in nature, to patriarchal urban cultures of conquest, whose Gods inspired and supported war" (1982, 5). Drawing explicitly on Karl Marx's concept of alienation, Starhawk writes: "I call this consciousness *estrangement* because its essence is that we do not see ourselves as part of the world. We are strangers to nature, to other human beings, to parts of ourselves. We see the world as made up of separate, isolated, nonliving parts that have no inherent value" (5). The concept of immanence counters this, almost term for term; it is described as "the awareness of the world and everything in it as alive, dynamic, interdependent, interacting, and infused with moving energies: a living being, a weaving dance" (9).

Although Starhawk does not cite Gilles Deleuze or Michel Foucault here (her philosophico-political references are largely to 1970s radical feminist theory), her use of "immanence" comes very close to the way that term was used in the radical French philosophies circulating around May 1968.[28] In *The History of Sexuality Volume 1*, for instance, Foucault writes, "It seems to me that power must be understood in the first instance as the multiplicity of force relations immanent in the sphere in which they operate and which constitute their own organization" (92). While Foucault's account hardly precludes this sort of reading,[29] it's important to underscore immediately that this is not merely a question of *human* relations. Jane Bennett's extension of Bruno Latour's "thing-power" in *Vibrant Matter* offers one of the more influential articulations of this "new materialist" proposition, shifting her understanding of power and agency to reconfigure even "human power [as] itself a kind of thing-power" (10). As it was for Starhawk, the human comes to be felt as part of nature or, more precisely, matter, understood not as "nonliving" (to return to Starhawk's word) but as vibrant and vital: "We *are* vital materiality and we are surrounded by it, though we do not always see it that way" (Bennett 2010, 14). For Starhawk—like Deleuze, Foucault, and Bennett—the entire world is animate (with differential capacities for agency; there is what Mel Chen has called an "animacy hierarchy" [2012]). And yet the present social arrangement—the one based on estrangement—works in manifold ways to disavow the consciousness of immanence.

For Starhawk, "Goddess religion, at its heart, is precisely about the erotic dance of life playing all through nature and culture" (1999, 20). Indeed, following Lorde's "The Use of the Erotic," Starhawk situates her account of the sensuous by distinguishing the erotic from the pornographic largely along the same lines of estrangement versus immanence. She writes, "In the empty world of the machine, when religious strictures fall away, sex becomes another arena of performance, another commodity to be bought and sold. The erotic becomes the pornographic; women are seen as objects empty of value except when they can be used. The sexual arena becomes one of domination, charged with rage, fear, and violence" (1982, 9). The present social world offers up, we might say, a highly particular configuration of sensuality—shot through with masculinist violence—as the whole of the "sexual," and witchcraft is part of a feminist project of attuning instead to the much wider world of erotics that surrounds and subtends the "estranged" (mal)formation.

For Starhawk, the shift from sexuality to erotics isn't just about a different way of conceptualizing human "bodies and pleasures" (to use Foucault's famous phrase), but is about a significant shift in understanding what a "human" is in relation to a more-than-human world of vital materiality. For her, witchcraft is "a religion of experience, of ritual, of practices that change consciousness and awaken power-from-within. Beneath all, it is a religion of connection with the Goddess, who is immanent in nature, in human beings, in relationships" (xii). This consciousness is the consciousness of a "bond" that the word "immanence," and its synonym "goddess," signals: "That bond, that deep connection, was the source of life—human, plant, animal, and spiritual. Without it, nothing could grow. From the power within that relationship came the ability to heal, to divine the future, to build, to create, to make songs, to birth children, to build culture. The bond was erotic, sensual, carnal, because the activities of the flesh were not separate from the spirit immanent in life" (xii). This "bond" is therefore not simply a psychic attachment: it is a material-semiotic web that constitutes the world from which any particular entity emerges and endures. And this emergence and endurance is conceptualized as *dance*. It is this erotic bond that courses through nature—and, although Starhawk doesn't go this far, through humans as a particular configuration of nature—and which names, for Starhawk, precisely what Bennett calls "vital materiality."

The politics of this erotics are sketched by Starhawk in the very next paragraph, where she posits that the sixteenth and seventeenth century witch hunts constituted one of the most dramatic and violent moments in the forced estrangement of people from this immanent, erotic bond. For her, the witch hunts "shattered the peasants' connection with the land, drove women out of the work of healing, and imposed the mechanist view of the world as a dead machine. That rupture underlines the entwined oppressions of race, sex, class, and ecological destruction" (xiii). Echoing the language of the Combahee River Collective Statement—which speaks of "interlocking oppressions" (2017, 15)—Starhawk proposes a conception of what we now call "intersectionality" that sees the intrahuman vectors of oppression (racism, sexism, and capitalism) as entirely entwined with extractive and destructive relations between humans and nonhumans.[30] And yet, in the context of the book, the rhetoric of Starhawk's list—beginning with "race" in its list of en-twined oppressions—seems to try to accomplish the work that the analysis largely avoids (the priority in sequence belies the text's "by addition race" approach). One could say that it's an attempt to solve a problem that adheres in the colonial grammar by shifting rhetoric (where one can ask about a list's climactic or anticlimactic sequencing, for example).

Starhawk's project would seem to want to rethink the human—and, cru-cially, bring that human into relationality with a more-than-human world that includes spirits—without articulating that subject beyond colonial gram-mars of the self. I suspect this problem has as much to do with the indicative tendency to think of history as the factual ground of the present as it does with its understanding of inclusion by addition within a settled grammatical field. Looking back at *The Spiral Dance* in a ten-year anniversary preface, Starhawk discusses the erotic in a paragraph and takes pains to distance herself from what now looks to her like an essentialist sex-gender binary at play in that early work. While I want to resummon here the theories of racial biopolitics I named above, I also note that Starhawk's more "inclusive" ac-count of the erotic works against human exceptionalism:

> Why are there two sexes? For the same reason we cut the cards before we shuffle the deck. Sexual reproduction is an elegant method of ensuring maximum biological diversity. Yet I would no longer describe the essential quality of the erotic energy flow that sustains the universe as one of female/male polarity. To do so enshrines heterosexual relationships as the basic pattern of all being, relegating other sorts of attraction and desire to the position of the deviant. That description not only makes invisible the reali-ties of lesbians, gay men, and bisexual people; it also cuts us off, whatever our sexual preference, from the intricate dance of energy and attraction we might share with trees, flowers, stone, the ocean, a good book or a painting, a sonnet or a sonata, a close friend or a faraway star. (1999, 20)

Starhawk exhibits an openness to moving away from philosophico-political positions, like an essentialist and binary understanding of sex, when those positions close down worlds that people interested in Reclaiming (and par-ticipating in the coven's) value. And it pushes the question of difference beyond the human toward "the intricate dance of energy and attraction" that is a world. But she also stops short of rethinking the sexed and gendered subject as the colonial subject, one consequence of which is a residual focus on sexual reproduction that elides how "reproduction is not a capacity located in sexed bodies" (Murphy 2012, 181), and that indeed most reproduction of biological (or "biocultural" [Frost 2016]) beings is asexual. Starhawk here encloses the erotic within the sexual despite other aspects of her thought that push against such enclosure.[31]

Still, in all its messiness, Starhawk's project allows us to feel the possibility of experimental, open-ended modes of education that refuse to be reduced to "universal" skills tied into the machinery of colonialist sorting, where this violence is only barely obscured by "meritocratic" rationality. Education can be esoteric worldmaking. The covens operate through specific methods of induction and initiation (1999, 38). While Reclaiming offers all interested parties opportunities for engagement, some of their communal and ceremonial practices are restricted. Rather than an exoteric education that offers "inclusion" to all (but only on condition of being subjected to the colonialist sorting of "life chances"), Reclaiming covens practice education as apprenticeship, where belonging is processual and conditional upon enduring, material care attachments.[32] This suggests that education—reoriented away from Man and its humanizing assemblages—could be thought and felt as a matter of specific, situated forms of more-than-human sociality that are processually composed in and by erotic knowledge practices that enact careful attention to a more-than-human world.

Thinking-Feeling through "Witchcraft" toward Endarkenment Esoterisms

Starhawk suggests that her practice of witchcraft is "akin in spirit, form, and practice to Native American and African religions" (1982, xii). As an indicative assertion, this is exactly the kind of homogenizing, colonialist claim that risks overrepresenting white "witchcraft" as if it were the whole of esoteric worlding. I am highly skeptical of the possibilities for settlers to think about the world from any particular Indigenous perspectives (in part because those perspectives are part of *land*), but I am trying to think about what it means to participate in decolonization as the abolition of Man.[33] If kinship could be articulated at the level of political orientation and haptic entanglements (that is, relations of care) instead of at the level of shared ontologies or ritual practices, kinship might not be something indicatively (and appropriatively) claimed but a subjunctive possibility that may guide (decolonial) tending. Against inclusion's homogenizing grammars, I want to move toward a consideration of esoterism that I have been trying to feel out *through* these histories of witchcraft. As I discussed more fully in the previous chapter, "witchcraft" is a term that appears in the colonial contact zone, where homogenizing enlightenment grammar encounters its constitutive outsides in other genres of existence, which means there is always a subjunctive (resistant and creative) excess attending the colonial grammaticalization.

If Haraway invites us to "make kin in lines of inventive connection as a practice of learning to live and die well with each other in a thick present" (Haraway 2016, 1), kinship might subjunctively name the political work of caring for each other in and as ways of living that arch toward decolonial futures. And this means caring for the borders that processually differentiate endarkenment, non-Man socialities too. We need to learn to be responsible to sociality-specific refusals to open practices to outsiders, such as when Marcus Briggs-Cloud writes, "Respecting the esoteric knowledge of Maskoke cosmology and medicine traditions, it would be unethical to expound on the subject here" (2020, 284). Esoterisms are not universally open or inclusive. They do not claim or strive to be universal in their applicability or truth claims. And affirming the pluriverse means affirming that some knowledges refuse my participation, or rather they invite my participation only insofar as they exhort me to tend my worlds in ways that do not diminish or disrupt these other worlds, these worlds that are not mine.

Discussing memories of such things of eating dirt, feeling waves, and noticing a piliated woodpecker, Anishinaabeg, Cree, and Métis scholar Melissa Nelson notes that "these eco-erotic moments make me feel connected to something outside and distant yet connected to my human skin" (2017, 230). While "these are encounters anyone can have anywhere on the planet" (231), Nelson moves from theorizing eco-erotics in general to the specificity of "Indigenous eco-erotics." In the more general sense—which refers to the commonality between Indigenous and esoteric practices—"eco-erotics is a type of *meta* (after, higher)-sexual or *trans* (over, beyond)-sexual intimate ecological encounter in which we are momentarily and simultaneously taken outside ourselves by the beauty, or sometimes the horror, of the more-than-human natural world. This means we are potentially aroused by *any*thing, meaning 'pan,' or all: pansexual" (230). This would seem to describe exactly what Starhawk calls the feeling of immanence associated with the goddess, or even what Bennett calls the feeling of "vital materiality." Indigenous eco-erotics, for Nelson, names a specific version of this wider set of practices, experiences, and affects: "Indigenous eco-erotics are maintained and strengthened through pansexual stories, clan and family identification, and a trans-human concept of nationhood" (232). In other words, Indigenous eco-erotics are always a matter of specific community and place via kinship understood as always already (an expression of) land. To anticipate the terms I will use in chapter 4, they are deictic.

A more-than-humanist, esoteric praxis that simply acknowledges its proximity with Indigenous thought (especially in general) runs an enormous risk of appropriation, especially if the thought in question "must be filtered through white intermediaries" in order "to be seen as credible" (Todd 2016, 11). There is, therefore, an obligation here for settlers such as myself to ask, in the words of Sebastian De Line, "How can one work with Indigenous philosophy who is not Indigenous without perpetuating appropriation?" (2016, 4). Many Indigenous theorists conceptualize land not as neutral space *on which* humans dwell with others, but as a way of naming the totality of life, which is to say "spirit" (Little Bear, cited in De Line 2016, 2), in all its internally differentiated manifestations shot through with always-in-flux relations; this way of thinking opens onto what feels to me like an inescapable answer: settlers cannot "work with Indigenous philosophy," precisely because of what Vanessa Watts calls "Place-Thought." "Place-Thought is the nondistinctive space where place and thought were never separated because they never could or can be separated. Place-Thought is based upon the premise that land is alive and thinking and that humans and nonhumans derive agency through the extensions of these thoughts" (Watts 2013, 21). Beginning with the idea of Place-Thought, we have to say that knowledge practices are not free-floating in the world, available to anyone. They are, rather, deictic and situated. Indigenous Place-Thought can only be practiced by those who understand themselves as part of the land in specific, material, spiritual networks of relationality; it cannot be "a gateway for non-Indigenous thinkers to re-imagine their worlds" if that means it is engaged in ways that "non-Indigenous peoples also keep control over what agency is and how it is dispersed in the hands of humans" (Watts 2013, 26). Selves here, if that word is even appropriate, are expression of land, of place. Any access to others requires complex negotiation of hospitality and apprenticeship, and that has to take place on situational grounds that are eventually, processually enacted, not imposed by homogenizing grammars of recognition (Couthard 2014; TallBear 2013; Simpson 2014).

There are crucial possibilities for new materialist, nonhumanist, and esoteric projects to participate in decolonization, but rather than simply "celebrating the convergence" of (enlightenment) science and Indigenous knowledge practices, we have to find ways to work against the drive to master—always a colonialist pursuit (Singh 2018)—and instead of incorporating (that is, appropriating) Indigenous knowledges into "critical" frameworks that are plotted in the homogenizing colonialist grammars of Man, learn to let such resonances guide us toward the political task of decolonization as the shifting of *all land-based governance* from settlers to Indigenous and ongoingly colonized peoples and the dismantling of the postenlightenment self. This will involve the events Wynter calls ceremony, in a nonmetaphorical sense, where worlds are tended in storytelling that modulate how participants tend worlds in materially embedded practices.[34] This is always a radically intimate (if dispersed) phenomenon, and it requires that settlers or arrivants approaching decoloniality through their esoteric practices participate in disarticulating coloniality in their mundane, everyday habits and patterns of relational living. It is a matter of (at)tending (to) how we participate in the tending of colonial homogenization and otherwise worlds.

An endarkenment practice in the pursuit of decolonization might begin with the agitation of settler affect, disrupting the grammar that enables settlers to approach Indigenous thought as something they can "use" and engage while avoiding or minimizing decolonial struggle.[35] What is needed is an everyday feeling for (de)coloniality, habits that tend (toward) the end of the world. As Imani Perry has argued, "The witnessing of alternative grammars for the moral universes in the act of creativity, in art or witchcraft, is an invitation to think in different ways" (2018, 174). What Perry senses is that witchcraft offers "alternative grammars" for articulating feminist futures, which is to say that it potentially carries a subjunctive, virtual field from which "alternative" modes of being human might arise and be sustained.

Citing Lauren, a poet-witch associated with Reclaiming, Starhawk offers that "we need to dream the dark as process, and dream the dark as change, to create the dark in a new image. Because the dark creates us" (1982, xiv). This statement of need slips close to the grammatical mood of the subjunctive, and it loops the weird temporalities of "the dark" around coven-practice. The dark is what "creates" us, but also an ongoing process, something that requires our "creation" of it in "a new image." Traditional causality and agency are baffled in and by the dark, at least as a process that is always being undertaken: "The turning dark: change" (xiv). Nothing suggests that Lauren or Starhawk are connecting this dark with the genres of existence "dysslected" in Man's colonial world, but we might push the light-dark metaphorics in Starhawk's language toward what Cynthia Dillard calls

Black feminist "endarkened epistemologies" and a politics oriented toward the abolition of Man and the racializing assemblages of colonial humanism. This politics is much more complex than the simple project of reclaiming "witchcraft"—a project that may not be able to escape colonialist grammars of self and history—and it poses questions of how we participate, exactly where we are, in the tending of esoteric worlds that aren't oriented toward Man as the post-enlightenment subject of science of history.

The feminist and gay liberationist histories I've read here reach toward a hazy, uncertain (even "discredited") past as they weave historical stories, and in this chapter, I have tried to modulate their indicative claims toward subjunctive potentiality. At stake in how we tend (to) such stories is, as Sylvia Wynter's work never ceases to remind us, the sociogenic proliferation of ways of being and performing the human in relation to more-than-human worlds. Stories world, and we are part of their worlding, even if we have (belated, and referred) agency for shaping the stories that move through us, including by attempting to indicativize those stories into history.[36] Storytelling reshapes us and our worlds, precisely because storytelling is worlding and we emerge and endure as participants in the ongoingness of these worlds.

Whereas enlightenment science dreams of universals and fabricates statements whose truth is not reliant upon immediate material context because it appears within the homogenizing gid of universal *nomos*, esoteric knowledges are inescapably linked with specific socialities (always more-than-human). "Witchcraft" as a concept mediates the esoteric energies that circulate across temporalities by charting them within colonial grammars. In shifting from the indicative to the subjunctive, I'm trying to turn away from grounding the present (and a *pluriversal* futurity) in claims about what was, while still tapping to the affects that circulate in these fraught erotohistoriographies. I am interested in how we feel the "past" energies (enduring as tendencies in the patterning of worlds in their ongoingness) such that they call us toward futures beyond homogenization, toward what Chela Sandoval calls "decolonial love" (2000, 144).

Feeling these pluriversal futures as subjunctive forces in our present can bring us together, participating in the collective dismantling of the homogenizing world of Man. Participation is not homogenizing, even if it may involve the orchestration of bodies together in time (Freeman, 2019), which means that the crucial thing is not that people share a "being" or a critical vision or even a tactical aim so much as that they all tend their non-Man genres of existence "together." This is what the Zapatistas call "one No, and many

Yeses." I think it's what Wynter means when she recalls the post–World War II social movements as an insurgency against Man:

> Now with respect to the *challenges* to the single biocentric model of liberal monohumanist Man, the sixties movements were really the first opening phase in which the series of "isms" (initiated by the black antiapartheid struggle for civil rights, women's rights/feminism, indigenous and other-of-color rights, gay and lesbian rights, and so forth) had erupted to challenge Man's episteme, its truth, and therefore its biocentric descriptive statement. And momentarily, they were making these challenges *all together*. Ah, but when you separate them, you retreat into the bourgeois order of things. (Wynter and McKittrick 2015, 23)

The challenge to Man's episteme does not require a single episteme that can be "critically" elaborated in order to authorize struggle, and Wynter's insistence upon genres (plural) of being human suggests that futurity itself must be dreamt multiply. But in our current moment of struggle against Man, we also need stories that affiliate or constellate those Roderick Ferguson calls "the bastards of the West" (2017, 60). We need *dehumanist* stories, ceremonies that turn us away from Man and its light toward the dark (Singh 2018). This cannot simply be a human(ist) task, since storytelling practice, like any other part of the world, is caught up in more-than-human assemblages.[37] Even as I have been attentive to commonality and shared fields of (eco-erotic) struggle, I want to underscore María Puig de la Bellacasa's provocation: "As blurred boundaries deepen entanglements and interdependencies, the ethico-political demand persists and maybe intensifies for elucidating how different configurations of knowledge practices are consequential, contributing to specific rearrangements" (2017, 28). What we can actually *care for* is not "witchcraft" nor is it "esoterism" or even "eco-erotics" in general, but some highly specific articulation(s) of it. Given Puig de la Bellacasa's extension of care beyond the human—it is "a force distributed across a multiplicity of agencies and materials and supports our worlds as a thick mesh of relational obligations" (20)—it seems imperative that we should say that endarkenment esoterisms would be knowledge practices that (at)tend more-than-human socialities, such that the entire assemblage is not oriented toward enlightenment projects of global, masterful homogeneity, but rather turned toward the deictic, toward the endarkenment proliferation of esoteric genres of dehumanist living (Singh 2018).

THREE

MAN'S RUIN

Hearing Divide and Dissolve

> You have to teach yourself how to listen.
> —Minori Sanchiz-Fung, "Reversal"
> on *Abomination* by Divide and Dissolve

> Metal delivers in darkness what has been
> historically disciplined as darkness.
> —Aliza Shvarts, "Troubled Air"

Divide and Dissolve play a particular mode of doom metal that tends toward drone, toward endarkenment. Doom metal, and metal more generally, is often said to derive, as a legible genre, from Black Sabbath, the English band whose sound was in turn derived—in a different way—from blues music, which is to say, Blues People (Jones 1963). The differences in these derivations have everything to do with the cluster of problems I've been tracking around tending: how worlds endure and collide, how we perceive that worlding (and our [non]selves as part of it), and how we care for the more-than-human socialities that make up worlds. These worlds—where more-than-human socialities are co-compositional with knowledge practices—are always bounded, nonuniversal, situationally specific. That is, they are esoteric: for some but not all, a refusal of homogenized world (singular) in favor of pluriversal ongoingness. My interest is in those esoterisms which tend away from Man as the overrepresentation of the human, and open onto more-than-human socialities, "genres of existence" (Brown 2021) tending toward worlds we might call feminist, queer, decolonial, abolitionist. I have been using "endarkenment" to mark these worlds that errantly tend away from enlightenment homogenization's colonial mastery.[1]

The question I want to ask here, in this chapter, is what endarkenment sounds like, what it feels like, what endarkenment hearing does to our situationally specific corporeal-material endurance in—and as parts of—worlds at the level of what we feel? It is a question of the affective politics of sound, or the sonic politics of affect: the ways that worlds form and deform in their sounding, where sound as acoustic phenomenon is about felt materiality vibrationally calling into being necessarily ephemeral territories, specific zones of ritual, of sacrality, of attunement to something beyond the surround, beyond space, beyond the body, but where this beyond is only ever apparent in the absolute hereness and nowness of the here and now, which is, when you really tune in, always already an elsewhere, a then and there, a yet to come.[2]

I want to follow the contours of this question by asking what it feels like to hear Divide and Dissolve, a Melbourne-based group whose members identify as Maori (drummer Sylvie Nehill) and Black and Tsalagi (guitarist-saxophonist Takiaya Reed)? Their slow, instrumental doom metal borders on drone, and at times on avant-garde jazz, and it opens onto what I eventually call a decolonial pedagogy of subjunctive space. A *Quietus* review of their album *Gas Light* puts it this way:

> The 90 seconds or so of pastoral sax dappling which opens "Oblique," thus the album, is like something you might expect to find on the ECM label. The guitar and drums, when they enter, are decidedly less so: Reed's riffs don't drone, exactly, but seem to melt into each other while sucking all the oxygen from the room. Nehill plays like a jazzer tasked with flattening their kit, snares leading a merry—if non-linear and skull-jabbing—dance. D&D's drummer has an especially singular technique, a Neubauten-like leaden clang cutting through 'Prove It' . . . and 'Denial' wielding cymbals like ancient weapons during its seven and a half-minute journey. (Gardner 2021)

It's not as stripped down as Sunn O))), a band who plays some of the most enormous yet most minimalist drone music in "Ritual Aktions" (that is, shows) wearing robes, only passingly visible onstage through dense fog seemingly emanating from the massive backline of Sunn O))) amplifiers.[3] But Divide and Dissolve aren't sonically that far off from adjacent groups like Teeth of Lions Rule the Divine, nor from certain iterations of Earth—the band who inspired Sunn O))) and whose career spanned a paragrunge US West Coast 1990s scene and a mid-2000s rebirth as dystopian Cormac McCarthy psychedelic rock played as slowly as possible.[4] Before *this* Earth, there was another: before becoming Black Sabbath, they were called Earth. Divide and Dissolve's Earth includes these Earths but does not derive from them so much as it taps into what was already "Earth" before these bands' names gestured in that direction. Reed says: "Aesthetically, our music is never gonna arrive at the same place a lot of other metal music does. I don't wish to pay homage to the same people [e.g., Toni Iommi] that a lot of people in metal do. We want to be honouring our ancestors, the earth, and every living thing. That's what's at the forefront of our minds when we play music" (Clarke 2021).

I noted above a difference of derivation: doom metal from Black Sabbath, and Black Sabbath from the blues. This shift from the blues to something else, something we have called "heavy metal" for decades, is also marked as the change of name, as the foregrounding of the black sabbath as ritual meeting of witches, as an inversion of Christian sociality, and as a mnemonic for a supposedly less enlightened moment in which "we" were still caught in superstition and irrationality's grasp. This shift in name from Earth to Black Sabbath, coincident with the shift from being a blues band to "inventing" heavy metal, not only helped to institute metal's particular semiological urges (grounded in various esoteric genres of "fantasy" fiction and eschatological dreaming), it cleaved Earth and (the) Black Sabbath as symbolic (and, for Divide and Dissolve, very material-political) registers. The sonic inheritance of Black Sabbath's inaugural moment—when Toni Iommi lost a fingertip in a sheet metal working accident and had to lower the tuning of his guitar strings to be able to play afterward—courses through doom metal (and many other forms of extreme metal) but so does the way this "inaugural" moment solidifies, or helps to solidify along with Rainbow, Led Zeppelin, and so forth, the association of heavy metal and whiteness. This is not to say that there have not always been people participating in metal who are not white, or that metal is not a global phenomenon that can at times be manifestly decolonial.[5] But extreme metal in particular and heavy metal more generally are seldom, almost never, framed explicitly as the sonic elaboration of the Black musics that have come to be called the blues.[6] The name Black Sabbath, through its conjuring of the figure of the witch and the transatlantic witch hunts of early modernity, muted any attribution of the music itself as an expression of Black people (Blues People), or indeed of Blackness as a paraontological fugitivity. It's love and theft (Lott, 1995). What's more, globally, metal has also been adjacent to or outright affiliated with all sorts of nationalisms and heterosexisms, some murderous. So extreme metal might seem a strange site from which to think about events of decolonial listening, another "deidealized object" (Amin 2017). Once again, that's what makes it a generative site from which to think about tending.

Divide and Dissolve play doom metal as Black music, as Earth music.[7] They draw, through extreme metal, from things that precede and subjunctively circulate in and around metal (metal's subjunctive "ghostly region"), and they express those things precisely as a sonic disorientation from settled, anti-Black, heteronormative living in its everyday ongoingness. I might say, following Julietta Singh (2018), that they play dehumanist doom, where doom is not an apocalyptic futurity but the general condition of enlightenment coloniality in our post-1492 moment. Overrepresenting the human "as if it were the human itself," Man's colonial homogenization—which includes homogenization of time and of listening—has ambivalently oriented much extreme metal. Metal dreams about death and decay and destruction but veers off toward nationalist heteropatriarchy in its tendings, keeping it oriented toward Man (Wynter 2003). Evoking the name of a crucial early 1990s doom metal record label and modulating it toward the subjunctive via Wynter's decolonial account of humanist modernity, I want to suggest that what sounds in and through Divide and Dissolve is nothing less than a ceremonial event that can de-tune subjects, enabling the feeling of Man's (subjunctive) ruin.

Hearing as More-than-Human Event: On the Spatiotemporal Specificity of Worlds

Hearing, as Aden Evans notes, is bound up with affect, with feeling (2005, xi). "To hear," Evans begins, "is to experience air pressure changing. . . . One does not hear pressure, but one hears it change over time" (1). Irreducibly spatiotemporal, sound is—as a change in *air pressure*—also irreducibly particular. Listening always happens in a situation, in a deictic specificity, where the space itself—and its volumes, apertures, temperatures, moisture, particulate dispersion, and so forth—participates in the sounding, in a more-than-human assemblage of "hearing," where this hearing is not something experienced by a subject (a "listener" hearing a "sound," as if that could refer to a bounded, stable thing).[8] I will riff on the subject differently than he does here, but Alexander Weheliye describes this particularly situated characteristic of hearing: "Music, and sound in general, roots subjects in their environment by making that environment audible, while the immersion that comes with the listening experience is always tied to a space from whence it originates, thereby spatially marking the sound. In other words, the listening event varies depending on the venue, so that the subject engages with music differently when at home, in a restaurant, or at a dance club" (2005, 112). Hearing or listening is a material, erotic happening in a milieu, a specific space with particular coordinates in social, psychic, and infrastructural grammars, and those spaces mark what hearing or listening to particular sounds *feels like* in that deictic situation.

While I would argue that worlds are evental "all the way down," I have also found it helpful to mark thresholds where perception and attention are agitated and shift. The question becomes how to shift our attention to what is happening in evental ontogenesis, thereby opening up the possibility of tapping into specific material possibilities for "otherwise" worlding. The distinction between situations and events is enormously helpful for this purpose.[9] Lauren Berlant writes that, "a situation is a state of things in which *something* that will perhaps matter is unfolding amid the usual activity of life. It is a state of animated and animating suspension that forces itself on consciousness, that produces a sense of the emergence of something in the present that may become an event" (2011, 5). Situations are the material-semiotic patterning of worlds in their becoming, and in our (anti-Black) world, we have to say that coloniality and its violences adhere in the mind-bogglingly diffuse encounters and "events" (in Alfred North Whitehead's sense [Debaise 2017]). But for many, this violence fades into the situation: things here are not hidden—although they can take place at scales that baffle "human" sensoria—but they largely exist in a zone of de-attunement. We might say, sticking with a word Berlant highlights in a reading of a John Ashbury poem, that the coloniality of the world constitutes, in most cases, something like a background *hum*: "the thing that resonates around me, which might be heaven or bees or labor or desire or electric wires" (33). Endarkenment (at)tending shifts this background to foreground, notices the hum. It is to have a sense (which will always only be minimally about consciousness or the volition of a liberal subject) of how the world's becoming allows what Massumi calls "freedom" adhering *in* the situation as a possibility to be played, a material spur to improvising otherwise worlds: "Our freedom is in how we play our implication in a field, what events we succeed in catalysing in it that bring out the latent singularity of the situation, how we inflect for novel emergences" (2015, 158).

Those situations are oriented, in their material patternings—their tendings—toward some probable outcomes rather than others; more specifically, they are oriented toward and around Man and its homogenizing violence. Sara Ahmed's work on the affective politics of orientation, which sees bodies and spaces as affectively co-compositional—attunes (us) to precisely the ways that spaces and bodies accumulate eventally: "Colonialism makes the world 'white,' which is of course a world 'ready' for certain kinds of bodies, as a world that puts certain objects within their reach. Bodies remember such histories, even when we forget them. Such histories, we might say, surface on the body, or even shape how bodies surface" (2006, 111). This readiness is inseparable from ongoing practices, where the continuance of a tendency—patterned movement through space(s)—takes the form of habit, of a backgrounding of evental ontogenesis into what phenomenologists call "the everyday." Ahmed writes that, "the habitual can be thought of as a bodily and spatial form of inheritance" (2006, 129). The everyday becomes, then, for feminist and queer theorists like Sara Ahmed and Ann Cvetkovich (2012), precisely the site of political and ethical (at)tending. Colonialism— what Ahmed calls whiteness and straightness—is *a tending through habit*, the generation of a singular world configured to make some parts of that world more "within reach" of some participants rather than others. And the decolonial question becomes how we tend other habits, habits that get out of line, deviate, get lost.

Ahmed thinks about this explicitly in terms of tending, and she ties that accumulation of tendencies in habit (where habits are an ontogenetic composition of worlds) to the question of education or pedagogy as a spatiotemporal problem, or even, more specifically, to a thinking about affective, evental pedagogy as the generative *tending* of inherited orientations that carry us away, lead us "off track," pull us toward otherwise, endarkenment worlds not oriented around Man. She writes (in terms that resonate through Butler and Wynter):

> Having tended toward what is within reach, the child acquires its tendencies, which in turn bring the child into line. The paradox of this temporality helps us to explain how orientations are the effects of work, at the same time as they feel "as if" they were like "handedness," as a way of being in the body, by being directed in some ways more than others. Bodies become straight by tending toward straight objects, such that they acquire

their "direction" and even their tendencies as an effect of this "tending toward." (2006, 86)

What Ahmed is tuning into here is a way of thinking about selves or subjects *as* tending, or the accumulations of tendings dispersed across scales that mark the deictic situation in its irreducibly multiple specificity. This subject can feel "as if" it is given, as if it isn't the effect of *hearing* as the doing of a more-than-human ceremonial assemblage.

Hearing is evental patterning of a world, and its deictic situation is always complex, which is to say, marked by the meeting of worlds in their differential ongoingnesses. In the wake of 1492, these events are modulated toward homogenization, an absorption of worlds into world (which includes through manifold violence). The question becomes, then, how hearing—and listening—can be modulated or attuned away from Man's colonial spatiotemporal grammars of worlding and toward non-Man tendings in and as hearing? This is where the question of the subject necessarily emerges: If specific modulations of listening or hearing tend the colonial world, what other kinds of listening or hearing are possible, and how do those differences (in patterning) make and unmake genres of "self"? This is also to keep asking, what kind of hearing happens when playing Divide and Dissolve?

Playing Divide and Dissolve

While seeing live performance may well fall within most people's everyday understanding of what an "event" is, playing a recorded album is an everyday thing, especially in an era of sound's endlessly more portable mechanical reproduction. This mechanical reproduction takes place through particular media—LP records, cassette tapes, CDs, MP3s, proprietary streams of binary code—which always involve complex spatiotemporal circuits in their material specificity. Evans's account is marked by the question of how the digital (mostly in CDs but increasingly in virtual information) differs from analog recording (and playback). In analog recording,

> time is transformed into space and pressure variation is transformed into the variation of a specific property of the recording medium. The wave may be etched into the grooves of a vinyl record or coated onto the surface of magnetic tape by varying the magnetic properties of the tape over its length in a pattern geometrically analogous to the original wave. In both cases the recording must be played back—its variations allowed to modulate

a loudspeaker thus producing an air pressure wave—to translate the variation in space on the recording medium back into a variation (of air pressure) over time. (2005, 12)

Digital recording, on the other hand, "works by sampling, taking a measurement of the air pressure at regular intervals, and storing those measurements as numbers. . . . The series of numbers that represent pressure measurements is used to recreate a wave of varying air pressure, which simulates the original sound" (12).[10] The differences between analog and digital can be (literally) amplified by sound in a particular situation, in large part because of the ways the specific space in which the sound is "played" participates as the surround of air pressure's fluctuation. "Sound," Evans tells us, "varies faster and more subtly than CDs can capture" (13). Handling a vinyl record and placing it on a turntable is also, as an erotic practice, considerably different from pressing play on a streaming service app or sliding a CD into a car's dashboard stereo. There are different embodied ritualities at play here, and incommensurate materialities. When clipped and compressed streaming files direct air intimately within ear canals through earbuds, there is a different spatial politics at stake than when an analog record is amplified so that the immensity of Divide and Dissolve's lower frequencies—including subbass—are physically felt impacting and passing through bodies.

I will not allow myself to linger too long on sonic materializations—which necessarily open onto questions of social, more-than-human labor sedimented "in" commodities circulating in complex networks stretching across vast scales—but I want to draw out how the material particularities of the medium—vinyl LP or online stream—shape what Ahmed calls the conditions of arrival (2006) of the sound, the listener, and the entire more-than-human complex of situated, situational hearing. Hearing Divide and Dissolve always happens, even when they perform live, in an assemblage that includes a specific place and a range of technical processes shaped by the agential participation of nonhumans (magnetic tape, vinyl, electricity, modems, earbuds). It is around these materialities that the economic questions of tending more-than-human sonic socialities gather: How do money and entities or actants circulate to make possible performance, recording, distribution, and playback? What lives and forms of material endurance are sustained and in what specific ways?[11] These material questions—which hover around Marxist critiques of commodity fetishism extended, following Ahmed, toward a feeling of more-than-human evental agency—necessarily return us to questions of how participation in tending happens, and how participation is a necessarily spatiotemporal problem. Divide and Dissolve put it this way: "We intend to decolonise the functions of space and time by altering the mechanisms by which people can measure these things. We intend to transform people's experiences of these variables with our music. The resonance of our music is felt by people long after we finish playing our instruments. People are shaken to the core of their body by our live performance" (Cory 2018).

"When we say that a thing resonates," Julie Beth Napolin tells us, "we say that a thing survives yet has been transformed, that it has been made to sound out in amplifying ways, and that it is no longer simply itself" (2020, 135). I might say that resonance is about what stays at play after playback (in the case of music recordings) or performance. And I mean this in the engineering sense as "give" or structural elasticity, but also as a capacity for maneuver, for taking improvisational advantage of the capacity for creative action. It's about what lingers as the waveforms spread out, decay, diminish, disperse, dissolve. As Napolin also insists, "when one listens to resonance," "one listens not to a source but to a relation, to a contact or touch" (125). Resonance is the name we give to the sonic—or as Ashon Crawley might put it, "choreosonic" (2017, 23)—perceptibility of the subjunctive: to what, beyond what "is" in an empirical sense according to human sensorial capacity, is still real, still *there*, *here*, affecting us, setting us in various kinds of motion.

David Cecchetto's concept of incommunication helps me amplify and clarify what I mean. "Incommunication," for Cecchetto, "names the world's incoherence with itself: it contours multiplicities of the seemingly systematic world that appear in and as this systematicity" (2022, 106). Implicitly pluiversal in its motivations,[12] Cecchetto's project similarly (at)tends (to) resonance:

As "resonance"—a key acoustic concept—describes the "patterned intensity of a flow, expressed as a rate or frequency ration," it seems naturally suited to the relational and distributed understanding of agency that incommunication develops, especially in its computational appearance. To listen in this environment is less to craft a stable subject/object relation and more to adopt a posture that acknowledges one's entanglement in ongoing processes of attunement and differentiation. (2022, 13)

Resonance is about how distributed agencies take shape, as patterns in the ongoingness of worlds, in situations of relation, of touch, of haptics that include the sonic precisely as a field that exceeds anything that might be simply called "listening," anything that might be as simple as what sound "communicates." Resonance is about how worlds take shape in and as feelings, even if those don't rise to any participant's conscious attention, which means it's also where subjunctive worlds begin to form, where they might move through us, and as us, even when we don't "know" that.

Drone

I would like to foreword here the proposition that Divide and Dissolve practices what Rizvana Bradley and Denise Ferreira da Silva call the "poethical": "Thinking the artwork as poethical, as 'a composition which is always already a recomposition and a decomposition of prior and posterior compositions,' requires being poised for the advent of becoming *as* matter, and its immanent interrogation of the temporality of forms" (2021). The temporality of forms is precisely the field within which the music of Divide and Dissolve sounds; within the language developed by musicology, the concept that may be most helpful here is "drone." As Marcus Boon writes in *The Politics of Vibration*, "A drone, in musical terms, is a sustained set of composite sound wave forms, in other words, a vibratory field. The world *field* conveys the way that the repetition of a set of waveforms opens up the possibility of exploring a tone cluster as a space that retains its form over time" (2022, 77–78).

Drone attunes, as a form, to the capacity for sound not just to take place within space, but to modulate temporality such that new spaces subjunctively manifest in and as resonance. Drone thus acts "on" bodies in strange and paradoxical ways (I might say in subjunctive ways that don't adhere to the logical coordinates of enlightenment grammars). Precisely in their incommunication, drone sonics modulate the perceptive apparatus of a listener, or—if listening presumes the conscious attunement and attempt to discern messages—hearer (which is to say "feeler" since this hearing need not be human or even animate). Drone envelops, surrounds, suspends (in the chemical sense): the hearer's borders blur and dissolve into the wider field—which might be an ephemeral one like a performance or playing a record. But this field continues to resonate, charging the present with a subjunctive, virtual field in which otherwise choreosonics might happen.

Boon theorizes a "modal ontology," and while from my standpoint, his account of cosmopolitics tends too much toward precisely the kinds of concordance that one might expect in musics that hover relationally with New Age knowledges and a serious investment in the mathematics of sound, rewriting this as "modal ontologies" helps me clarify what compels me in drone. Modal ontology, for Boon, proposes that "what something is can be best described by the way (mode) in which it vibrates, and this vibration as a change of shape. But, in order to recognize this possibility, we need to in some way be open to the possibility that we ourselves are modal beings, that is, not entirely fixed but subject to structural principles, that is, modes and their functional determination of us as entities" (2022, 153).

Working from this, but shifting it toward the pluriversal, I might say that drone is a modulating of a world such that participants are opened toward some kind of encounter—a touch, a feeling, an affect—with their own existence as patterns in the mattering of worlds, which is to say as tendings. This is almost precisely the opposite of enlightenment conceptions of subjectivity and self. Crawley writes: "Enlightenment thought constructed its conception of the subject through a desire for reducing openness and vulnerability[.] Enlightenment's subject was one created by the shoring up against movement, created a subject through containment and enclosure. Enlightenment's subject is one that can withdraw into an absolute silence, unbothered and unconcerned by the ongoing verve and noise of worlds" (2017, 44). If enlightenment hearing shores up a subject, endarkenment hearing tunes in to what Crawley calls "endarkened logics of otherwise sociality" (209). I hear something of this sociality in Jayna Brown's reading of Sun Ra's music: "Ultimately, we are no longer human at all but radically decentered, destabilized, dispersed as particles, energies, and vibrations" (2021, 156–57). That is, instead of colonial subject shored up against noise, Divide and Dissolve attune us to how we are nothing but noise as it is modulated into the spatiotemporal affective patterns we call worlds. Recalling John Dewey's provocation that "we never educate directly, but indirectly by means of the environment" (1916, 19), I want to suggest that Divide and Dissolve's drone opens up a specific spatiotemporal field in which that (deictic) attunement happens, offering a decolonial pedagogy of subjunctive space.

Noise

Divide and Dissolve's music sounds out of sync with itself, blurry. And this happens in a way that feels quite distinct from the kind of explicitly drug-oriented disorientations one hears in adjacent doom metal groups like Sleep (especially on *Dopesmoker*) or Electric Wizard (on *Dope Throne*). Part of this comes from each musician playing in a different time signature, from their preference for dissonant chord progressions that don't resolve according to traditional "Western" musics, from the ways they blur doom metal and jazz, which puts their music in the same musical universe as more ritualistic groups like Ascend (a duo of Sunn O)))'s Greg Anderson and Gentry Densley, leader of the heavy free jazz ensemble Iceburn) and Spain's Orthodox (especially on *Amanecer la puerta oscura*). Doug Wallen writes that "the almost eight-minute single 'Denial' revels in similar extremes: the song slows and stretches, establishing a brutal inner peace before the saxophone again leaves us haunted in the aftermath . . . [and] the menacing 'It's Really Complicated' fully commits to an overdriven, swarm-like effect." This "swarm-like effect" might be referred, as Wallen does, to "transformational effects" (presumably guitar pedals and technical apparatuses of recording), which participate in the music. However, one might explain this nonconvergence of the music with itself, its sonic pluriversality, as the effect of a specific, and specifically affective, unsettling of hearing that underscores the colonial capture of spatiotemporality and temporospatiality. The band says: "Our music is nonlinear and asymmetrically grounded. We are driven to create heavy music, in whatever form it takes. We aren't loyal to any particular genre." The passive construction here locates agency elsewhere than in their first-person plural subject "we," which cannot be the source of this drive.

In *Parasite*, Michel Serres proposes that systems, what I'm calling worlds, are always relational with other worlds, and the borders where those worlds meet and collide are tended in specific practices, most of them habitual, everyday (like pulling out an iPhone and clicking play on Spotify). At these thresholds, "the systems interfere with one another" (2007, 69). From within one world—and its signals, its messages, its descriptive statements (Wynter 2003)—this other world sounds like "noise." "A noise," for Jacques Attali, "is a resonance that interferes with the audition of a message in the process of emission. A resonance is a set of simultaneous, pure sounds of determined frequency and differing intensity. Noise, then, does not exist in itself, but only in relation to the system within which it is inscribed" (1985, 26). Serres, from whom Attali is largely drawing here, writes about this with the adverb "more" marking what I'm calling a tendency adhering in attention: "Whoever belongs to the system perceives noises less and represses them more, the more he is a functioning part of the system" (68). This allows me to pose the question of Divide and Dissolve's music very directly: How can hearing them *lessen* the participation of the listener or hearer as a "functioning part of" Man's world?

Divide and Dissolve, as I said, play something else *through* doom metal.[13] As their iconic T-shirts proclaim, the primary concerns of the band are to "destroy white supremacy" and "dismantle colonial borders."[14] This is a question of sonic tending. Clarke writes: "Their primary mode of communicating those aims is via physical sensation, the way a big rush of overdriven noise and stampeding drums can quite literally rattle your core. 'I love having more amps than everyone else, I love taking the longest to set up,' says Reed. 'I love shaking a room, when the ceiling is crumbling into people's hair. I love when the electricity flickers before we start playing'" (2021). I want to think about what it means to "rattle" a listener's "core," and to think of that as a question of the temporal and spatial capture of worlding into homogenized world. Reed's attention to crumpling ceilings and electrical flickering reminds us that the decolonizing event of hearing Divide and Dissolve is always about more-than-human participation in ways that could be thought in the field imaginaries of new materialisms and scientifically attuned theories of affect, but it's also a questions of spirits: "The heaviness comes from our ancestors," says guitarist and saxophonist Takiaya Reed. "I am Black and Indigenous. There's been so much that has happened to us, and I feel this. I carry this with me, and if I decide to have children, they will carry this with them too. I don't feel like I could not make heavy music" (Clarke 2021).

To consider what it means to say that Divide and Dissolve's music "comes from [their] ancestors"—the colonized and enslaved—I return to Aisha Beliso-De Jesús's concept of copresences, which I engaged in chapter 1's reading of *I, Tituba, Black Witch of Salem*. Beliso-De Jesús writes: "Copresences are not mutually exclusive. Energies of nature, death, different ancestors, and humans are constantly transgressing in and out of energetic intra-actions. The momentum of these energies electrifies the bodies of practitioners in close proximity, as they pull (*jular*) other copresences down (*bajan*) into and emerge through other bodies. This spiritual current is measured, rated, and experienced by practitioners in a qualitative differential of feeling ritual power" (2015, 70). This feeling of ritual power might be another name for the affect born of participating in and as droning, decolonial noise. Reed and Nehill's ancestors are copresences *in* and *as* the sonic field, the modulation of timespace that vibrates and resonates even after the event of hearing a "source" or "performance." Indeed, it becomes impossible to locate Reed and Nehill as authors of this music in any simple sense, although without their participation—the care they bring to tending their worlds—this music would not arrive. And when it arrives to us, we are invited not just to revel in the dissolution of self, but to (at)tend to how that temporally and spatially bounded event of dissolution—in the rituality of playing music—is not yet enough to abolish the enlightenment self. In the resonance of their music, we have to attune to how we tend toward enlightenment in our daily practices, our often-backgrounded sense of spatiotemporal existence, our active contributions to the persistence of some worlds (even world, singular) rather than others.

Participation

The question of will—of agency (or agencies) in the event—snaps to attention. For Reed, ancestors provide "heaviness" to their music—or rather, Divide and Dissolve's music is the "carrying" or tending of those ancestral spirits, and it disarticulates the question of agency or volition: Reed cannot not participate. Thinking about this participation requires a different notion of subject or self than the one presumptive in post-enlightenment rationality. Noting that "a more accurate theory of listening might consider the dissolution of subjective boundaries" (2005, 61), Weheliye notes that "once the sonic is introduced into th[e] mix, the category of the subject transmutes into a multifarious constellation that does not rest on mutual exclusives but instead enables particles to bounce off one another and bring to the fore their vortexes" (50). What colonial grammars capture as a "subject" is material resonance and vibration, a patterning of worlds in their ontogenetic becoming. Evans rethinks the subject as a "channel," which helps to amplify Reed's feeling of not being able to *not make* heavy music: "One must will the loss of one's self, the dissolution of the will, to find an equanimity that will just let the music be, let the music come, without the need to force it along" (2005, 134).

One of the modalities of such channeling that Evans turns to is "spirit possession," and his explanation calls our attention to not just the blurriness of Divide and Dissolve's music, but also their slowness. He writes, "rhythmic drumming or music pervades [the musician's] senses, creating a seamless background that fills the host's subjective space, blanking her concentration or possibly shutting out distraction" (134). Reed says "We need to be up there resonating with the frequencies of everyone on earth. . . . Making people feel what we feel" (Clarke 2021). Combining low frequencies and, by the standards of rock and roll music generally, very slow tempo(ralitie)s, Divide and Dissolve perform live at extremely loud volumes so that hearing is a more-than-aural phenomenon, one where sound as the modulation of air pressure in a *specific space* impresses the listener as evental surround. This is about participation: a "performer shapes but does not finally determine the sound" (Evans 2005, 83).

Fred Moten's *In the Break* can hone our attention further. Thinking about a resonant temporal and spatial unsettling in Black performance, he writes, his attention on Amiri Baraka's poetry, "we might look at that temporal-spatial discontinuity as a generative break, one wherein action becomes possible, one in which it is our duty to linger in the name of ensemble and its performance" (2003, 99). In this space of ensemble—of assembly and assemblage in the more-than-human(ist) sense—worlds sound that exceed the homogenizing world and its grammars, including the grammar of the subject: "That breakdown is not the negative effect of grammatical insufficiency but the positive trace of a lyrical surplus" (38). This is the musical break as an *event* of worlding, one where the colonial subject who listens might start to dissipate or dissolve, registered first, as Serres argues, as a kind of oscillation between worlds. (At)tending to noise, "the noise temporarily stops the system, makes it oscillate indefinitely" (2007, 14). The subject comes to feel itself as more-, less-, and other-than subject, as a patterning in the evental ongoingness of worlds, and this happens in events of hearing involving the participation of a differentiated more-than-human ensemble.

Dylan Robinson's work on settler listening, which he calls "hungry listening," attunes to this differential participation in the tending of (endarkenment) worlds.[15] He writes, "Decolonizing musical practice involves becoming no longer sure what LISTENING is" (2020, 47). Listening for Robinson, I might aver, is tending: "Listening itself may become an act of confirming ownership, rather than an act of hearing the agonism of exclusive and contested sovereignties" (13). Hungry listening—as settler appropriation, as the presumption that everything in the world (singular) should be "within reach" (Ahmed 2006) for Man—might encounter, in specific scenes of hearing, a kind of blockage, a refusal, an esoteric boundary event. Robinson makes two moves that are crucial to how I'm trying to hear Divide and Dissolve as the sonic tending of Man's abolition (which is to say, pluriversal decolonization, or, the end of the world): he feels out a finely grained intersectional approach to thinking differential participation and he proposes the political necessity of settler participation in decolonization through an affirmation of Indigenous refusal of settler participation in Indigenous worlds. And, like Divide and Dissolve, he thinks about both in terms of slowness.

Part of *Hungry Listening* is about articulating "a decolonial practice of critical listening positionality" (2020, 62). In his primary field of interest—encounters where Canadian settler musics and their institutions include Indigenous musics in programming only through violent colonial homogenization—what's at stake is how the colonial grammars of state "recognition" politics situate Indigenous musics on the plane of culture, removed from the political (which is to say, ontogenetic) questions of worlds. In these scenes, Indigenous musics are rent from particular scenes of landed participation—and rewritten through colonial grammars as "music" in the post-enlightenment sense of aesthetics. And these ungrounded aesthetics are then recoded, in a feedback loop, as demanding cultural appreciation and empathy grounded in a liberal settler subject. Robinson writes, "Many of the contributions by settler participants addressed the need to cultivate harmonious relationships with First Peoples, while discussions regarding the need to establish political nation-to-nation relationships remained conspicuously absent" (206). This "harmony" of the homogeneous (but still hierarchically policed) human world is grounded in the violence of the scene's very grammar, which mutes the decolonial politics of hearing but also and in the same gesture—which locates agency in Man-as-subject—disattunes to nonhuman (sonic) participation. Robinson writes that *"Hungry Listening* focuses on the intersubjective experience between human and nonhuman actors in music performance by considering object agency in non-representational and new materialist theory alongside Indigenous knowledge regarding nonhuman relations" (79).

The particulars of how Robinson stages this consideration guide how I hear Divide and Dissolve, but they also open the questions about participation in evental ontogenesis that I am trying to consider in this book with the concept of esoterisms as bounded, nonuniversal, more-than-human socialities sustained by knowledge practices, which is to say, by specific, deictic modes of attention and care. Rather than try to articulate some critical framework that could responsibly bring Indigenous worlds and Indigenous hearing together into the same frame as hungry listening—a project that participates in grammars of homogenization dreaming of universal intersectionality—Robinson amplifies Audra Simpson (2014) and Glenn Sean Coulthard's (2014) work on "content refusal" to propose what he calls "structural refusal." In "content refusal," Robinson writes, "Indigenous scholars have resisted the Western imperative for all knowledge to be accessible at all times, acknowledging that Indigenous epistemologies uphold context-specific knowledge sharing" (2020, 21). Robinson tends these forms of refusal—cares for them and participates in carrying them—by thinking about "formal and aesthetic strategies that impede Indigenous knowledge extraction and instrumentalization" (23). This leads Robinson to propose that his book's reading requires the kind of differential participation he theorizes. That is, Robinson calls settlers to participate in reading his book, but also modulates that participation toward an esoteric refusal to include the settler: parts of the book "are for you [the settler] and also not for you" (25). He then asks his settler readers to *not read* the next section:

> If you are a non-Indigenous, settler, ally, or xwelitem reader, I ask that you stop reading by the end of this page. I hope you will rejoin us for chapter 1, "Hungry Listening," which sets out to understand Indigenous and settler colonial listening. The next section of this book, however, is written exclusively for Indigenous readers. (25)

Setting up this paragraph, Robinson explains that it is an affirmation of "Indigenous sovereignty" to follow the "injunction." For settlers, participation in decolonial listening involves evental hearing that affirms the *pluriversal* ontogenesis of worlds that are barred from settlement, where settlers cannot travel and extract, where setttlers might participate in evental hearing by *not* listening.

The Slowness of Man's Ruin

I did not read the next pages. What Robinson has to say to Indigenous readers is not something I know or should know. Referring to "the participatory call of music to foment modes of identification that transform perspectives slowly over time" (225), Robinson cites Cvetkovich, who is citing Berlant: "For Berlant, an object of knowledge becomes a (productive) impasse when it slows us down, preventing easy recourse to critique or prescription for action and instead inviting us to see it as 'a singular place that's a cluster of noncoherent but proximate attachments that can only be approached awkwardly, described around, shifted'" (Cvetkovich 2012, 20). In this participatory modulation of spatiotempoarality, Divide and Dissolve's slow doom is the noise of other worlds blurring the borders of world, exposing the subject (Man) to its more-than-human, more-than-secularist intimate or immanent outsides (Massumi 2019). Divide and Dissolve do this by attuning to the sonic tending of world's colonialist capture of space and time, which is the material surround of their decolonial tending. This slowing down is also resonant with what Tiffany Lethabo King calls "the Black shoals"—the contact zone where Black and Indigenous worlds are frictionally co-composed—which begins by noting that "as a geological and oceanic formation, shoals force one to pause before proceeding" (2019, 2).[16] At stake in this friction and its "unpredictability" that "exceeds full knowability/mappability" is "a site where movement as usual cannot proceed" (3).

Slowness—the disruption of "movement as usual"—is not the same as an absolute refusal, a rigid border construction. It is about the modulation of what Serres calls the subject's oscillation. When I listen to Divide and Dissolve, it's either by putting a record on the turntable—which is itself an important part of the ritual character of doom metal listening[17]—or by streaming their music in my earbuds as I walk, which is to say, while I move about the space in my vicinity and think-feel. According to Cory, "They were drawn to playing slow, heavy, and crushingly loud music because of the effect it would have on the bodies of their listeners, not because of any desire to pay homage to the riff lords of the past" (2018). The heaviness moves in and through the body in ways that far exceed anything that might be called consciousness—Sunn O))) produced a T-shirt that asks "ever breathe a frequency?"[18]—and the slowness is a way of feeling the transhistorical endurance of non-Man worlds, worlds marked for homogenizing violence by enlightenment grammars. In what Sunn O))) calls breathing a frequency, we can attune to the self as constitutively open to worlds, as an expression of those worlds and their vibrational patternings. Hearing here is the production of an "oscillating" uncertainty or disorientation, an interference in the subject's endurance (and with it, colonial tending) that allows something else to be felt, to exert a pull, a claim, a call to participate. I might think of this as affectively modulating the subject such that it slows down to the point at which its "functional participation" causes it to sputter and dissipate, to the point where things in the surround have timespace to haunt that subject, returning it to its evental conditions of (subjunctive) potentiality in the contact zone of pluriversal worlding.[19]

Hearing Divide and Dissolve while sitting at home or walking the alleys of the neighborhoods where I live, I feel how my sense of place is structured by grammars oriented toward coloniality's evental endurance, how the things I do to tend my life directly participate in the ongoing theft through settlement of Powhatan land, how the resources that accumulate around me as a subject (and in me, including intellectual resources) are inseparable from the extractive and gratuitous violence of transatlantic slavery. These grammars of listening overrepresent the sound of coloniality as the sound of the world, where the subjunctive feeling of Man's ruin is a background hum (Berlant 2011) beyond habitual notice. Their music draws me toward sonic participation in worlds that move through the colonial world (subjunctively) without making those worlds available to me as things I can inhabit or own, settle or master. Divide and Dissolve do not ask me to participate in (their) Black worlds or Indigenous worlds, but they call me to feel how my everyday world participates in the homogenizing violence from which those worlds have to be protected.[20] This is, perhaps, most audible in the words of Minori Sanchiz-Fung, whose spoken word poems appear on many of the band's albums (as the only human voice). On *Gas Lit*'s "Did You Have Something to Do With It" (2020), Sanchiz-Fung says:

> We are tethered to a circuit that excludes nothing
> A song the dead can hear
> Something resilient forming all
> Something that makes time small
> So old, that language can't dispose of it
> Still gold over the violence
> Don't forget, this too, this too, is our time
> Our spirit is not weaker
> It is waiting on us to decide
> What it is, that we will honour
> While we are alive

Here, spirit attends our participation, and "our time" is not universalizing homogeneous settler time, but the time of evental participation, where tending is at stake.

In hearing Divide and Dissolve (a more-than-human event), I feel how my everyday world tends (toward) coloniality, how "I" am an effect—a co-composition—of that tending. Cultivating what Julietta Singh (2018) calls "vulnerable listening" to the sounds of other worlds, this feeling of our evental participation in coloniality resonates with the feeling of other tendencies that mark our situations—in all their deictic particularity—which opens up participation as the improvisational playing of endarkenment (subjunctive) worlds outside of and beyond settler spacetime; worlds where what is at stake is hearing—as a more-than-human event of worlding—Man's world come to ruin as we tend our worlds elsewhere, otherwise. In words the band used on Instagram, referring to *Gas Lit*: "This album is a prayer that land be given back to Indigenous people and that future generations no longer experience the atrocities and fervent violence that colonization continues to bring forth" (December 1, 2020). The question is how we modulate hearing to participate in that prayer, that ceremony that dreams the end of the world.

FOUR

CEREMONY

Participation and Endarkenment Study

> The sacred is nothing less than the experience
> of sociality through and as infraction given in
> "interaffective" excess, given in and as "collec-
> tive ecstasy." The sacred here manifests as the
> experience of innovation and improvisation...
> —J. Kameron Carter, "Other Worlds, Nowhere
> (or the Sacred Otherwise)"

> How do those of us laboring in the complex
> environments of an academy indifferent and
> even hostile to spirit make our professional
> work into a form of spiritual practice?
> —Gloria Anzaldúa, *Luz en Lo Oscuro*

In this final chapter, I want to think about tending as a complex problematic of participation in worlding, in evental ontogenesis as the patterning
of worlds in their ongoingness, by lingering with the everyday context of
the university. I follow Sandy Grande in thinking that the university is, first
and foremost, *"an arm of the settler state*—a site where the logics of elimination, capital accumulation, and dispossession are reconstituted" (2018,
47). What Grande calls "reconstituted" here marks the evental ontogenesis
of coloniality, where elimination, accumulation, and dispossession are not
things that happened "in the past" as the primitive accumulations of land

and resources that enabled universities to emerge and endure. Rather, these are all ongoing processes, processes that structure the university as a site of everyday, banal violence, where teaching, research, and campus life tend to be organized around the production of Man (what liberal arts advocates have long called "character development") in such a way that this ongoing tending of coloniality is rendered a kind of background, folded into the everyday experience of going to and teaching at a college that is unremarkable, almost inaudible.[1] For some: the further you are from what Sylvia Wynter calls Man as the human's overrepresentation, the louder this violence sounds, the more you hear it as part of participation in the university as a "technology of social stratification" (Chuh 2019, 11) within the singular, colonial world.

My primary aim here is to think about the university as a site of everyday ontogenesis through Wynter's concept of ceremony: rituals that participate in the sociogenic production of genres of the human. In the post-1492 event of coloniality, much of this ceremony—which happens throughout every sociality, not only "in" the university—is oriented toward the processual enactment of Man as that human's overrepresentation. As Stefano Harney and Fred Moten say, "The Universitas is always a state/State strategy" (2013, 32), and it has been configured, as Roderick Ferguson puts it, "as an institution fundamentally antagonistic to everyday people in general and people of color in particular" (2017, 84). Letting these two quotations resonate together, I am trying to think about the university as the site of the evental production *of the everyday*, where there is a statal, Man-centric everyday of colonial tending, and other everydays tended by "everyday people" who don't belong, who might be "in but not of" the university (Harney and Moten 2013, 26).[2]

The university is not a technology singular, perhaps, so much as "an assemblage of machines" where "its machinery is always being subverted toward decolonizing purposes" (paperson 2017, xiii). It's a complex field, one that Julietta Singh and I have tried to theorize as a specific ecology we call "educational undergrowth." Taking as our point of departure the university's evental production of Man, "we look to the undergrowth thriving in the colonial milieu beneath this Man or outside his reach, to the forms of disbelonging that infiltrate and subtend the university, to the ways education that bears little resemblance to the official accounts of it takes place" (2021, 4). This chapter elaborates this by thinking with tending as a capacious concept. There are, we might say, two opposing tendencies (and tendings) at stake in the university as an ecological assemblage of evental ontogenesis: on the one hand, a colonial tending toward the production of Man (through accumulation, dispossession, and elimination), toward the post-enlightenment subject (da Silva 2007), toward neoliberal homini oeconomici (Wynter 2007) whose praxis is oriented in a homogenous world. On the other hands (as this always becomes a question of collectivities and more-than-humans without hands), we have study as the evental, ceremonial articulation of non-Man worlds, other "genres of existence" (Brown 2021); endarkenment worlds; worlds where there may not be subjects of colonial grammar so much as specific, felt, haptic "non-selves" (Moten 2017) that hang together in and as patterns of participation in worldly ongoingness.

Another resonance I am trying to hear—which is to say to participate in—is between what Wynter calls "ceremony" and what Harney and Moten call "study." I need to quote *The Undercommons* at length, precisely because their language (at)tends to the everydayness of study, its necessarily co-compositional relationality with worlding, to the esoteric orientation of study as evental everydayness. Moten writes:

> When I think about the way we use the term "study," I think we are committed to the idea that study is what you do with other people. It's talking and walking around with other people, working, dancing, suffering, some irreducible convergence of all three, held under the name of speculative practice. The notion of a rehearsal—being in a kind of workshop, playing in a band, in a jam session, or old men sitting on a porch, or people working together in a factory—there are these various modes of activity. The point of calling it "study" is to mark that the incessant and irreversible intellectuality of these activities is already present. These activities aren't ennobled by the fact that we now say, "oh, if you did these things in a certain way, you could be said to be have been studying." To do these things is to be involved in a kind of common intellectual practice. (2013, 110)

Study names something far more diffuse than what happens in classrooms, or in study hall, something more ordinary and more improvisational, more subjunctive. Study is esoteric worlding as the collective intellection of its own ontogenesis, and it happens everywhere, all the time, in as many keys and time signatures as there are worlds, and study often involves the coming together co-compositionally of many worlds at once. Study is where the utmost potentiality of improvisation (epitomized, sonically, by texts like Ornette Coleman's *Free Jazz*) and the haptic, erotic rhythms of the everyday are indistinguishable. The everyday is a site of subjunctive excess where a potentiality for otherwise, endarkenment worlding is part of what moves through us, and our participatory tending, as part of the endurance of the colonial world and the simultaneous continuance of other worlds.

Wynter's concept of ceremony (always resonant with study) returns my attention to evental ontogenesis and the ethicopolitical questions of differential participation that guide my theorization of tending. Before getting to those philosophical meditations—which emerge from thinking about Christina Sharpe's *In the Wake*, which means they emerge in that very wake—I am going to situate myself not at "the university" in general but at the university where I teach, where I work, which is to say, the site of my "everyday" participation in worlding. I attend to three events that happened (in the sense of "hap": an aleatory improvisation of worlding) on this campus in April 2019. For reasons that will become apparent by the middle of the chapter, I might think about these events as something like raindrops on a surface of the ocean, where the drops themselves are singular in the sense of taking a particular pattern (where their "breaking" the surface of the water sends a pattern radiating outward). This participatory patterning—where events generate waves that interfere with other waves in ways that amplify or diminish particular patterns—works because the drops are materially "the same" as the surface they interrupt and modulate. Pattern is immanent worlding, material articulation of socialities that endure for some time but not forever, in a deictic situation and not anywhere. The three events I am here going to dwell with—which is also to say tend—are never discrete; they resonate with each other and across spacetimes toward other events. They are patterns at a particular level—a level I am thinking here as the everyday—that enfold events happening at much smaller and faster levels (micro processes of matter's energetic patterning) and can be enfolded into events at much larger, almost unfathomable scales.

On April 1, 2019 my undergraduate literary theory students and I walked into a building named after the first president of the university. We were here to discuss Toril Moi's "'Nothing Is Hidden,'" an essay that intervenes in the literary studies "method wars" by proposing that there are no "methods," we just look at details and think, asking, "Why this?" As we entered the building, we all noticed a sign, posted on a stake in the ground, that offered "Our University's True Story," highlighting the entanglements of the building's namesake, Robert Ryland, with transatlantic slavery (he both enslaved people and wrote in defense of slavery). The sign ends by calling for a "complete and unvarnished portrayal of Rev. Ryland's legacy." This sign was a disruption to a certain trajectory in our study, but also an event catalyst, one that modulated our collective but distributed attention so that when we asked "Why this?" with Moi, the "this" that impressed itself on us was the sign, and more broadly, this "legacy." The first president's legacy would have to include this building and what transpires inside of it, which means that this class participates in that legacy, and we faced the task of thinking about how the pedagogy unfolding takes up this inheritance and is taken up by it. What does it mean to study, today, in *this* place?

The following week, we began to study Christina Sharpe's *In the Wake*. This pedagogical scene—reading *In the Wake* in the building by (at)tending to the sign—is the second event. The wake that we studied with Sharpe was not abstract, was not something "outside" of the classroom and our encounters. It was in the walls, in the deep structure of the university we inhabited, in us. The vertiginous way that Moi's question guided our attentions from the most abstract level of a question's enunciative force to the most precise attunement to a specific detail we could muster left us searching for language to slow down and attend to the manifold, diffuse, and largely ignored ways those levels are mediated in and by bodies, objects, texts, spaces, and specific conditions of emergence and circulation. To give us some traction—to put us in a space of friction, as Anna Tsing would say—we found another question, this one from Sara Ahmed: How does this thing arrive, what are its "conditions of arrival"? Ahmed's queer phenomenology begins with an encounter—the writer at her table—and then elaborates a Marxist critique of commodity fetishism hyper attuned to both the affective politics of racialization and heteropatriarchy, and the world-constituting agency of nonhumans. Asking these two questions together—why this? and what are its conditions of arrival?—led us back and forth between the language of the texts we read and the specific situation of our study.

The third event was an official university ceremony, on April 12, celebrating the fortieth anniversary of the university's feminist student life organization, *will*. This "feminist" ceremony was articulated, in some obvious ways, around the university's grammars of coloniality, toward Man, but it also included a performance—part poetry reading, part storytelling, part conjuring—by Alexis Pauline Gumbs, who modulated a presumptively indicative and homogenizing event toward subjunctive, endarkenment worlds. And her performance leads me to Octavia Butler's *Parable of the Sower* to think about ceremony as an erotic poethics of evental ontogeneisis. What I'm interested in across the chapter is how our on-campus study involved unsettling questions that modulated our (at)tending and how that tending was amplified and (re)orchestrated by Gumbs in ways that foreground the erotic, evental matter of participation.

Letting these events resonate together, this chapter tunes in more carefully to evental ontogenesis, which I elaborate here through the concept of "ceremony." I do this by thinking about Gumbs's practice in *Spill, M. Archive,* and *Dub* of ceremonially conjuring what she calls "scenes," which I want to call esoteric worlds. These books practice a specific kind of study, reading with Black feminist thinkers—Hortense Spillers, M. Jacqui Alexander, and Sylvia Wynter—and conjuring, from the subjunctive force of their words, everyday otherwise worlds, worlds Gumbs thinks of as poetry, which might also be what Wynter calls "autopoiesis" (2007), or what da Silva calls the "poethical" (2014). This is poeisis as worlding, as participating in erotic, haptic evental ontogenesis of endarkenment worlds. In pluriversal contact— the necessarily ensemble practice of study as everyday worlding—there are always possibilities for improvisation, where instead of generating selves acting in history (Man), other patternings of worlds might be played, heard, participated in. It is finally a question of how we live together in the everyday coloniality of the university, which captures study in homogenizing grammars of Man as subject, where, as Alexander puts it, "one of our tasks as committed feminist, antiracist intellectuals is to figure out how *not* to reproduce the racial regimes of the academy" (2005, 113). This necessarily involves a rethinking of what the human is, a turn away from Man as the organizational logic of the university and study because "liberal humanism," Kandice Chuh tells us, "posits the sovereignty and autochthony of the human even as—or precisely because—it justifies the conquest and dispossession, enslavement and eradication that constitute the course of liberalism in its intimate partnership with capitalism" (2019, 3–4).

Ceremony and Sociogeny

In her genealogy of the present order's "descriptive statement" of the hegemonic genre of the human (Man), Wynter articulates a complex ontology where storytelling, bodies, and relationality (spreading beyond the human) mutually co-compose each other. Her 1984 essay, "The Ceremony Must Be Found," articulates this genealogy by situating her in a particular context— shaped by the institutionalization of Black studies and other fields of minority knowledge in US universities following an explosion of demand made by radical social movements[3]—that turns on three threshold moments. In the first moment, she analyzes "the founding heresy of the original *Studia Humanitatis*" (21) in the "site" we now describe as the hinge between the Middle Ages and early modernity's Renaissance. The *Studia* authorized a fundamental mutation and reversal in the order of things, putting "Natural Causality" in place of "Divine Causality" (33). In this mutation, the newly constituted field—which retroactively posited itself in history—of "literature" plays a privileged role. Of this moment, Wynter writes: "It was to be an utterly new way of feeling, of imagining Self and World, and a mode of imagination that would no longer find its referential figurative *auctoritas* in the great religious schemas and symbols, but rather in a new referential figurative *auctoritas*, that of the fictional poetic/dramatic schemas of the phenomenon we call 'literature'" (33). Wynter's second threshold takes shape in the eighteenth and nineteenth centuries, ultimately being marked by both the institutional codification of disciplines including "the literary humanities" as part of the "nineteenth century's reordering of the episteme" (45), and by the same moment's reorganization of the sciences (Foucault, 1994). Together these shifts would authorize what Wynter here calls "a new bio-ontological form" (36) and her later work will call the human's "biocentric descriptive statement" (2003). This threshold's mutation in the work of ordering done by constitutive outsides appertains to "new plantation orders" of coloniality (37). Specifically, this descriptive ordering statement about the human requires "the 'active creation' of the type of Chaos, which the dominant model needs for the replication of its own system" (37). Hierarchical, differential modes of a "universal" humanization are ordered not exactly through exclusion of constitutive outsides, but through their production as particular limits *within* taxonomies of humanness. Zakiyyah Iman Jackson argues that "animalization is not incompatible with humanization: what is commonly deemed dehumanization is, in the main, more accurately interpreted as the violence of humanization or the burden of inclusion into a racially hierarchized universal humanity" (2020, 18).[4] Here, those Fanon would called *les damnés* function as the liminal subjects consigned to violence upon which the ordered stability of "the universal human" depends (1963, 321). As King argues, for Wynter "the epistemological revolution of Enlightenment Man requires the Negro as an irrational and sensual human Other" (2019, 18).

The third threshold moment for Wynter is speculative or, as I would prefer to put it here, subjunctive. It is the "not yet" toward which we always reach in our praxis (Muñoz 2010). Conceptualized under the heading of "ceremony," I want to approach it by backing up to describe the *mechanism* that Wynter theorizes across several essays that allows "descriptive statements" to have the power to overrepresent Man as the human, since that will be the power ceremony must access in order to turn away from Man.

In the 1984 essay, Wynter draws on cybernetics—the work of Chilean biologists Humberto Maturana and Francisco Varela (1998)—in order to argue that discourses, or "descriptive statements," enter into human (and, presumably but ambiguously, more-than-human[5]) autopoeietic life. Referring to the "normative defining of the secular mode of the Subject," Wynter insists on the present participle: "Defining, rather than definition, because the latter does not exist as a reality except by and through our collective system of behaviors, systems which are themselves oriented by the ordering modes of knowing or epistemes of each human system" (22). Which is to say, that for humans, the "environment" each of us responds to as an autopoeietic system includes an ensemble of discourses constituting a social world that becomes part of the human's bioaffective apparatus. A human being "bring[s] that specific normative template of identity into living being" (22). Wynter here uses the concept of "psychogeny" to signal how "this self-imaged, self-troping Self now came to function as the Final/Formal cause which determined behavior for the human, as the mode of genetic speciation had determined behaviors for other biological organisms. For the hominid-into-human, psychogeny replaces philogeny as the determinant of its cognitive mechanisms or ratiomorphic apparatuses" (24).

By the time she published her 2001 essay, "Toward the Sociogenic Principle," Wynter would drop "psychogeny" in favor of "sociogeny," a concept she takes from Frantz Fanon's *Black Skin, White Masks* (1967). She writes, "The proposal here is that Fanon's thesis, that besides phylogeny and ontogeny stands sociogeny, reveals that the cultural construction of specific 'qualitative mental states' (such as the aversive reaction of white Europeans and of blacks ourselves to our skin color and physiognomy), are states specific to the modes of subjective experience defining what it is like to be human within the terms of our present culture's conception of what it is to be human" (2001, 46). By theorizing what David Chalmers calls "underlying physical processes," Wynter uses cybernetics to reconfigure Fanon's psychoanalytic claim into one about how specific biocultural individuals come into being in a climatological *and* social environment. Here, subject formation takes place in shifting material conditions that include the discursive, and the global production of narratives is plugged directly into the autopoeietic systems of human beings and their affective apparatuses. The stories circulating that describe the human *materially* configure our humanness, and our experience of what "it is like" to be human.

In "The Ceremony Must be Found," Wynter takes up what Julietta Singh (2018) would call a dehumanist perspective that is situated in the nonbelonging of being "in but not of" the university. Wynter writes that "the view from the Black Culture Center [on the edges of campus, accessible only by climbing muddy hills] therefore insists, heretically, that far from 'literature having no function,' as it is assumed, it is we who are the function. It is as specific modes of imagining subjects of the aesthetic orders which literature's figuration-Word weaves in great feats of rhetorical engineering that we come to imagine/experience ourselves, our modes of being" (1984, 50). Since literature, or more broadly, "stories," create us as "functions," the political future Wynter writes toward turns out to adhere in heretical storytelling events, events she calls "ceremony." Ceremony names events in which stories articulate shifts in our naturecultural functioning, opening us toward different futures and, hopefully, worlds in which different genres of the human (or what Jayna Brown calls "new genres of *existence*" [2021, 9])—not just Man as overrepresentatiaon—can flourish in relation to specific knowledge practices.

These ceremonies can be geared toward the evental tending of Man and Man's singular world, where "settlement is a terrifying ritual that purportedly transforms profane land into sacred world" (Winters 2021, 248). Against Man's homogenizing "sacred" world, we might instead cultivate "modes of ecstatic-erotic vitality that are excremental to the theopolitical order" (Carter 2021, 175), which might be thought of as "an alternative practice of the social, a poetics of improvisational sociality under constraint" (152). There are enlightenment ceremonies tending *Man's world*, and endarkenment ceremonies that tend *otherwise worlds* (and often things are quite muddled with many tendings colliding at once). As King argues, "Wynter pursues a way to mark a ceremony or ritual act that can usher in the heretical, the unthinkable, and the unfathomable without trapping it/them once it is/they are conjured" (2019, 187). At stake for Wynter, then, isn't a question of whether education—wherever it happens, in or outside of the university or school—is ceremonial or not, but of how those ceremonies tend worlds. We need to tend, in the everyday, ceremonies authorizing different, non-Man genres of the human through the production of stories and through evental, ceremonial lingering with new (and old) stories. These storytelling ceremonies would no longer articulate a universal, "global" human internally rent by anti-Black, colonialist, ableist, and (cis)heterosexist hierarchies, but would instead articulate a proliferating field of knowledge practices, which are always co-compositional with more-than-human socialities, and which animate differential modes or genres of existence. Ceremony can be endarkenment tending.

Why This?

Let me return now to the classroom on April 1. Toril Moi offers the question "Why this?" to short circuit the often acrimonious "method wars" circulating in literary studies with two polarized positions. On the one side would seem to stand the hermeneutics of suspicion where interpretive practices hinge on exposing hidden truths or ideologies governing the structures of utterances (including complex utterances like poems or novels or art objects) (Sedgwick 2003). This camp would include psychoanalytic and Marxist traditions of analysis, and the many "critical" projects that developed in relation to them (including much feminist and queer criticism). These writers understand interpretive practice to "be" political insofar as the critical aim is to make transparent ideological structures that, by virtue of being explicitly theorized, can be resisted. On the other side are those who want to read surfaces instead of depths (Best and Marcus 2009), repair rather than unfurl paranoid critiques (Sedgwick 2003), and clear space in the field for something other than critique to flourish in our classrooms and writings.

Since a good deal of what we read in the course would probably be considered "critical" or suspicious, I wanted to give students a sense of how current disputes may be shifting the presumption of critique as a guiding logic for curricula in literary studies. I assigned parts of Elizabeth Anker and Rita Felski's *Critique and Postcritique* to raise questions about my own course design, and the kinds of assumptions we bring to thinking about what "theory" is and what it means for undergraduate study. While Anker and Felski's introduction offers a careful overview of the shape of the method wars (unlike my reductive one above), Moi's chapter—the first in the book—effectively cries foul, noting that the entire argument feels like a distraction from acknowledging that there is no method in literary studies beyond one that can be stated plainly: we "simply look and think" (2017, 35).

Arguing that there is a gap between how literary critics talk about method (as in the method wars) and what they do, Moi posits that texts don't really have depths or surfaces and that the entire problem hinges on a "need to think of texts and language as hiding something" (34). In the method wars, some readers want to bring to light what is hidden while others want to look at what is not hidden, but Moi insists that no matter what kinds of theories and political commitments one brings, "in the encounter with the literary text, the only 'method' that imposes itself is the willingness to look and see, to pay maximal attention to the words on the page" (35). To develop this claim, Moi turns to two canonical suspicious readers: Sigmund Freud and Sherlock Holmes. Taking up Holmes (not the character as seen in Arthur Conan Doyle's stories but the version in the BBC television show *Sherlock*), Moi underscores how the show frames Sherlock's reasoning skills as strange and extraordinary; but for Moi, that lesson isn't about Sherlock Holmes so much as it is about a particular intensity of attention: "The other characters—the police detective, Watson—simply fail to take an interest in the features that grab Sherlock's attention. It's not that others look at the surface, whereas Sherlock looks beneath it. It is that he *pays attention* to details they didn't think to look at" (42).

Economies of attention, not "methods," are what are at stake in literary analysis.[6] And Moi borrows the deceptively simple question "Why this?" from Stanley Cavell in order to shift the debate away from binaries of surface versus depth, reparative versus paranoid, critical versus postcritical reading to questions that aren't about "how" we read so much as about how we handle "matters of response, judgment, and responsibility" (47). In our class discussions, Moi's question put me on the spot as the instructor: I had to account for why I thought "literary theory" was a thing that was worth engaging (especially given its perceived "difficulty"), and for decisions that I had made during syllabus construction about what questions, disputes, and theories to assign, as well as specific choices about texts that would serve as representatives of those conversations in the field. These are, in a way, anticipatable calls for responsibility, ones I prepare myself to engage every time I teach. But Moi's question kept arising in other places, ones that weren't part of the "planning" any of us did before the course began. And the most obvious concern on our minds while discussing Moi's chapter was: What about *the sign*? While Moi's question moved our attention there, we also butted against its abstract universality: as she writes, "We can ask Why this? about anything" (46). The question's generality is one reason it works: one can always start there, in any context or situation. But the trouble becomes translating "this" into the specific demands of "looking and thinking" Moi calls for (which will often not be "looking" but differently sensuous and erotic affective contact). Once our attention snaps into place, what exactly does it mean to "think" here, especially when that cannot be reduced to a method or even something agentially done by a self-conscious subject because, as Erin Manning has argued, "it is urgent to turn away from the notion that it is the human agent, the intentional, volitional subject, who determines what comes to be" (2016, 3)?

What Are Its Conditions of Arrival?

Moi's "Why this?" question is grammatically minuscule—just an adverb indicating a shift to the interrogative mood and an indexical adjective. The force of the question (and its usefulness in shifting conversations about method) lies in the way that minimal grammar attaches deixis to wonder. *This* can be anything, but whenever it is uttered it is *this very specific thing and no other* that demands our attention. Once we notice a thing, what are we to do? The sign spurs an event, sets conditions for an emergent relationality we might call study (Harney and Moten 2013). When I arrived in the room, students were already there talking. No one knew who put up the sign, although they shared rumors circulating on GroupMe and other social media. And students immediately made the metonymic link from *How did this sign get here?* to *How did I get here?*; that is, students immediately began to account for their own anxieties and disorientations on campus, talking about the ways that their experiences—marked by capitalist inequalities, racialization, heterosexism, ableist infrastructures, and international visa protocols—had made them feel already like things here were *off*, sometimes without being able to say what exactly or how.

Because we had touched on some of Sara Ahmed's ideas when they came up in our discussions of Julietta Singh's *Unthinking Mastery*, I turned toward Ahmed in this moment. Most of us felt out of place on campus (although in very different ways) and Ahmed reminds us that "we only notice the arrival of those who appear 'out of place.' Those who are 'in place' must also arrive; they must get 'here,' but their arrival is more easily forgotten" (2006, 9–10). Ahmed's *Queer Phenomenology* is a summons to attend to these conditions of arrival: to the ways that "here" is always constituted by a confluence of arrivals, and the conditions of that transit and circulation turn out to also influence the conditions of the encounter. Taking up the example of the writer at a table (in Husserl's phenomenology but also, for example, in Virginia Woolf's *A Room of One's Own*), Ahmed writes that "attention involves a political economy, or an uneven distribution of attention time between those who arrive at the writing table, which affects what they can do once they arrive (and of course, many do not even make it)" (32). This "political economy of attention" is exactly what our class was trying to articulate as we asked "Why this?" of ourselves, our course texts, and *the materiality of our meeting*. And her analysis provided a whole range of questions we might ask as corollaries of "Why this?," questions that sent us looking from our deictic situation to the circuits, forces, networks, and structures that made "being here" something that happens for each of us.

Ahmed's account of the table begins in phenomenology: How does this table appear to me, the writer? But she quickly realizes that "we may need to supplement phenomenology with an 'ethnography of things'" (39). This means, first, retooling phenomenology with a kind of attention Marxists bring to critiques of commodity fetishism: What kinds of labor in what kinds of conditions were required for this table to come into being in the world and find its way *here* (39)? Ahmed pushes through what can often seem like an anthropocentric tendency in Marxism to locate labor solely in humans toward a more expansive account of the affective possibilities of things (she asks "how does the 'matter' of paper matter?" [26]). In the process, Ahmed hits on orientation as a necessary concept: it is not the case that bodies exist as such and spaces exist as such and then orientation names the ways bodies circulate in pregiven spaces. Rather, orientation points toward the unfolding of worlds in their tendencies. Bodies and spaces are shaped by these material, affective encounters, and economies of affect lead to accumulations such that certain spaces are more available to some bodies than others, some bodies can reach more or different things than other bodies. Ahmed argues that whiteness is best understood as a logic that shapes how bodies and spaces co-compose each other: "Whiteness becomes a social and bodily orientation given that some bodies will be more at home in a world that is oriented around whiteness" (138). Whiteness is less a property of bodies, or of spaces, than it is the affective sedimentation of "white" bodies and spaces as co-emergent across time. Ahmed looks at the specifics of a table and thinks with phenomenological questions we might consider of as part of the psychology of affordances (what does this object allow me to do?), Marxist questions about the sedimentation of human (but not just human) labor in objects that circulate, and decolonial and queer questions about how worlding unfolds in ways that make some feel "in place" because others are "out of line."

This gave us a set of orienting queries that helped us turn from Moi's provocative question to the seminar table around which we sat, where our conditions of arrival made *this* table feel different to each of us. This table turned out to make specific demands: I had to earn a PhD and be hired to teach in the English Department. The students had to be (competitively) admitted to the university, and then find their ways to English, whether as majors or not, enroll in the class and pay relevant fees to hold their seat. And those institutional demands often uneasily met our individual needs as people trying to move through a world shaped by coloniality such that while we are all inescapably shaped by colonial inheritance, "shaping" takes many forms.

The sign noted something about "the past," about someone who lived when slavery was legal, when Richmond, Virginia, was a thriving scene of the chattel slave trade, and who enslaved people and justified slavery, even if other parts of his life can be read as signaling different kinds of (quasi) anti-racist beliefs (he preached at a Black church). For many who have arrived at the university since its founding in the 1840s (just two decades before the city became the capitol of the Confederacy), little about Ryland's slave own-ing would have seemed out of line, nor would it have made them feel out of place. But most of us in *this* room would not have been allowed here in the not-very-distant past. Learning together how to ask the kind of questions we asked in Modern Literary Theory while in a building whose name honors an enslaver became a difficult prospect, a "brick wall," as Ahmed put it else-where (2017), that keeps us from feeling "at home" (which may not be what we want to feel anyway). This feeling was one we had all experienced before, maybe even most of the time, but it wasn't one we brought to our conversa-tions, especially in literature classes. Once the sign snapped our attention to it, though, we couldn't *not* think: How did we arrive here, in this place that only itself arrives via the (present and ongoing) theft of Powhattan land and the wealth accumulated from enslaved labor? This was and is to feel that the "the past" is not past, or rather, that homogenizing linear time is only settler time's overrepresentation (Rifkin, 2017). Another inescapable question: How is it that so many can look at this campus, this building, and *not* see this, not feel this, not attune and ask why? These questions emerge in and as the event, and their force (dis)orients us.

The Wake as Event

Christina Sharpe's *In the Wake* is clearly addressed to a Black readership as she elaborates a theory of "wake work," a particular approach to attentive living in the wake of transatlantic slavery. Marking the address, located in the first-person plural, I quote at length here in order to tease out a problem our class hit on as we took up Sharpe's book just a week after the sign appeared outside our door: What does it mean to live "in the wake" for those of us who are not Black? Note, as you read, the deictic insistence. Sharpe writes:

> Living in/the wake of slavery is living "the afterlife of property" [Saidiya Hartman's phrase] and living in the afterlife of the *partus sequitur ventrem* (that which is brought forth follows the womb), in which the Black child inherits the non/status, the non/being of the mother. The inheritance of a non/status is everywhere apparent *now* in the ongoing criminalization of Black women and children. Living in the wake on a global level means living the disastrous time and effects of continued marked migrations, Mediterranean and Caribbean disasters, trans-American and -African migration, structural adjustment imposed by the International Monetary Fund that continues imperialisms/colonialisms, and more. And here, in the United States, it means living and dying through the policies of the first US Black president; it means the gratuitous violence of stop-and-frisk and Operation Clean Halls; rates of Black incarceration that boggle the mind (Black people represent 60 percent of the imprisoned population); the immanence of death as a "predictable and constitutive aspect of *this* democracy" (James and Costa Vargas 2012, 193, emphasis mine). Living in the wake means living the history and present of terror, from slavery to the present, as the ground of our everyday Black existence. (2016, 15).

This long quotation is meant to offer a sense of the book's style of proliferating, asterisked elaborations of thought, one where the "terror" of "everyday Black existence" is a ground or "the weather." Anti-Blackness here names a totalizing, enveloping *scene* that endures in ways that make clear distinctions between historical modalities of anti-Blackness and present institutional, economic, legal, carceral, and educational operations impossible. Anti-Blackness, as the reference to the Afro-pessimist concept of "gratuitous violence" makes clear, is *the world* in its tending. But the tending of worlds for Sharpe is not ever thinkable only as anti-Blackness. Wake work attends to the ongoingness of anti-Blackness as it shapes the ongoing mattering of the world at levels and scales that we are taught to see as distinct, but it also includes practices that disrupt it, stall it, steer away from routes that would leave the materiality of its "wake" in the same shape. Sharpe writes, "I mean wake work to be a mode of inhabiting *and* rupturing this episteme with our known lived and un/imaginable lives. With that analytic we might imagine otherwise from what we know *now* in the wake of slavery" (18). Wake work, we might say, is both critical and affirmative. It attends to social death, yes, but also to what Kevin Quashie (2021) has recently called "Black aliveness."

One of Sharpe's key "events" is the ship Zong, which left Africa carrying "442 (or 470)" people in its hold, and arrived in Jamaica four months later with only "208 living Africans on board" (35, 37). Most of the slaves were thrown overboard—although many jumped into the sea—as a result of fear of losses of "property" that had to be settled in an insurance claim: "The deposed crew recounted that it was lack of water and the insurance claim that motivated the throwing overboard. They recognized that insurance monies would not be paid if those enslaved people died 'a natural death'" (35). Weaving historical and genealogical work on the Zong with analysis of M. NourbeSe Philips's poem *Zong!*, Sharpe explicitly theorizes this ship and everything it tells us now about "the wake" as an event: "*The event*, which is to say, one version of one part of a more than four-hundred-year-long event" (37).

Sharpe's nesting of events within an event suggests that there is something like an evental ontology of the world: the world is always becoming in and as events. We can name one of those events—happening at a scale of centuries—as anti-Blackness, slavery and its wake. And we can also name more discrete events *within* larger events, like the Zong. I might begin to sketch the importance of this claim by reading it against an extremely influential claim in settler colonial studies: Patrick Wolfe's "invasion is a structure not an event" (2006, 388). Wolfe is here getting at the crucial idea that we cannot think of settler colonial invasion as a "one-off (and superseded) occurrence" in the past (388), a claim that seems similar to what Sharpe is after with the concept of the wake of slavery. The difference, however, is not exactly in the larger claim about the historical ongoingness of violent dispossession, but in the understanding of what an "event" is. For Wolfe, that concept evokes something temporally bounded, over and done at a locatable moment. Events would be discreet. Yet for Sharpe, discreteness is a function not of events themselves per se but how they can be felt and lived through from particular deictically marked locations ("here," in "*this* democracy"). This ontoepistemological difference is immediately soldered to a political question, for a structure leads to critical practice: the labor of uncovering how a system works so that it can be known in turn suggests the ability to imagine an alternatively conceptualized system. Critical analysis, we are told, matters because in imagining what's wrong with the world, one can plan a new one; the political task is dismantling or overthrowing the current system so that a better one can be erected. "Critical" politics tend to be imagined playing out at large scales, with "the people" rising up in revolution. That is, even if invasion is a structure, its undoing will still often be imagined as an event that founds a new structure, one that has to be planned and orchestrated.

Sharpe's wake work is different. The very concept of "the wake" resists critical closure: it proliferates, held open by an asterisk. And the response to it cannot be a question of getting everyone to affirm a single critique so that large numbers can be orchestrated to enact an imagined better world. The political response adheres, precisely, in the evental nature of the world. As Brian Massumi argues, "the event" is "the primary unit of the real" (Massumi and Manning, 2015, 147). Massumi develops this theory of the event through a reading of Alfred North Whitehead's process philosophy where, as Didier Debaise puts it, "each event is a passage, inherently unique in its moment, different from all others" (2017, 35) and the world is made up of such events happening at all kinds of scales. For Whitehead, there is a tendency coursing through such events toward patterning: matter tends, in events, to hang together in particular ways. In each event, entities enter into a distributed becoming where a whole panoply of possible outcomes are virtually present and the passage of a *specific* event selects some of those outcomes rather than others.

Whitehead uses the name "society" to describe particular configurations of matter (a crystal is, in his lexicon, a society; this is not a question of anthropomorphism). As Debaise explicates it, "The sole aim, the sole goal of a 'society' is to maintain its historic route, the movement of its inheritance, the taking up, the transmission of the acts of feeling that comprise it" (73). Singular instances of anti-Black society are not "examples" of larger, macro-level events. Rather, what one viewpoint sees as a four-hundred-year-long event can be, from another viewpoint, innumerable events with different conditions, possibilities, and outcomes. Nothing is "given"; history does not "determine." Rather, in every event where bodies and spaces co-compose, there adheres a tendency, in this anti-Black world, for events to emerge that pass on anti-Blackness. Indeed, this is the expected outcome of most events, a kind of statistical or probable endurance of coloniality.[7] There is no "outside" to the wake, but there is, and must be, possibilities for disruption, for tending what Sharpe calls the "otherwise." These possibilities adhere in matter:

> But even if those Africans who were in the holds, who left something of their prior selves in those rooms as a trace to be discovered, and who passed through the doors of no return did not survive the holding and the sea, they, like us, are alive in hydrogen, in oxygen; in carbon, in phos-

phorous, and iron; in sodium and chlorine. This is what we know about those Africans thrown, jumped, dumped overboard in Middle Passage; they are with us still, in the time of the wake, known as residence time. (Sharpe 2016, 19)

I read the movement from Sharpe's "like us" to "with us" as suggesting a shift in scale, a zooming in, that might tend toward "in us," "as us." Our own wakefulness, attentiveness, is an articulation of the molecules that make up, and disrupt, the wake in its ongoing evental patterning.

Sharpe elaborates this evental ontogenesis through a focus on Black aspiration in the wake, thinking through, among other things, M. NorbeSe Philip's *Zong!* and Eric Garner's last words, uttered as refrain and plea, "I can't breathe." Sharpe writes, "I've been thinking about aspiration in the complementary sense of the word: the withdrawal of fluid from the body *and* the taking in of foreign matter (usually fluid) into the lungs with the respiratory current, *and* as *audible breath* that accompanies or comprises a speech sound" (2016, 109). Aspiration, here, is the material process—the event—in which the atmosphere (the weather of anti-Blackness) gets inside us and becomes us, and it is also the same event in which our living (our breath) (re)constitutes that atmosphere. Aspiration names a kind of tending, and, to get a little ahead of myself, I want to frame aspiration, following Gumbs, as a matter of ceremony that might unfurl from the force of an interrogative (always blurring into the subjunctive too). Gumbs writes, of *Dub*, that "it is structured to ask, what if you could breathe like whales who sing underwater and recycle air to sing again before coming up for air? What if you could breathe like coral from a multitude of simultaneous openings connected to one source built upon the bones of all your dead? What if you could breathe like cyanobacteria who made the sky into oxygen millions of years ago and sent their contemporaries to a world of sulfur deep under ocean and ground. What then? And by then I mean now" (2020, xiii).

The pedagogical task is to (at)tend to the tendencies of worlds in their ongoingness and bring what you can to your participation in the *event*: to attune (which will always only be partly about consciousness or the volition of a liberal subject) to how the world's becoming allows what Massumi calls "freedom" adhering *in* the situation as a possibility to be played, a material spur to improvising otherwise worlds: "Our freedom is in how we play our implication in a field, what events we succeed in catalysing in it that bring out the latent singularity of the situation, how we inflect for novel emergences"

(2014, 158). This play doesn't belong to an "I" so much as to the erotic, evental field itself: "This does not . . . mean that there is no 'I.' It just means that the 'I' cannot be located in advance of the event" (Manning 2016, 37). Breathing is not really the voluntary action of a subject, but a mode of (nonvolitional) participation, one that tends the colonial world or tends other(wise) worlds as those words (literally) move through us and (re)create us as we (re)create worlds.

Modulating Endarkenment Ceremony

> Breathing gifts us with an attention to wonder.
> —Marquis Bey, *Black Trans Feminism*

Not two weeks after walking past the sign, I attended the fortieth anniversary celebration for the WILL program (founded as "Women In Living and Learning"), an undergraduate life program at the University of Richmond that predates, by a few years, the program in Women's Studies (which today is named "Women, Gender and Sexuality Studies"). The event was held in the lavish Jepson Alumni Center—a building I had never been in but which synecdochally signals the enormous wealth of the university and its endowment—and included a catered dinner. Guests were faculty and students, but also alumni and donors. The event began with an address from the university president: its first Black president, a cellist by training, who favored libertarian politics and whose signature policy objective is something he called "inclusive excellence," a phrase that may well work as exemplary of Man's homogenizing logics. The entire scene—its situation in a particular space, with particular food, particular guests, and particular speakers—unfolds within colonial grammars. It presumptively celebrates the university's tending of Man in the sense of generating the kinds of citizen-subjects who become leaders (even "feminist" ones) and then "give back." The event is structured to suture everyone there to participation in Man's tending through what Ferguson has called the university's "new techniques of management" of minority demand and knowledge production (2012, 25).[8] In the wake of reading *In the Wake*, the logics of capture here were palpable, and, as I ate my salad, I felt the everyday banality of Man's overrepresentation of the human.

There was a litany of thank yous—sometimes to people who ambivalently tended coloniality by also seeking out improvisational openings that amplified the cracks in Man's heteropatriarchal capture so that that those other than white cismasculine subjects could participate in the university and the kinds of study it allows (if only because it captures that study's energy as Harney and Moten might say). Then something else happened, something Manning might phrase as a shift from major to minor tending: "The major is a structural tendency that organizes itself according to predetermined definitions of value. The minor is a force that courses through it, unmooring its structural integrity, problematizing its normative standards" (2016), 1). Alexis Pauline Gumbs took the podium to read sections of her book, *M. Archive*, and to intersperse those readings with storytelling: she told one story about each of four feminist ancestors: Audre Lorde, June Jordan, Toni Cade Bambara, and Octavia Butler. Each story—a story of the unexpected, of the everydayness of ontogenesis—led to a quotation from their writing, a quotation that Gumbs spun into a spell, a collective incantation and invocation, a sounding-together that is also a hearing of a collective that is not separable from its present incantatory improvisation.[9] This was an event in which, as Ashon Crawley puts it, "everyone is held within breathing as process" (2017, 85).

After a story about the possible, subjunctive, disappearance (or extraworldly eccentric existence) of Octavia Butler's gravestone (or perhaps both), Gumbs hit on the poem of Lauren Olamina's that opens *Parable of the Sower*: "All that you touch you Change. / All that you Change Changes you."[10] She drew the audience in, orchestrating our voices, demanding more sound, different sound, differently paced sound. It was a means of conjuring evental participation at a level that isn't about individual selves or their psychology in the first instance—she didn't explain a critique of the world and call for rational decisions of commitment to that intellectual-political telos. Instead, she worked directly on air pressure as the materiality of sound, on (more-than-human) bodies that breathe, and where the air (and water) moving in and out of these bodies mixes into a general evental atmosphere, one where everyone is participating in the same air, an air saturated with water vapor (and much more as we can't forget thanks to COVID-19). Air, for Crawley,

> is an object held in common, an object that we come to know through a collective participation within it as it enters and exits flesh. The process by which we participate in this common object, with this common admixture, not only must be thought about but must be consumed and expelled through repetition in order to think. (2017, 36)

Gumbs's practice is an enactment of precisely what Butler's words would seem to say: in the chanting together in that room, we touched and were touched by each other (and on the "inside" of us: our sinuses, our lungs, the entirety of our bodies' molecular tendings through the in- and excorporation of energy).

As we said "all that you touch," our breath sent air out into the atmosphere even as our eardrums were touched, intimately, by the differentiating pressure of the air modulated by my voice and everyone else's in the event. What Butler's words do when incanted by an ensemble orchestrated by Gumbs is attune us to precisely the way worlding happens in the very instant of its evental ongoingness. The event generates, here, a kind of intensity where levels—molecular, sonic, aesthetic, political, and spiritual—resonate through and off each other, a massive vibratory, material happening in which participation is highly unequal. "Within such ecologies," Jean-Thomas Trembley avers, "breathing is revealed as . . . a conduit through which imperialism, colonialism, and sexism are felt and negotiated" (2022, 93) in differential ways. Gumbs's role, as poet and poethical conjurer of worlds, is not the same as mine as a faculty member, or the students', or the alumni's, or the donors', or the caterers' and servers,' or the animals whose cooked bodies were on the meal plates, or the material structures of the building that sediment settler colonialist extraction and anti-Black enslavement and its afterlives.

What this improvisational incantation—this sociogenic tending of a pluriversal world, a minor world—does is make palpable how coloniality resides in what we feel, how the space feels, how it feels to be with each other, to practice worlds together. The minor world of Gumbs's (and Butler's) ceremony is an affective patterning of world, a felt participation in evental ontogensisis. Riffing on Wynter's concept of ceremony, Myra Rivera writes that "ritual is the means by which feelings are embodied, transmitted, and transformed" (2021, 77). Ceremony can bind us to Man; Rivera notes that what is at stake for Wynter are "the possibilities of refusing the imposition of the Word of Man as the mobilization of affective energies and bodily performance in specific sociomaterial contexts" (77). But there are undercommon ceremonies of endarkenment, of tendings away from Man that are felt, haptic: "Hapticality, the touch of the undercommons, the interiority of sentiment, the feel that what is to come is here. Hapticality, the capacity to feel through others, for others to feel through you, for you to feel them feeling you, this feel of the shipped is not regulated, at least not successfully, by a state, a religion, a people, an empire, a piece of land, a totem" (Harney and Moten 2013, 98). At stake in this haptics, this erotic biopolitics of touch, this affective participation in evental ontogenesis, is a kind of hearing, an (at)tending (to) worlds as they are improvised by more-than-human socialities. For Manning, "minor sociality is a listening-with the array of potential socialities in our surrounds. Lively with the forces of the outside, it asks that sociality be invented anew each time, that the world, and worlding, become the occasion for study" (2020, 227).

Ceremonial Scenes: Conjuring Everyday Endarkenment Worlds through Study

A hap care would not be about letting an object go, but holding on to an object by letting oneself go, giving oneself over to something that is not one's own. A hap care would not seek to eliminate anxiety from care; it could even be described as a care for the hap.... In time, we attend. To attend to something that has become more easily breakable is to attend to its history, with love, and with care.
—Sara Ahmed, *Living a Feminist Life*

Gumbs's trilogy of Black feminist study—*Spill*, *M. Archive*, and *Dub*—helps me think about what I mean when I say that study, ceremony, and endarkenment participation in evental ontogenesis are resonant ways of signaling the more-than-human, other-than-Man, spiritual worlding (always plural, always esoteric) that can always happen, might always be happening, should always be happening. It's about the subjunctive adhering in the hap, outside of what's captured by homogenizing grammars. The three books emerge from a very particular practice, a tending. Gumbs calls the practice "ceremony" (2020, xiii) and also describes the project, particularly *Dub*, as "an artifact and tool for breath retraining and interspecies ancestral listening" (xiii). What this listening (at)tends to, by thinking about evental ontogenesis as a matter of participation, is the subjunctive articulation of pluriversal, esoteric "kindred beyond taxonomy" (xii).[11] Elaborating this toward the entire trilogy, Tiffany Lethabo King proposes that "listening in the mode of Gumbs, Spillers, Alexander, and Wynter exceeds the sonic and reorganizes and unmoors the sensorium something akin to the haptic" (2020, 1); I would call this mode or mood the subjunctive.

What Gumbs does is read Spillers, Alexander, and Wynter care-fully and slowly. When she finds herself resonating with a particular word or phrase— not necessarily the concepts that academic readers tend to gravitate toward and (at)tend to, including myself—she writes a "scene," which is to say she conjures a minor world. "They are poems, surely," as Marquis Bey puts it, "though poems not as objects but as *events*" (2022, 116). Describing how such scenes are a matter of "finding ceremony," Gumbs says:

> I think of the pieces on each page as scenes. I think of the book as a whole as a poem (#epic) and I think of every scene as poetic. And I think of it as an index and an oracle and a meditation. My intention is for the technologies of Black women poets, fiction writers, hip-hop artists, priestesses, singers, mamas, fugitives, stylists, and literary theorists to converge in the same space. Sylvia Wynter says, "After humanism—the ceremony must be found," and I wanted to find a ceremony where we could be together, and where I could be with the revolutionary work of Hortense Spillers and with everyone else I love at the same time. Finding ceremony is a poetic act. So it is poetry. (KMT 2018)

I will return, in a moment, to how these scenes, inspired as they are by Spillers, are about the fugitive disruption of colonial grammars, including grammars of the self as (raced, gendered, sexual) subject. But first, I want to mark here a particular kind of esoteric collective in her language—a "we" that can "be together"—that opens onto an intersectional and evental meditation on material-spiritual ceremonial participation and helps us think of these scenes as tending (toward) endarkenment esoterisms where participation and poet(h)ics aren't separable.

In Gumbs's study, reading is a kind of listening, a more-than-human hearing. Asked by Joy KMT what she was listening to working on *Spill*, Gumbs says something I need to quote at length:

> I needed to hear the phrase. I had written down the phrases [from Spillers's work] and I would open up the notebook that had the phrases outside of their context, and I would work with the one my eyes fell on. Then I would cross it out after I worked with it. I was distilling it in that way because I had to look at the phrase and not then go, well here's what she meant by that. Here's what I think about it. I had to not let my brain fill the space. I had to leave a space and listen to where the phrase took me. Who is this? What is the scene? Where? As I was hearing it and writing it and seeing it, the rhythms were very different. Sometimes there was a breathlessness at the end of writing it. Sometimes I would reread it and be like *woo!* Sometimes the experience was like *um-hm*. Sometimes it was a feeling of being transported and traveling back into my actual life. Who has the

actual expertise to tell this actual story is who I had to listen to, and understand that I'm in relationship to who that is through my intimacy with Black women's writing, and that legacy of listening. Listening to storytellers and also listening beyond, listening to the silence of a room, that those writers have been doing. And realizing that it was all there. (KMT, 2018)

Listening is participation, (at)tending. There is a haptics, a particular rhythm to each world, an irreducibly spatiotemporal affective consistency of patterning. Storytelling generates worlds by modulating, sociogenically, the rhythms and participatory patterns of ontogenesis. Gumbs doesn't invent these worlds, these scenes, so much as she participates in them by tending them as patterns of world. She finds ceremony as the sociogenic arrangement of words, phrases, and pauses for breath—where the irreducibility of spirit to language outstrips even deconstruction's attention to phonologocentrism—where reading is always incantation and is always ensemble (or assembled) participation in events. Haptics can be dispersed; intimacies transpire across scales.

Let me offer one specific scene from *M. Archive*. Reading Alexander's *Pedagogies of Crossing*, Gumbs comes across the sentence I italicize in this paragraph, which concerns precisely the problem of participation, of how different worlds come together and diverge in their ongoing tendings, and how that pluriversal worlding encounters Man's homogenizing logics in and outside of contexts of institutionalized education:

> Are there not fissures of class, skin color, shades of yellow and brown, within our respective nation/communities? Linguistic and regional differences that have created their own insiders and outsiders? *At what historical moment does heterogeneity become homogeneity—that is, the moment to create an outside enemy?* Neither of us as African American nor Caribbean people created those earlier conditions of colonialism and Atlantic slavery. Yet we continue to live through them in a state of selective forgetting, behaving now as if they have ceased to be first cousins. (Alexander 2005, 273, emphasis "mine" but only because I am participating in Gumbs's emphasizing).

I will resist here the urge to amplify all the resonances of this passage with arguments I have been making throughout the book, arguments I will return to below. For now, what I want to consider is how Gumbs, to recall Maryse Condé's word, (re)creates Alexander's sentence, how she studies it, how she participates in it *as study* and conjures the possibility of our participation in it too. I quote this too at length, knowing that to do so opens up the scene to your participation, your (at)tending, and the particular ways this ceremony lands in your decitic situation. Gumbs writes:

> some people said they had felt it in early twenty-first-century New York City after the financial towers fell for the first time. but that wasn't it. that was the false feeling of being "American" which didn't even include all American citizens. not even then. especially not then. some Black artists in the twentieth century had claimed a feeling of global citizenship when they fled to Europe in the early part of the century. it was short lived. some Black activists felt it when they fled to Africa in the second part of the century, but their feeling of being human was relative and fed by enduring imperialism externalized. don't count that.
>
> there did come a moment when the species was united on the planet as human, but it was not what anyone had dreamt. and it was too late to truly benefit those of us who had been called alien. we who had nonconsensually generated the human across time. it was what the Black speculative feminists called "the Butlerian moment." the more musical among them said "Octavian Overture." that moment when it was time to leave. when the true others finally arrived. (2018, 171)

Here, again, I feel an impulse toward explanation, toward a kind of authorial pedagogy oriented toward making connections explicit, ensuring that felt resonance takes the form of conceptual, linguistic articulation. What might it mean to forgo this, let go of the impulse to interpret? Sarah Jane Cervenak, writing about teaching after and teaching about the events in Ferguson, Missouri (where Ferguson came to be a synecdoche for racialized state violence following the police's murder of Michael Brown): "I think the time of the classroom, as with writing itself, needs to reorient itself out of respect for those gaps—to put off the 'aboutness' of the educational exercise so as to make room for grief, moments of silence, what moves as a modality of life that agitates for some privacy, for a damn moment against understanding" (2015, 224).[12]

One of the things about Gumbs's scenes is that they refuse the convention of capitalizing the first word of each sentence, a convention that is immanent in Microsoft Word's autocorrection. To type the scene, I had to first type and then edit every single first letter of every sentence to capture Gumbs's 'incorrect' grammar.[13] My typing—which is a technologically mediated form of incantation, of speaking and breathing along with Gumbs and Alexander—

was slowed down in precisely the sense I was interested in in chapter 3, where slowness undoes the obviousness of colonial orientations and invites leaky, delinquent, errant, fugitive improvisations. To get Gumbs's words right, I have to (at)tend the deviations from colonial grammar. Her worlds can only happen outside of Word's grammar, which is the world's grammar, which is the grammar of Man. Bey calls this writing "experimental," which "means a kind of writing that violates grammar and disallows 'normality' in terms of reading and encountering" (2022, 117). The point of this violation and disallowance isn't negative, but a necessary work of subjunctively presencing other worlds: "Gumbs presents what other worlds, after the world, under the world, might be, and who we might be in those worlds" (Bey, 117).

Gumbs talks about this as a Black feminist fugitive poetics, where what's at stake, again via Spillers, is precisely the ungrammatical, the anagrammatical, the other-than-grammatical, which is to say the rhymes that can be felt, as subjunctive worlds, that "spill" beyond the boundaries of colonial grammars. Gumbs says:

> For me, the repetition of rhyme is the fugitivity. The arrival at the urgency that's asking for your own revelation. Fugitivity for me is like, okay, so we have this flight and we're compelled and propelled and the momentum of the pieces of *Spill* is evoking that through the rhythm. What does that embodied experience give and demand? It demands ceremony in a particular way. Fugitivity demands many ceremonies. One of the things I talk about in the beginning note is, "we have to create the space now we gotta leave." The rhythm shapes that movement. (KMT 2018)

Hearing Gumbs's—and Wynter's, Spillers's, Sharpe's—fugitive poetics, the question is how we (in our semiboundedness as nonselves) participate in that poeisis, that worlding. "Her scenes are glimpses of what life might become if we listen to the fugitive whispers begotten by black (trans) feminism," as Bey argues (2022, 120). Gumbs differentiates this into primary and secondary ceremonies: "The primary ceremony I think *Spill* calls for is for Black women, all of us by the way, cis and trans, to recognize ourselves, each other, our ancestors and what we've been through. And to recognize the love and life-making that has also been there the whole time and is still there. And the secondary ceremony is for everyone who doesn't identify as a Black woman to also understand that their healing is bound up with ours too" (KMT 2018). Gumbs choreo-sonically gathers in the event both "black pneuma" (Crawley 2017) and other modalities of breathing, modalities that can at times even be orchestrated as the refusal of Black breathing, as the asphyxization of otherwise breathing particular to Man's coloniality.[14] As Trembley might say, this is about "respiration's imbrication of vitality and morbidity [which] is differently felt by differently situated people," and where the questions we have to ask are about "registering and partially, only partially, diffusing the risks of breathing" (2022, 9). Being led by Gumbs to feel "bound up with" Black women, materially entangled with them in the manifoldness of tendings, is an affective spur to the question of participation. For those of us participating in this secondary ceremony (I cannot speak to what it is to participate in the primary), it means learning to feel how our everyday worlding tends the colonial world that visits endless harm upon Man's dysslected, disqualified others. Which means that tending (toward) endarkenment, decolonial worlding is a question of how I participate in my deictic situation, not something I do "for others."

Care and Participation in the Wake

Ahmed notes, in *Queer Phenomenology*, that "contingency is linked . . . to the sociality of being 'with' others, to getting close enough to touch" (2006, 103). The questions I have been proposing as spurs to open up an evental pedagogy proceed from this axiom: "contingency" names the possibilities of reorientation, disorientation, disruption, refusal, failure, and delinquency. If the crushing weight of the wake proceeds through the tendings of manifold events, so much so that coloniality and anti-Blackness can come to *feel* like just "the world," then our task is to feel out spaces of contingency where its endurance or perseverance breaks down. Rather than a large-scale, planned revolution following on knowing critique of structures of dispossession and accumulation, an attunement to the evental becoming of the world suggests smaller, seemingly "minor" forms of decolonial agitation.[15] We don't necessarily (or only) need conscious understanding of what is wrong with the workings of this world, so much as we need to participate in economies where we come to *feel* (that is, to perceive and pay attention to) the immanent, ongoing, becoming, where this feeling might lead us to seek a simple aim, one that, like Moi's question, is simultaneously abstract and precise in its deixis: How can we disrupt *this* event's tending toward coloniality?

The word Sharpe gives us for this perception and attention is "care," and for her, it is simultaneously emotional and material: in short, it is "affective." She writes, "I want to think 'care' as a problem for thought. I want to think care in the wake as a problem for thinking and of and for Black (non)being in the world. Put another way, *In the Wake: On Blackness and Being* is a work that insists and performs that thinking needs care . . . and that thinking and care need to stay in the wake" (5). The forms of perception and attention Sharpe elaborates in her book—including the asterisk, redaction, and annotation—are indexed to what it means to perform this care *for her*, and she generalizes to what that work may entail for Black people. Reading this book from a different perspective (but fully convinced of her claims about the historically and ontologically evental nature of worlds) in the Modern Literary Theory seminar, we wondered what it means to feel the wake from our own deictic perspectives in the situation.

Erin Manning's concept of "event-care" answers to this, and it points us toward an evental pedagogy that is simultaneously hyperaware (in a "critical" register of how histories of coloniality and heterosexism have marked us) of differences we usually note in grammars of identity, but also always alert to tapping into something else, into the more-than, perhaps into what Mel Chen has recently called "emergent being" that is belatedly "summed" into the forms identity can capture (2023). Manning, hitting on "care" as a concept, writes: "Here I don't mean the subjectivity of human-to-human care, but rather how an event produces an environment that can sustain different kinds of participation which include different affective speeds, including the slownesses that we perhaps associate with depression, or the speeds we associate with anxiety. With event-care perhaps there is a kind of collective tending that comes close to the sense that Guattari gave to the word 'therapeutic'" (165–66). Event-care is hyperindexical, oriented toward exactly what is happening *here*, *now* without assuming or requiring that the deictic situation is or could be homogeneous. The question for us as we hone attention and perception—by utilizing operators like Moi and Ahmed's questions—is how to care for *this* event such that whatever it is we bring tends somewhere otherwise than coloniality and anti-Blackness.

This care is an everyday matter, and one of the things *Tendings* has been trying to think through is that this requires refusing the politics of disqualification. This is to ask, with Anzaldúa: "How do those of us laboring in the complex environments of an academy indifferent and even hostile to spirit make our professional work into a form of spiritual practice?" (2015, 92). This spiritual practice is precisely what I am thinking, with tending as a concept, in the site of the everyday: "Even if this form of spiritual experience also partakes of the transcendent and extraordinary, it is also rooted in the ordinary.

It is about paying attention to what is immediately present and hence about valuing the ordinary and the detail. If the spiritual is about a connection with something beyond or outside the self, the route to that form of utopian feeling is the simple act of observing or noticing what lies in one's immediate vicinity" (Cvetkovich 2012, 192). Spirit is breath—re-*spir*-ation—and sprit is tending; it is the "art of noticing" (Tsing 2015) that accompanies participation. Participation, ultimately, has very little to do with "identity" or even subjectivity. This is why Massumi can say (to people considering what participation in an event means), "don't bring your products, bring your process. . . . Don't perform yourself, co-catalyze a collective event with us" (171). In events, what we call identity would seem to be part of the beginning coordinates for any occurrence; identities are modulated by the *tending* of events in particular directions with particular orientations. Tapping into evental conditions moves us away from such coordinates, instead opening up ways to feel out how colonialist tendencies can be blocked, diverted, and simply dropped.

But it doesn't mean we ignore the necessarily differential and differentiated care required in, by, for participation. Sharpe's book is written toward a Black readership that might crystallize around her first-person plural, and some of my students found, and find, themselves in that grammar. For the rest of us, especially in what Laz Lima calls "White Serving Institutions," we might linger with what Syd Zolf writes about reading Sharpe in *No One's Witness*: "Encountering the 'monstrous intimacies' (Sharpe's term) of transatlantic slavery and its afterlives demands that white viewers/readers look directly at Medusa's obliterative head and listen to what is said and unsaid in the monstrous duration, not as voyeurs or spectators but as participants in an ongoing disaster" (2021, 12). How do we participate in this disaster? How are the taking place of *this* very class and the hearing of Gumbs at *this* institution modalities of that participation? Our study is an event in which the wake of transatlantic slavery conditions our environment, is our weather. Our concern—what Puig de la Bellacasa calls a "matter of care" (2017)—is how we tend colonial endurance or seek out possibilities for disruption.

In our seminar room reading Sharpe, and on the campus more broadly, we had to reckon with all of this. Indeed, she explicitly includes "the school" in her asterisked elaboration of the hold of Middle Passage, noting "the reappearance of the slave ship in everyday life in the form of the prison, the camp, and the school" (21). Asking our questions alongside Sharpe tuned our attention to the deictic force of the sign, and we realized that the name of the building says everything, hiding nothing (except through our own laziness and disinclination to ask of names, "Why this?"); this building, these grounds, this institution aren't just historically implicated in anti-Blackness, we are (differentially) oriented in relation to *this* ship. Some of us are in the hold, while others load the ship or work on it; others are investors in its endeavors, or passengers hopefully scanning toward futures of opportunity they can sense *only because they are on the ship*. Anti-Blackness affects every single one of us. Situations are where anti-Black tendencies accumulate as orientations—habitual movements through spaces—that extend and continue anti-Blackness. The colonial rupture of worlds into homogenous world is our inheritance in the materiality of our situations. And the question for us, in this event, is: Feeling what we can now feel of the wake because of Sharpe and Gumbs (and Wynter and Spillers and Alexander in ensemble), the wake that is in us and moves through us, what can we do? "Why this?" and "What are its conditions of arrival?" are questions that open the present to (often other-than) conscious attention to the deictic. In thus shifting the background hum to the foreground, their combined asking creates conditions for feeling the sign not as a question of the "past" but our the present and of the future, or rather, futures. And this answering is inseparable from another question: What can we do, now, *here*, to break the homogenizing pattern so those futures might arrive?

I would like to end with two ways of amplifying the force of this question and its subjunctive tendencies. The first concerns Man's homogenizing grammars of the classroom which secure a threshold—using tuition, debt, admissions, and degree progress metrics but also police, teargas, tazers—separating the class from the outside world, an "ivory tower" from the "real world," a space of learning in the statal sense from the more informal study that eventually tends worlds. The grammar provides an order—what Erin Manning calls an "order-word" (2020, 228)—that modulates study toward enlightenment learning. This grammar distributes subjects (teachers who know and profess) and objects (students as passive recipients who bank this knowledge) in ways that can be binary (my language here comes from Paulo Freire) but can also accommodate differentiation within this homogenizing grammar: students can be "active listeners" or "active learners," for example. This may be legible in the conversation if markers like "Professor" or "Doctor" are used as honorifics, but colonial grammars mark the fields of affective relationality far beyond that verbal discourse. This includes the orientations of physical space (around a teacher's desk or podium, white boards or projection screens presumptively controlled by the teacher) and of the particular psychic spaces of pedagogical transference in the colonial university (students' need, in order to tend their own identities, for performance recognition, including in the form of metrics like grades[16]). Because this order-word courses through the entire world of the classroom as part of Man's homogenizing capture of worlds, it's enormously difficult to dislodge, to baffle, to disrupt.

Fred Moten, in *The Undercommons*, offers a speculative question that opens up precisely this space of (im)possibility for endarkenment study. I again quote at length:

> What's totally interesting to me is just not to call the class to order. And there's a way in which you can think about this literally as a simple gesture at the level of a certain kind of performative, dramatic mode. You're basically saying, let's just see what happens if I don't make that gesture of calling the class to order—just that little moment in which my tone of voice turns and becomes slightly more authoritative so that everyone will know that class has begun. What if I just say, 'well, we're here. Here we are now.' Instead of announcing that class has begun, just acknowledge that class began. It seems like a simple gesture and not very important. But I think it's really important. And I think it's important to acknowledge how hard it is not to do that. In other words, how hard it would be, on a consistent basis, not to issue the call to order—but also to recognize how important it would be, how interesting it might be, what new kinds of things might emerge out of the capacity to refuse to issue the call to order. (2013, 126)

A "simple gesture" is the modulating switch between Man's order and something else, something that's already been going on, that precedes and exceeds the class's order, something that's called study. Calling the class to order is an interference in study, study's disruption, the channeling of differential worldings into homogeneous worlding. Refusing that gesture, that call for a *particular* kind of participation, would be to acknowledge that we come to the classroom already tending our studies, our worlds. Study is captured, ordered, by the university classroom. Endarkenment education refuses this call, this enclosure, situating study immanently in worlds. Or, perhaps, given the difficulties bordering on impossibility for Moten's "simple gesture" (a "minor gesture" in Manning's sense too [2016]), study in a classroom might differently participate in tending. We might think of endarkenment pedagogy as seeking everyday ceremonies that tend study—esoteric worlding—even in the university's extractive, appropriative, homogenizing structures. And this means we don't necessarily need to think of this in the way Moten seems to here, as the generation of "new kinds of things," we just need to feel how our pedagogical encounters might improvise otherwise worldings (some of them quite old) precisely because Man's pedagogy is ever only the colonialist capture of everyday study. Noting that "intelligence in this context [Nishnaabeg intelligence] is not an individual's property to own" (2017, 156), Leanne Simpson writes that "within the context of humility and agency, decisions about learning are in essence an agreement between individuals and the spirit world," where "to gain access to this knowledge, one has to align oneself with the forces of the implicate order through ceremony, ritual, and the embodiment of teachings one already carries" (2017, 155).

This brings me to the second way I want to amplify Moten's question, which is to let sound one last time that instead of post-enlightenment, liberal subjects (Man), who inhabit colonial world and its grammar, we might think of education as the milieu of everyday storying which improvises otherwise modalities of being, other "genres of existence." Thinking in ensemble with Spillers and Wynter (and Aimé Césaire), J. Kameron Carter writes of ceremonies that might amount "to a nonegoic ritualizing of self, the performance of a self in excess of the sovereign subjecthood of the racially individuated ego and the imposition of a body of singular, bordered meaning" (2021, 178). I want to think about this anagrammatical, improvisational subject in relation to what Manning calls the "more than" of events, where "the individual is, at the very most, the expression of [power's] passage, not its operator" (2020, 217). This is to think of the self as participation, as a kind of affective patterning in the tending of worlds that works through the self but cannot issue from a self or subject as ground. This is something other than Man, other than the "transparent" post-enlightenment subject (da Silva 2007).

Fred Moten has called this ceremony "diasporic prayer" (2017, 232), a kind of attention that sends "what's left of me—dispersed, disbursed, all through its folds and creases" (232)—from event to event in a participatory tending of what sounds through those events, most of them here sonic or visual events. Moving in this blur, Moten begins with a particular feeling arising from an encounter, an erotic and haptic and ceremonial one, with a painting by Chris Offili called *Blue Rider*. Moten writes: "I can't handle it, can't grasp it, can't quite reach it but it's precisely that aeffect, that getting to in being gotten to, that I'm after. I mean to say that I am after that but also that 'I' is always and only ever after that, as emanation, as emissary, as evangelist" (230). This is participation: evental emanation that sends us.[17] We tend what sends (what's left of) us, we send worlds in (at)tending to how they arrive to us. In this prayer, this ceremony, there is no "I" that can be said—in an exhale of breath that is always collective—but only "differential being," the evental ontogenesis of worlds in their ongoing patterning. We don't participate "in" that so much as we "are" participation: a verb, a praxis, a process, a performance, a tending: all that we touch we change, all that we change changes "us." This is the prayer for "the End of the World as we know it" (da Silva 2014), the end of world singular, and it is only ever spoken by speaking along, by adjoining one's breath to the ongoing atmospheres of worlds in their emergence and endurance. Endarkenment ceremonies have always already begun. They don't await a call to order. So let us instead listen, pray, study, tend.

CONCLUSION

On Deictic Participation in/as Tending

Throughout this book, I have been developing "tending" as a variegated concept that might help us account for the ontogenesis of worlds (always plural) as they take shape, persist, and sometimes perish, as well as our participation in those (our) worlds. And I have been using the enlightenment-endarkenment distinction to mark what I see as crucial differences in the orientation of tendings. There are tendings—modes of material patterning, attention, care, and anticipation—that prop up and contribute to the continuance of coloniality. And there are tendings, arriving from an elsewhere that I often call the subjunctive, that draw us in other directions, toward otherwise worlds. If the colonial tendency is toward universal mastery, toward a single, homogeneous world that is nevertheless internally rent by violent hierarchies, endarkenment tendings sustain non-Man worlds, worlds whose flourishing is inseparable from what Denise Ferreira da Silva calls "the End of the World as we know it" (2014).

The book's attention to the politics of tending has often moved through my concept of esoterisms: bounded forms of more-than-human sociality where that sociality is co-compositional with deictic knowledging practices. There is no participation in worlds without knowledging, and no knowledging that is not irreducibly entangled with a(t least one) world. Esoterisms, for me, refer to those socialities where borders are processually tended: *some* participate, but not all. In the introduction to *Tendings*, I sketched this more substantially in relation to Antoine Faivre's enormously influential account of "Western esotericisms," noting that the primary divergence between my understanding and his is concerned with what he calls "concordance": the postulate of a single world knowable via some master, if occult, knowledging.

I have come to see this drive toward concordance in the "esotericisms" Faivre gathers, and those that derive from them in our contemporary moment, as a crucial point of convergence between esoteric practices and the practices we usually call "sciences." Both sciences and many "Western esotericisms" ultimately presuppose the singularity of the world, and they view knowledge—whether magic, alchemy, deism, physics, or chemistry—as presumptively or asymptotically *universal*. My interest in the decolonial politics of pluriversality—which is to say, interest in the abolition of Man as the colonial overrepresentation of the human—leads me toward a very different axiom: there *is* no single world, except insofar as colonialist assemblages leverage ontogenesis to keep something approximating it operating *in practice*. The pluriversal vastness of worlding is, at every moment and in events happening at highly dispersed scales, aspirationally (which is to say, asphyxiatingly for many) reduced to world (singular) by coloniality, by the violence of homogenizing grammars. This sometimes happens in spectacular ways, but mostly in this book I've been focused on the everyday, on practices and habits: all the little things that make up a modality of worlding. While tending can name enormous geological, climatological, or cosmological patterns that persist, in its iterations as attention and caring, tending signals everyday practices.

In the introduction, and then again in chapter 2, I noted that this project arises from having noticed what seemed to me like a striking divergence in contemporary feminist practice, where explicitly esoteric—or occult or woo or witchy—feminisms are proliferating online and in mass paperback publishing, while feminisms oriented toward scientific practices—including new materialisms, some posthumanisms and affect theories, and feminist science studies—have become enormously influential within academic feminist spaces. To conclude, I want to return to this divergence and pose a few questions. Specifically, I think what's at stake is two different modalities of *participation*, one that is explicitly esoteric in orientation and one that is pluriversal. And I think feminist and queer esoterisms, especially when oriented toward the abolition of Man, have something crucial to offer as we "imagine ourselves in the first place as participants, each immersed with the whole of our being in the currents of a world-in-formation: in the sunlight we see, the rain we hear and the wind we feel in" (Ingold 2011, 139). Tim Ingold's formulation here begins to shift agency from a human subject to a wider situation, a more-than-human "world-in-formation," and much of what I have to say about participation here presumes that it's something we are always already doing because participation is what we are, even *all* that we are: a pattern of worlding that moves through us, where that moving through also opens up space for us to tend. Erin Manning summarizes this as artfulness: "Artfulness depends on so many tendings, so many implicit collaborations between intuition and sympathy. And so more than all else, it depends on the human getting out of the way" (2016, 63). What I want to ask, at the end, is about how the deictic—the indexical, the grammar of pointing to a specific situation of utterance—might shape how we tend our various and manifold worlds.

How Can We Keep Our Esoteric Practices Deictic?

When Tituba's transatlantic travel delivers her into enslavement as settler colonization, Condé's novel offers Tituba a narrative voice that not only theorizes this experience in (proto)intersectional terms, but also gives Tituba space to reflect on the problems for knowledging that such displacement produces. Some of her trusted spiritual copresences (Beliso-De Jesús 2015), but not *all*, could pass over the ocean, and many of the flora Tituba's knowledgings (or care and healing practices) required were no longer to be found. She has to learn, experimentally, how to tune into the specificity of Massachusetts, which is rather different from Barbados, in order to continue her healing and worlding practices.

Needing herbs for an abortion, which Tituba rather consistently calls "murder," she narrates: "In Barbados, where I knew every plant by heart, I would have had no difficulty getting rid of an unwanted fruit. But what could I do here in Boston? Less than half a league outside Boston grew some thick forests that I decided to explore" (1992, 50). Knowledging here is more-than-human, and Tituba's question is how to participate in a deictic situation, how to access and tend an agency that is not "hers" so much as it is the capacity of a world. Places, situations, worlds: that is where "thinking" happens, whence it comes. It comes to us, moves through us, moves us, and indeed makes "us" even as our attentions, actions, decisions in turn contribute to "making" a world.

Let me amplify this by recalling, too, Elissa Washuta's attention to how white feminists who burn sage as part of their "witchcraft" practices participate, directly but via the occultations of commodity fetishism, in the disfuturing of Indigenous worlds. That is, the *material* use of sage by settlers creates an economic, agriculture situation in which Indigenous worldings *with* sage, understood as itself a participant in those worlds, are disrupted. Something analogous is at play in what Eva Wiseman might call "blood crystals" (2019).[1] If you open many contemporary guides to witchcraft and other esoteric practices, including most explicitly feminist and queer guides, you are likely to find suggestions for rituals involving various crystals (Michelle Tea's *Modern Tarot*, for instance, requires crystals for most of its rituals). While I have no difficulty at all in believing that different crystals have material, which is to say, spiritual, properties that matter in all their specificity, Wiseman's journalism makes clear that these crystals arrive to the global market drenched in blood. The vast majority of such crystals turn out to be mined in conflict or war zones, often by minors, usually through processes that are ecologically devastating, and in ways that funnel profits toward the global 1 percent.

The use of such crystals, then, is another site from which to think about what I call tending, and especially its modality as deictic attention. When one buys a crystal from a New Age shop to practice a feminist or queer ritual of self-empowerment, one is likely directly participating in the ecological and economic violence of coloniality (some might call this "globalization"). The feminist ritual only takes shape because of this colonial violence (Malatino 2022). Wiseman's account for the *Guardian* turns to an owner of one of these shops, Stephen Wells, who underscores that this violence is *in no way* separable from the material-spiritual specificity of the crystals: "For Wells, the importance of ethical crystal mining is not solely about the impact on the planet, but also on the crystal itself—he believes the mining of a stone affects its healing properties. 'Taking something by force, destructively, has an effect on any living thing. Crystals are archetypal pure frequencies, nature's perfect geometric tuning forks. Can anyone imagine the shockwaves of explosions having no impact?'" (quoted in Wiseman 2019).

The question I have for practitioners of esoteric rituals—especially feminist and queer practitioners—is how we might cultivate more deictic tending. My suspicion is that the questions I gathered in chapter 4—"Why this?" (from Toril Moi, who borrows it from Stanley Cavell) and "What are its conditions of arrival?" (from Sara Ahmed)—give us just the kind of spur we need. The second question pushes us to notice how the use of blood crystals might saturate any ritual—however feminist or queer in its aims—with the colonial violence of extraction and expropriation. But the first question ends up having to track similar things, precisely because for most feminist and queer practitioners the answer to the question of why they are using a particular crystal (probably bought from a New Age shop) is because they came across that crystal in one of the host of guides to witchcraft and esoteric practices that can be found in any well-stocked bookstore today.

As I argue in detail in chapter 2, these guides tend to inherit the "reclaiming witchcraft" projects of the 1970s and '80s, when second-wave feminist and gay liberationists constructed "big tent" histories of witchcraft that strove for universal inclusion but ultimately ended up enacting colonialist modes of violence precisely because of this drive toward inclusion. While many feminist and queer esoteric practices take up this drive, reclaiming the witch as a blazon instead of an epithet, my reading of *I, Tituba, Black Witch of Salem* gives me pause, slows me down. For Tituba, "witchcraft" is a discursive construct in the colonial field, arising when homogenizing violence of colonial grammaticality encounters non-Man worlds and worldings. Witchcraft is not a name for knowledges that precede and may endure despite colonial violence, it is an index of precisely this *contact*, this contest, this site of encounter. For this reason, I described my approach to Condé's novel and to the feminist and gay liberationist histories I analyze in chapter 2 as an attempt to read "through" witchcraft to the esoterisms that subjunctively haunt that (colonial) concept. I recall this here to say that these guides don't present noncolonial, non-Man knowledges—they don't present esoterisms in the sense I use that term—they instead present a kind of homogenized, grammatically flattened "tradition" that purges "witchcraft" of its colonial complexity.

I am not suggesting that we don't read these books, or that we don't practice whatever ritualities find us and call out for our participation. But I think anyone who has not come to an esoterism through initiation processes set by that esoteric sociality itself has to be very, very careful. At best, the results are cultural appropriation, and usually "practicing witchcraft" according to what's offered in these books is a summons to buy blood crystals, or to destroy Indigenous land (understood a more-than-human relationality) by burning sage. If we read these books, we might try not to take anything as an imperative or a set of recipes (even if some of these books are explicitly marked as grimoires) so much as an invitation to think about subjunctive ceremonies that must be ceaselessly supplemented by deictic attention. I think it's possible to subjunctively read colonial complexity back into homogenized accounts, thereby allowing a more care-full tending. In this, I have been inspired and informed by *I, Tituba*'s (and Tituba's) modulation of the indicative to the subjunctive, but my attention has been no less shaped by its (and her) insistence on the deictic.

If these feminist and queer esoteric books could call us to tune in where we are, now, *here*—which includes (at)tending (to) how we participate in vastly asymmetrical ways in keeping the colonial world humming—then they might enable us to improvise and compose, together with all the nonhumans in our situations, worlds that exceed Man's world precisely by tapping into the specific subjunctive field (the "ghostly region" as Wai Chee Dimock puts it) that haunts every deictic situation. And for those of us—especially white people or settlers—who approach a knowledging that is not "ours," we have to ask, with as much care as we can muster, how *our* practices contribute to the violent disruption of other worlds. Rather than being summoned to participate in knowledges that don't belong to us, we might instead, perhaps more modestly, learn to tend practices that, at the very least, don't disrupt those other worlds.

How Can We Gather without Disqualification?

If my first question is posed to participants in "esoteric" knowledgings, my second is addressed to those of us who move in spaces that are, constitutively, *not* esoteric, spaces that are configured for pluriversal gathering. As I traced in chapter 4, I primarily think about this in terms of the university, but chapter 3's exploration of the politics of extreme metal worlds is, in part, meant to mark that such spaces aren't merely (or even mostly) in schools. What I mean when I say pluriversal, here, is that when I enter such spaces—say, the classroom—the situational encounter is or might be configured, in important ways, toward a queer, decolonial hospitality as unsettling or unsettled openness to difference(s).[2]

I mean something beyond what is usually meant by "inclusion," which universities have tended to frame in narrow, homogenizing ways. That is, scholarly discussion is meant to be, in principle, open to anyone—demographically speaking—who is willing to submit to the homogenizing frame of secular (and secularist) rationality, in either a scientific (or logical) universalism or a universal criticality. Universities, and classrooms, are spaces where differences are welcomed, even sought out, provided that they do not challenge the possibility, even the necessity, of a prior presupposition about the right (proper, "scholarly") modalities of participation. This modality might be held up mimetically as a kind of guide to education, even taking shape as a learning outcome: we can learn how to be more rational, more critical in our deliberations. In other words, even when that universalizing frame is not presumed at the outset, it is still an orienting telos of the (statist) pedagogical project.

Guided by Gloria Anzaldúa, I have been wondering what happens when, or if, we welcome "those who carry conocimiento," who "refuse to accept spirituality as a devalued form of knowledge and instead elevate it to the same level occupied by science and rationality" (2015, 119). What I'm trying to think about is what it might take for a classroom to *not* presume universal secularist rationality and to invite participants to bring their spiritual and other disqualified knowledgings to bear in whatever capacity they wish. Put more simply, what if we could gather to study without having to check large parts of what and who we care about at the door?

This question has led me to the field of religious studies, where this question gets asked with a peculiar intensity, and I've even come to see this book as, I hope, a modest contribution to the project Eleanor Craig, Amy Hollywood, and Kris Trujillo call "the desegregat[ion of] religious studies and theology from the humanities more broadly" (2021, 2). But before getting there, I should say right up front that in asking us to be more welcoming to non-enlightenment and other-than-secular modes of knowledging, I am keenly aware that not all of these will be ones I can affirm, or even tolerate. Given the often explicitly secularist and logicist bent of the university, I am sure some, maybe many, of my readers will be skeptical of inviting creationist, literalist, or "fundamentalist" knowledgings, or "conspiracy theories" like QAnon. And I am keenly aware that writing a book questioning feminist field attachments to science while welcoming in knowledgings that may seem not just cringey but actually dangerous in a moment of global COVID-19 pandemic is going to strike many as problematic. So let me slow down.

At some point in the time of the forty-fifth US president, I began to notice signs in yards proclaiming a set of beliefs ("In this house we believe . . ."). The wording varies, and particular designs shifted as MeToo, Black Lives Matter, the No DAPL at Standing Rock movement, and COVID-19 captured people's attentions. One of the commonly proclaimed beliefs, at least around me, is "Science is real." While I suspect that the obvious banality of that phrase was meant sarcastically as a response to some of the president's (but obviously not only his) most egregious claims about the virus or healthcare or bodies, the phrase also strikes me as delimiting, in its elegance, the paucity of liberal, homogeneous pedagogy. When a large portion of the humans in a sociality are denied an education that would offer scientific literacy, and powerful nodes of discursive power (like the White House) spread scientifically dubious information constantly, and the actual situation and all of its affects are scary and draining and confusing, it doesn't seem particularly surprising to me that many people were hesitant or resistant to things like masking and vaccination. In the face of this, it seems to me that the yard sign says just about the only thing that the progressive avatars of state biopower have to say: science is real. This is a matter of belief, and it can be refused, but if you refuse you are disqualified. There is one world, one set of laws, one science: anything that deviates or doesn't acknowledge this is "not real."

I'm not saying that I have a better rhetorical strategy if the goal is something like high vaccination rates—that's really not my field of expertise[3]—but I do know this: we have to be able to do better. I don't even need to get into the way that sciences become Science (as Bruno Latour often put it) to point out that this is basically a version of "because I said so" uttered by a parent when a child, often rightly, contests their bullshit. If nothing else, I think we need to find much better ways of engaging with each other, including across differences of worlding and knowledging, that have something offer beyond an insistence that there is a single world, "we" (secularist or scientifically or logically oriented thinkers) know how it works, and you can take it or leave it.

In some ways, I could mark this in a contemporary activist language of calling out and calling in, but let me instead turn to religious studies. Even here, as Tyler Roberts puts it, there is often a requirement to delimit "secular *academic* thinking about religion from *religious* thinking about religion" (2013, 4). In that context, there's a gravity to the field imaginary such that Roberts writes: "We become suspicious of religion—and of scholars who are not suspicious enough" (4). In this sense, what I'm calling for is us to begin with less suspicion. At the very least, we might be able to hold off such disqualifying judgment at the outset, reserving space for encounter that might still require different kinds of critical engagement, but where those aren't given in advance of the event.[4] In other words, what if matters of spirituality, of esoteric worlding, of ghosts, of magic, of faith don't have to remain confined within the colonial grammar of "objects" but might instead shape, in ways that we don't have to be embarrassed by or suspicious of, our approaches, our methods, our knowledgings?

The very last sentences of Marisol de la Cadena's *Earth Beings* refer to "a proposal for a partially connected commons achieved without canceling out the uncommonalities among worlds because the latter are the condition of possibility of the former: a commons across worlds whose interest in common is uncommon to each other. A cosmolife: this may be a proposal for a politics that, rather than requiring sameness, would be underpinned by divergence" (2015, 286). These sentences sum up what I think we might learn to practice, together, in pluriversal gatherings like classroom encounters. And what I want to suggest is that in these meetings, our primary aim should not be the imposition of a homogenizing frame—a transcendent given we require at the outset or a telos of study—but rather the immanent labor of pluriversal worlding as the ephemeral, deictic, testing of grounds for encounter that don't enact disqualification. That is, the primary aim of any study is to tend *this socialitiy*'s modality of study: how can we care for *us, here, now*? This has to be posed ceaselessly, each time anew even with "the same" group, and I suspect there is at least as much possibility here for frustration and confusion as there is for joy and the transformative bliss of learning. But any study that hopes to avoid the colonial logics of disqualification has to be able to begin there, with that welcome to worlds that don't interface with enlightenment world in frictionless ways. Which doesn't mean, once we get going, that we have to be relativist to the point of affirming the knowledge of everyone who shows up.

I have been working with the concept of endarkenment to signal the differences that matter politically within the vast field of nonenlightenment knowledgings, and I have needed this concept to feel out the possibilities for maneuvering away from enlightenment, colonialist homogenization that subjunctively haunt our scenes of engagement. Some of the knowledges that might enter the classroom, even if they violate some tenets of enlightenment knowledging, are still oriented toward Man and its overrepresentation. Not all esoterisms, even in the sense that I give that concept, are oriented toward endarkenment. So we might (at)tend (to) those ceremonial events such that we can feel how they carry, subjunctively, the force of otherwise worldings. Ashon Crawley reminds us, writing in an adjacent context, that "Blackpentecostal aesthetics resist the conceptualization of the purely new, of western time's forward propulsion. Blackpentecostal aesthetics, rather than a turn to the new, is the production of an otherwise, shows the sending forth of otherwise possibilities already enacted, already there" (2017, 34). Amplifying such "endarkened logics of otherwise sociality" (209) is precisely what *Tendings* has been concerned with at the level of our everyday practices, including our sociogenic, ceremonial storytelling practices.

This book opened on the words of Anzaldúa, and it will end with her words too: "Changing the thoughts and ideas (the 'stories') we live by and their limiting beliefs (including the national narrative of supreme entitlement) will enable us to extend our hand to others con el corazón razón en la mano" (2015, 20). What is crucial about Anzaldúa's account, for me, is that by welcoming spiritual knowledgings—and thinking about the absolute indifference between matter and spirit—she, like Wynter, Gumbs, and Butler, foregrounds the capacity of this collective storytelling to change the world. She writes, "We revise reality by altering our consensual agreements about what is real, what is just and fair. We can trans-shape reality by changing our perspectives and perceptions. By choosing a different future, we bring it into being" (21). This choosing isn't "mine," it doesn't issue from a self so much as it is the force of a world, perhaps several, that take, for this moment, the shape of a self, a self that is little but pattern, eventually tended and in turn having some specific, limited, but nonetheless miraculous capacities to change. This is what I have come to think about tending: that we can feel out, in our deictic situations, the potentiality to improvise worlds, futures, realities, by paying more careful attention to what arrives to events with us, what moves through us, what calls us to the event, the ceremony.

Acknowledgments

This book is another elaboration of the ongoing queer worlding I began with Julietta Singh in graduate school, which is not a life's work, but, more simply and crucially, *a life*. What I have to say about tending in this book emerges from living as a participant in what we came to call, during the COVID-19 pandemic's moment of "podding," Grey House. Grey House includes some so-called humans (Julietta, Isadora Singh, and me Chase Joynt), some four-legged furry creatures (Mars, Spirit, and Dosa), and also a dizzying array of entities, "living" and not, that constitute a particular scene of living. The intensities, frustrations, pleasures, dreams, affordances, and costs of this more-than-human relationality made this book possible in so many affective, intellectual, spiritual, and material ways. Crucial "staycation writing retreats" gave me time to think about and draft the book's first iteration in the wake of my father's death in the fall of 2020.

As the last chapter of the book makes very explicit, this book is very deeply connected with my classroom practice at the University of Richmond, and I would not have been able to think of much of what's here without the incredible students I have studied with over the last decade. In particular, students in the spring 2019 section of Modern Literary Theory—the class at the center of chapter 4—enabled me to give expression to a lot of the questions that I had been accumulating across years of reading toward what I often vaguely called my "witchcraft project." I would like to acknowledge the intellectual contributions of students in that class: Nathan Burns, Logan Etheredge, Sabrina Garcia, Joyce Garner, Krishna Lohiya, Katherine Murbach, Tracy Naschek, Claire Tate, Olivia Tennyson, Madeline Tolsdorf, Will Walker, Daniel Williams, and Yang Yang. I was reading Christina Sharpe's *In the Wake* in a "Care, Touch, Collectivities" seminar with Ngan Bui, Olive Gallmeyer, Kenedi Gallogly, Shira Greer, TaShira Iverson, Sam Mickey, Julia Nalecz, Kelly

Saverino, Lily Von Spreckelsen, and Alison Zhang when I drafted chapter 4, and their critical engagements made it possible to clarify the stakes of the chapter and the book more generally. Many other students were part of my thinking at crucial moments of drafting this book, including Miquell Shaw, Doro, Eva Steinitz, Gabriel Mathews, Lauren Oligino, Pamira Yanar, Katiana Issac, Kristin Santana, Katherine Walker, and Ananya Chetia.

I lack the words to express my debt to the students and faculty who participated with me in the 2022–2023 Humanities Connect program at the UR: Alan deClerck, Ny'Asia Flowers, Josie Holland, Anthony Russell, and Doug Winiarski. The conversations that emerged from this group, including with the whole crew participating in the Shakers at the Center Symposium, not only shaped the introduction and conclusion to this book, but have been among the most exciting, I'd even dare say enchanting, I've ever been a part of on or off campus. Beyond this group, I want to extend a tremendous thanks to Jenny Cavenaugh and Manuella Meyer in the A&S Dean's Office for everything, and to the entire English department and everyone around Women, Gender, and Sexuality Studies for their unceasing support.

Many conversations, explicitly about the book or not, shaped my thinking over the last few years, and I want to acknowledge Melissa Adler, Aren Aizura, Jessie Beier, Jane Bennett, Brenton Boyd, Vivienne Bozalek, Chris Breu, Mel Chen, Kandice Chuh, Ashon Crawley, Ann Cvetkovich, Daryl Dance, Rita Felski, Asilia Franklin-Phipps, Erica Fretwell, Sandy Grande, Jules Gill-Peterson, Alexis Pauline Gumbs, Nora Hanson, Zakiyyah Iman Jackson, jan jagodzinski, Eileen Joy, C. Libby, Natalie Loveless, Chris Martin, Toril Moi, Tavia Nyong'o, Wendy Truran, Matthew Richardson, Erin Manning, Brian Massumi, Nancy Lesko, Dana Luciano, Ela Przybylo, Derek Ryan, A. Marie Sairsingh, Donovan Schaefer, Kyla Schuller, Kyla Wazana Tompkins, Sarah Gerth v.d. Berg, and Boni Wozoleck. When I was ready to share early drafts, Matthew Arnold and Maura Finkelstein's generous and incisive comments transformed the project, as did comments from Hil Malatino, A. J. Lewis, and David Cecchetto at a later stage. The engagements of three anonymous readers for Duke University Press led to significant changes to the book's arguments and structure at least twice, and I remain the most grateful for those engagements when they felt the "hardest" and pushed me the most.

While COVID made the initial drafting of this book feel rather solitary, I knew Rebekah Sheldon and A. J. Lewis were working on adjacent projects, and their interest in collaborating and thinking together across time—even when it's mostly a history of plans that didn't come to pass—animated me through those quiet hours at the computer. I am overjoyed that in these late, which is not to say "post-," pandemic days, our plans to gather and study have taken shape.

Greg Seigworth and Carolyn Pedwell offered not only encouragement and edits but, most importantly, the original idea for what became chapter 4, which appears in slightly different form in the *Affect Theory Reader 2*. Jane Ward and Soma Chaudhuri's comments on the portion of chapter 1 that will appear in the *Witch Studies Reader* helped me clarify the stakes of that chapter and its importance to the overall project. Both of these books are published by Duke University Press.

I want to think Kristen Schilt for inviting me to the University of Chicago's Gender and Sexuality Studies Working Group in the Center for Study of Gender and Sexuality, where I met S. J. Zhang and Kris Trujillo. That conversation, and especially my encounter with Kris, catalyzed a turn toward the field of religious studies in my thinking. Supported by a grant from my Provost's office, Kris organized a workshop on this book in manuscript form at the Harvard Divinity School with Amy Hollywood and Eleanor Craig. The intensity of their ongoing collective study (in the strong sense I offer in chapter 4) was immediately apparent to me, and the generosity they offered by allowing me to participate in that ongoing study for a day not only animates the conclusion of the book (which I wrote in my hotel room the day after our workshop) but has reoriented my career in the most unexpected and energizing way.

Liz Ault's encouragement of this project—which I first described late at night at an affect studies conference hotel before *Animate Literacies* was even out yet—has kept me focused and inspired throughout its writing, which was interrupted at so many turns. I can't imagine working with another editor. Ben Kossak's care with details and management of my anxieties throughout the process with clear communication also kept me steady. I want to extend a tremendous thank you to the entire (now unionized!) staff at Duke University Press, including Bird Williams, Chad Royal, and Aimee Harrison. I remain humbled to get to work with the copyeditors, production managers, typesetters, designers, and marketing staff, plus the people at the printing presses and binderies who make Duke University Press books the erotically animating objects they are. My next big project is, in part, an effort to amplify and honor all those kinds of labor, so consider this thank you a down payment on a more extended celebration of everything you make possible.

Notes

Preface. In the Cards

1. Natasha continues to offer tarot readings in a variety of modalities, including a weekly single-card reading by text that has sustained me throughout the process of finishing this book. https://www.moonhanded.studio/.

2. Rather than a kind of nationalism, this spell simply uses the "American Dream" as a deictic point of reference before using a thread practice to guide reflection: "The thread forms a net to catch us. As we affix, we think about everything and everyone that supports us. We think of the thread as hands reaching out, forming a network, offering our support at the same time as receiving it."

3. Beyond all the excitement of SSASS itself—an enormously generative event that has, so far, also given rise to at least one other book: Hil Malatino's *Trans Care* (2020)—it was on SSASS's opening day that I received my first physical copy of my book *Animate Literacies*. The entire week felt magical, like a world opening up before me.

Introduction. Tending Endarkenment Esoterisms

1. Languages differentially distribute agency through their animacy scales (Chen 2012), which in English (and most of the other colonial languages) involves grammatical markers of subject and object status through which agency is emplotted. Subjects act and objects are acted upon. Subjects shape an inert, passive world of matter: "When rewriting reason as the secular regulative force acting on every existing thing, the framers of science transform nature into the holdings of a power that acts solely as law, that is, universal *nomos*" (da Silva 2007, 47). In da Silva's account of the colonial grammar of homogeneous worlding, the "world" is affectable and lawful, while the subject at least asymptotically achieves self-determination (what she calls "transparency"), a masterful movement through the world that is about control of self *and* control of the (outer) world by manipulating its laws. This is the post-enlightenment subject, the

subject of (Western techno)science and history, the subject Wynter calls Man. As I try to notice how this subject structures world, I am also trying to feel out other patternings that are possible beyond subjects, patternings that may not even take legible form as "selves," at least within colonial grammar. Rather, these "non-selves" (Moten 2018, 187) are particular, semistable patternings within worlding, and they endure in and as tending endarkenment, non-Man worlds. What's at stake here is thinking the absolute intimacy between the axiom that all matter is vital or animate (which upsets the purported inertness of objects) and the necessity of thinking outside of the grammars of knowing subjects, since those grammars articulate Man's world, even if such subjects "critique" it.

2. In *Ontological Terror*, a "black nihilist" reading of the ontometaphysical tradition that reaches a certain point of inflection in the thought of Martin Heidegger, Calvin Warren suggests "Being" and even the human will prove unworkable concepts, and he turns, instead, to "spirit." Warren writes, "I would suggest that this thinking lead us to spirit, something exceeding and preceding the metaphysical world. We are still on the path to developing a phenomenology of black spirit, but it is an important exercise. I will continue this work in subsequent writing, but I can say for now, the aim is to shift emphasis from the human toward the spirit" (2018, 171).

3. I conceptualize endarkenment as the improvisational patterning of worlds that don't presume the form of the (colonial, enlightenment) subject, or necessarily even of the self. Throughout this book I attend to the colonial production of the subject, but also to its subjunctive outsides, the virtual potentialities for otherwise being that haunt its articulation, what Fred Moten calls "an improvisatory suspension of subjectivity" (2018, 51). For Marquis Bey (2021), race and gender are part of a structuration that creates an ontological cut or marking which makes "the subject" possible, and they too are interested in different ways of being than subjecthood and subjectivity. Which is to say that we can cultivate—or tend—a reading practice that feels out what might be happening "beyond, beneath, and beside" the subject (Sedgwick 2003, 8), where the patterning of worlds, what Mel Chen calls "differential being" (2023), happens in ways without pregiven shape and texture, where colonial tendings are disrupted by other tendings, where worlds frictionally relate.

4. My thinking about pluriversal politics is also informed by Marisol de la Cadena's *Earth Beings* (2015); Marisol de Cadena and Mario Blaser's edited collection *A World of Many Worlds* (2018); Escobar's newer *Pluriversal Politics* (2020); and Martin Savransky's *Around the Day in Eighty Worlds* (2021).

5. My use of "otherwise" is inspired by what Ashon Crawley calls "otherwise possibilities": "The urgency of our times, times that began *before* the inaugural events of Christopher Columbus's 1492 blue oceanic colonial expansionist mission, demands a thinking about what we might call '*otherwise*' possibilities, *otherwise* inhabitations, *otherwise* worlds. The *otherwise* in all its plenitude vibrates afar off and

near, here but also, and, there" (2020, 28). I am also inspired by Kandice Chuh's *Imagine Otherwise*, where she argues that "to imagine otherwise is not about imagining as the other, but rather, is about imagining the other differently" (2003, 9).

6. Rebekah Sheldon finds a "dark correlationism" or "new critical occultism" (2016, 139) running through object-oriented ontology and new materialist thought, which is one of the primary reasons I would include those as, at least subjunctively, esoteric projects. It matters that this occult influence is itself occulted, an acknowledgement of the politics of disqualification governing most of the academy.

7. For work on biology, see Haraway's *Primate Visions* (1989), *Simians, Cyborgs, and Women* (1991), *When Species Meet* (2008), and *Staying With the Trouble* (2016) and Willey's *Undoing Monogomy* (2016). For work on physics see Barad's *Meeting the Universe Halfway* (2007), Daggat's *The Birth of Energy* (2019), Kirby's *Quantum Anthropologies* (2011) and Stengers's *Cosmopolitics* (2011). On chemistry, see Frost's *Biocultural Creatures* (2016). On neuroscience, see Pitts-Taylor's *The Brain's Body* (2016). On geology, see Yusoff's *A Billion Black Anthropocenes or None* (2018).

8. It is worth noting that in all the attention to biology and physics in Coole and Frost's introduction to *New Materialisms*, it's easy to miss this sentence: "In this monolithic but multiply tiered ontology, there is no definitive break between sentient and nonsentient entities or between material and spiritual phenomena" (2010, 10).

9. Taking up and reworking Bruno Latour's work (1993), Isabelle Stengers sees modern science as a practice of confrontational dialectical distanciation: "In order to present themselves as scientific, they *need* to disqualify the opinions, the beliefs, of others, the nonmodern practices of which some claim to serve as rational substitutes" (2011, 285). This disqualification takes place in experimental "purification" of knowledge claims (over and against "fetishistic" knowledges) (329), and, although Stengers does not often put it in precisely these terms, a directly colonialist mastery of the world (Singh 2018). Stengers's proleptic formulation of a cosmopolitical science conjures the ghosts of this colonialist violence: "If other peoples know how to keep watch over their ancestors and restore their voices through the worlds they create, the history we have invented for ourselves is haunted by the ghosts of those it has crushed, vanquished, or bowed, and by the shadow of everything our reasons, our criteria, have destroyed, or reduced to silence or ridicule" (398). The violence of disqualification renders non-Man worlds and their knowledgings legible within colonialist grammars and the accompanying homogenized frame of temporality but only by disqualifying the affective, material, spiritual conditions of their thriving as worlds (Savransky, 2021). Haunting is a kind of tending (Gordon 1997; Young 2006).

10. The kinds of depoliticizing claims about queer nature Jordy Rosenberg (2014) worries about adhere in one version of this tendency to ground feminist

and queer politics in nature, matter, becoming, and so forth as if the ontological claims about how worlds work self-evidently lead to feminist and queer politics.

11. It might be worth noting that both Donna Haraway's "Cyborg Manifesto" (1991) and Isabelle Stengers's *Cosmopolitics* (2011) make direct but *uncited* reference to Starhawk. See also Rebekah Sheldon's (2016; 2019) work on the occult influences on object-oriented ontology. Josh Ramey's *The Hermetic Deleuze* (2012) is relevant here too, although I don't think anyone would classify Deleuze as a scientifically oriented thinker.

12. My understanding of secularism is heavily informed by Talal Asad's *Formations of the Secular*, which argues that "secularism doesn't simply insist that religious practice and belief be confined to a space where they cannot threaten political stability or the liberty of 'free thinking' citizens. Secularism builds on a particular conception of the world ('natural' and 'social') and of the problems generated by that world" (2003, 191–92). Asad notes one especially crucial axiom of the secularist project: "Beliefs should either have no direct connection to the way one lives, or be held so lightly that they can easily be changed" (115).

13. Throughout modernity, esoterisms have been aligned with projects of colonial empire such as John Dee's renaissance magic. See Frances Yates, *The Occult Philosophy in the Elizabethan Age*. Dee "identified completely with the British imperial myth around Elizabeth I and did all in his power to support it" (2001, 100). They have aligned with political visions that affirm patriarchal and fascist social formations. See Eileen Joy's talk, "Building a Tribe Outside the System: Allen Frantzen, Jack Donovan, and the Neomedievalist Alt-Right," Annual Humanities Lecture, University of Richmond, Richmond, VA (March 2018). On occult currents in accelerationism (including the fascistic "dark enlightenment" of Nick Land), see Rebekah Sheldon, "Accelerationism's Queer Occulture" (2019). In *The Ahuman Manifesto*, Patricia MacCormack notes that esoterisms show up in "a nostalgic right-wing return to tradition" both in "neo-fascist occultism" and in some less obviously troubling esoterisms (2020, 102). But they have also aligned with anticolonial struggles on occupied lands and throughout the Black Atlantic. See the collection *Sorcery in the Black Atlantic*, edited by Luis Nicolau Parés and Roger Sansi (2011).

14. Foucault's essay "What Is Enlightenment?" ends with an admonishment to those who would conflate enlightenment with humanism, arguing that at least as far as the eighteenth century is concerned, he is "inclined to see Enlightenment and humanism in a state of tension rather than identity" (1998, 314). Moreover, Foucault proposes that however we conceptualize it, we have to be wary of "everything that might present itself in the form of a simplistic or authoritarian alternative," a form of "blackmail" (313).

15. Kant's short 1784 text zeroes in on relations between freedom, authority, and knowledge, locating Enlightenment as "man's emergence from his self-imposed immaturity" (1970, 33) in precisely the possibility of free, intellectual

exchange *in public*, which is to say, in print. Enlightenment is thus inseparable from what Benedict Anderson (1983) calls print capitalism, and the possibility of suturing a "nation" to affective forms of belonging that exceed material interpersonal contact. Rejecting a notion of authority that would oppose it to freedom of thought, Kant instead wants to ground public obedience to state power precisely in the free circulation of critical thought. This grounding makes crucial use of a distinction between the public and the private, where in their positions as private individuals playing specific roles, "one must certainly not argue, instead one must obey" (42). But, "the *public* use of one's reason must always be free, and it alone can bring about enlightenment among mankind" (42).

16. Zakiyyah Iman Jackson's *Becoming Human* similarly thinks about Man's homogenization working through differential ontologization (where that overwrites evental emergence as "being" in what she calls "ontologized plasticity"). Analyzing logics of what we often name dehumanization, Jackson writes, "animalization is not incompatible with humanization: what is commonly deemed dehumanization is, in the main, more accurately interpreted as the violence of humanization or the burden of inclusion into a racially hierarchized universal humanity" (2020, 18). Inclusion within humanity, or homogenization around Man, actually requires the production of the non-, in-, and less-than-human as constitutive insides that are ultimately *within* the evolutionary frame of Man's "biocentric descriptive statement" (Wynter 2003).

17. Dillard explains her "'endarkened' feminist epistemology" by anchoring it in the specificity of Black women's experience (and more specifically their experiences as school leaders), and laying out its six key assumptions: "Assumption #1: Self-definition forms one's participation and responsibility to one's community" (2006, 18); "Assumption #2: Research is both an intellectual and a spiritual pursuit, a pursuit of purpose" (20); 3: "Only within the context of community does the individual appear (Palmer, 1983) and, through dialogue, continue to become" (22); 4: "Concrete experience with everyday life form the criterion of meaning, the 'matrix of meaning making' (Ephraim-Donker, 1997, 8)" (23); "Assumption #5: Knowing and research and both historical (extending backwards in time) and outward to the world: To approach them otherwise is to diminish their cultural and empirical meaningfulness" (24); and 6: "Power relations, manifest as racism, sexism, homophobia, and so on structure gender, race, and other identity relations within research" (26).

18. My sense of "implication" here is indebted to Michael Rothberg's *The Implicated Subject* (2019) which theorizes the implicated subject as a nonhomogeneous field of responsibilities that fall outside of a binary model of perpetrator and victim.

19. Tavia Nyong'o writes, of recent posthumanist moves toward "dark ecology," "In this sudden profusion of darkly vibrant speculative realisms, too little

time or real patience is given to the dark precursors to these blacknesses and darknesses in the red record of genocide, slavery, and colonialism out which this new world was worlded" (2019, 108). The performance Nyong'o turns to as a counterforce to this lack of patience is by Guatemalan artist Regina José Galindo, *Piedra* (2013). Nyong'o's reading carefully attends to the specifics of the situation, in which a naked body crouches on the ground, covered in charcoal paint, becoming "like" a stone in ways that dramatize histories of racism and extractivist capitalism. Nyong'o ultimately discovers a kind of tending I would call endarkenment in that it gathers feminist projects without homogenization: "Something no more wondrous, no less pedestrian, as a small black stone sitting, warming, in the Brazilian sun, can be a seed around which the crystal image of Black and Latina feminist recollection unfolds in the singular plural" (108).

20. José Esteban Muñoz writes that "to become attuned to the brownness of the world is to see what is here but concealed. It is a sustained practice of seeking, finding, and, again, touching an aspect of being with and in the world" (2020, 118–19). He finds an apt instantiation of this attunement in Ricardo Bracho's 1997 play *The Sweetest Hangover (and Other STDs)*, which conjures "a world without white people" (18). In the play, Thing 2 suggests to Thing 1 that "he get over whiteness by simply blinking his eyes and letting in darkness. This ritual thus magically expels whiteness from the play, leaving a brown world of feeling, organized by affective belongings between people of color" (18–19). While my primary understanding of whiteness is a diagram that organizes affective worlds—a part of the homogenizing grammar of colonial modernity— Muñoz's references here to "white people" and "people of color" refuses the abstraction of "systems" from material, corporeal entities that are intra-active with them. Such abstraction would locate darkness as an idealist horizon, a kind of symbolic or merely metaphorical orientation that is absolved from engaging ongoing histories of violence as they structure material situations. For Muñoz, though, darkness is a matter of "the brownness of the world."

21. On the paraontological, see Moten's *Stolen Life* (2018) and Bey's *The Problem of the Negro as a Problem for Gender* (2021), both of which elaborate the work of Nahum Chandler.

22. Tim Ingold writes, "Rather than thinking of ourselves only as observers, picking our way around objects lying about on the ground of a ready-formed world, we must imagine ourselves in the first place as participants, each immersed with the whole of our being in the currents of a world-in-formation: in the sunlight we see, the rain we hear and the wind we feel in. Participation is not opposed to observation but is a condition for it, just as light is a condition for seeing things, sound for hearing them, and feeling for touching them" (2011, 129; cited in Escobar 2018, 87).

23. This sentence is informed by Jennifer Christine Nash's *Black Feminism Reimagined* (2019) and Julietta Singh's *Unthinking Mastery* (2018).

24. La paperson writes, "Everywhere land refuses and resists—whales that destroy ships, bees that refuse to work, bombed islands that reconstitute themselves. The land also resists in the form of people; Indigenous peoples' resistance is the land's resistance. Indigenous people continue to subvert legal and capitalist technologies as part of that resistance. And technologies and technological beings resist too" (2017, 21).

25. Anticipating chapter 4, Christina Sharpe's *In the Wake: On Blackness and Being* proposes what I want to call an evental ontology of worlds, or, more specifically, a sense of worlds as eventally ontogenetic: events make worlds; worlds are evental. We might say, summoning Sara Ahmed, that worlds are "hap": "Caring about what happens, caring whatever happens. We might call this a hap care" (2017, 266). Caring for and about what happens animates the practices Sharpe calls wake work (2016, 5), where, as I will draw out more in chapter 4, the wake of transatlantic racial slavery is part of *all of our* situations, which means the question becomes how we think our differential participation in that wake, how we tend it in ways that enable its endurance or how we tend other, endarkenment worlds. Sharpe focuses on the ship Zong (along with cultural and theoretical work that returns to that ship) as a participant in Middle Passage and the site of the emergence of insurance as part of global capital's extraction of value from lives rendered fungible. Sharpe writes, setting up the turn to Zong, "*The event*, which is to say, one version of one part of a more than four-hundred-year-long event . . ." (37). Events within events, part(ial) events, version of events: for Sharpe, as it were, it's events all the way down. The world is evental; there is no stable ontology or material substrate upon or against which things "happen" (to again hear Ahmed); worlds are processual, they emerge in and from events, they *are* events. If "the wake" of slavery is a way of naming our world, it's only because at every single moment—where moment might include time spaces that far exceed the human in their molecular speed or their geographical and ecological slowness—it is recreated, reaffirmed, reinstantiated. Man's world is not the aftereffect of the ontological rupture of Middle Passage (and European colonization) so much as it is a world that is continually remade (I might say practiced or performed) in anti-Black (and anti-Brown, anti-Indigenous, heteropatriarchal) ways, within colonial grammars. The colonial, enlightenment world tends to maintain its historic route.

As Sharpe puts it, "At stake is . . . antiblackness as total climate. At stake too is . . . recognizing an insistent Black visualsonic resistance to that imposition of non/being" (2016, 21). In "the hold" of Zong—as one part of an event that is in turn within the centuries-long event we can call colonial modernity (and its totalizing homogenization)—there is always this resistant excess, a "Black aliveness" (Quashie 2021) to mark just one of many names for the animating darknesses I'm turning toward in the book, that emerges from and tends the endurance of its own subjunctive possibility. Quashie's book—perhaps one of the most beautiful examples of close reading I have ever encountered—opens with the invitation to "imagine a black world," where I would mark that indefinite "a" in contradistinction to the (definite) singular world of Man. He writes, "we have to imagine a black world so as to surpass the everywhere and everyway of black death, of blackness that is understood only through such a vocabulary . . . a world where blackness exists in the tussle of being, in reverie and terribleness, in exception and in ordinariness" (2021, 1). While I am drawn here to Quashie's "black world" because of the precise questions of *In the Wake*, I might constellate it with the ongoingness of what Leanne Simpson calls "radical resurgence": "Radical resurgence means an extensive, rigorous, and profound reorganizing of things. To me, resurgence has always been about this. It has always been a rebellion and a revolution from within. It has always been about bringing forth a new reality" (2017, 48–49). Quashie and Simpson tend different esoteric worlds, but they resonate in their insistence that such worlds endure *despite* coloniality's crushing violences.

26. I am using terminology from science studies: "intra-action" is Karen Barad's (2007) way of conceptually marking how bounded, discrete entities are produced in, by, through, and with their articulation in apparatuses (technological apparatuses of measurement in physics, or conceptual apparatuses in theory). Entities do not preexist their articulation (2007). Actant is Bruno Latour's (2004) word for any participant in knowledge, human or non.

27. While not explicit in the text, I also hear in tendings "tender," not as a modality of exchange per se ("legal tender" is money) so much as a kind of tenderness, a word that has a particular resonance in recent queer discourse, and that has important ties to vulnerability.

28. Didier Debaise writes that "each event is a passage, inherently unique in its moment, different from all others, according to a rekindling of the principle of indiscernibles, but there are elements that do not pass" (2017, 35). Events emerge and perish; they are bounded both temporally and spatially, even if they might have shapes that look blurry or diffuse according to certain postenlightenment logics. And their perishing sets the conditions for the next event. This conception of worlds as (generated from) events thus introduces a particular potential for evental *disruption*. Worlds—as more-than-human socialities made up of "societies" in Whitehead's sense—will tend to endure in their evental ongoingness. This tendency could be said to be probable: heteropatriarchal coloniality—and its anti-Black, anti-Indigenous, anti-Brown, extractivist logics—works by modulating the most likely outcome of these events at all kinds of scales. Coloniality itself, then, is, considered from the standpoint of what has been called ontology (as the study of what "is"), a tendency in the patterning of worlds. Decolonization is about differential, otherwise, endarkenment patterning (which includes material and political land relations). Because there are "elements that do not pass," there's an opening to practice tendings toward the

End of the World as we know it (da Silva 2014). How might we participate in practices such that Man can no longer (come to) pass?

29. In my book *Animate Literacies* (2019b), I propose that we think of literacy as a more-than-human phenomenon, a practice that unfolds relationally in all situations, which means that human storytelling (what we call "literature") is a *version* of a wider field of literacies or more-than-human meaning making processes.

30. While I will engage with specific conceptions of care throughout *Tendings*, my general sense of the feminist, queer, trans, decolonial, and abolitionist politics of care has been shaped by Joan Tronto's *Moral Boundaries* (1993); Leah Lakshmi Piepzna-Samarasinha's *Care Work* (2018); Hil Malatino's *Trans Care* (2020); and the Care Collective's *Care Manifesto* (2020). I would especially like to sound Mel Chen's "wish" in the afterword of *Animacies*: "Well beyond rejecting secularism or spirituality, I wish for an ethics of care and sensitivity that extends far from humans' (or the Human's) own borders" (2012, 237).

31. Brian Massumi foregrounds play in evental emergence, at least for those entities within worlds that we think of as vital. He writes, "Our freedom consists in how we play our implication in the field, what events we succeed in catalyzing in it that bring out the latent singularity of the situation, how we inflect it for novel emergence" (2015, 158). There is, in the wake (Sharpe 2016), not just a continuance of colonial, homogenizing logics, but also a kind of surplus, what Massumi calls here "the latent singularity, " Deleuze calls the virtual, and I might call the subjunctive.

32. I return to touch and haptics many times in this book, but I should note my thinking about this is heavily informed by Erin Manning's *Politics of Touch* (2006).

33. My use of "grammar" to signal this complex follows Hortense Spillers's "Mama's Baby, Papa's Maybe: An American Grammar Book" (2003), an essay that thinks anti-Blackness as a structure of worlding that articulates the (white) subject through complex assemblages of (un)gendering that preclude the grammatical, juridical, "human" possibility of a Black "subject" within the colonial and heteropatriarchal world. My thinking about grammar is also always in conversation with Saidiya Hartman's *Scenes of Subjection*, in particular her attention to how "the particular status of the slave as object and subject" (1997, 54) requires a rethinking of the entirety of the political, because its grammar precludes the possibility of a Black subject since "those subjects removed from the public sphere are formally outside the space of politics" (65). As Tiffany Lethabo King puts it, "Hartman's theorization of fungibility represents a Black mode of expression, screaming, or utterance that exceeds the narrow humanist and settler grammars of labor (and land as property)" (2019, 22). In this expanded sense, grammar may be something like a synonym for what Foucault has called an "episteme," "the pure experience of order and its modes of being"

(1994, xxi). Epistemes are historical in the sense that they, like everything else in worlds, are constantly becoming, and this becoming's overall tendencies are something like aggregate outlines of microencounters happening across societies (in Whitehead's more-than-human sense) at multiple differential scales. They are "anterior to words, perceptions, and gestures" (xxi), where ordering logics immanently pattern worlds by patterning practices that tend worlds. Grammar is about the ways that our attention to worlds takes place *within* the ongoingness of worlds that carry, as tendencies, previous patterns which shape the field of possible (and probable) worlds we think, feel, and participate in.

34. Saidiya Hartman has called this, with a beautiful use of the subjunctive, waywardness: "an ongoing exploration of *what might be*; it is an improvisation with the terms of social existence, when the terms have already been dictated, when there is little room to breathe, when you have been sentenced to a life of servitude, when the house of bondage looms in whatever direction you move" (2019, 228).

35. Building on Moten's attention to grammar in *In the Break*, Christina Sharpe writes, "I arrive at blackness as, blackness is, anagrammatical. That is, we can see the moments when blackness opens up into the anagrammatical in the literal sense as when 'a word, phrase or name is formed by rearranging the letters of another'" (2016, 76).

36. Returning to and extending Spillers, Frank Wilderson III has thought this in terms of the "structures of US antagonisms" between white, Black, and Indigenous worlds as they differentially participate in the homogenizing anti-Black and anti-Indigenous singular world of coloniality in the North American context. Wilderson's account, like that of Orlando Patterson, foregrounds how "the imaginary of the state and civil society is parasitic on Middle Passage. Put another way, No slave, no world" (2010, 11). The colonial grammar that presumes Man as the post-enlightenment subject is inseparable from the anti-Black and anti-Indigenous violence of enslavement and elimination, violence that Afro-pessimists call "gratuitous violence" as opposed to the contingent violence that attends contacts among groups where we imagine violence may be avoided through changes, however radical, within the structure of world singular. What he dreams of is the end of the homogeneous world, then, but he's also skeptical of certain kinds of alliance or affiliation. There is thus a lot of conversation about the incommensurability of justice movements (Tuck and Yang 2018), which have often turned on tensions between Indigenous and Black futures, or between decolonial and abolitionist projects.

37. I follow Wynter in extending "tending" to a wider field than gender performance (as I explain in chapter 2), but Judith Butler's *Gender Trouble* signals precisely the distributed, participatory agency I am trying to think in *Tendings*: "Gender is always a doing, though not a doing by a subject who might be said to preexist the deed. . . . There is no gender identity behind the expressions

of gender; that identity is performatively constituted by the very 'expressions' that are said to be its results" (1990, 25).

38. In *Provincializing Europe*, Dipesh Chakrabarty writes, "I would suggest that the idea of a godless, continuous, empty, and homogeneous time, which history shares with the other social sciences and modern political philosophy as a basic building block, belongs to this model of higher, overarching language. It represents a structure of generality, an aspiration toward the scientific, that is built into conversations that take the modern historical consciousness for granted" (2000, 75–76).

39. See my discussion in chapter 4 of the "order-word" in Erin Manning's *For a Pragmatics of the Useless* (2020). It is, however, worth noting that these categorical modal differences are backformations (that become pre- and pro-scriptive) belying how the imperative leaks into the subjunctive in practice. As Kris Trujillo reminded me, especially hortatory subjunctives, and especially in certain contexts, can affectively function more as imperatives than anything else. And these imperatives in the grammatical form of subjunctive utterances can be linked to struggles over the universal "correctness" of specifically white and middle-class expectations (Delpit, 1995). Which is to say, Man's subjunctives can still function imperatively.

40. See Gilles Deleuze and Félix Guattari, *A Thousand Plateaus* (2002); Didier Debaise, *Nature and Event* (2017); and Steven Shaviro, *Without Criteria* (2009).

41. There is, as Dipesh Chakrabarty (2009) notes in the context of the ongoing anthropogenic climate catastrophe, a generative grammar within what we call "historiography" that presumes a particular kind of subject (of knowing and acting) that writes itself into futures which are *always imagined* as materially continuous with the legible "past" that is the (ultimately very tiny) past of *homo sapiens*, which also turns out to be (although Chakrabarty doesn't put it quite this way) a specific effect of the aggregate worldings we gather under the geological nomenclature of the "Holocene." History links the past and future not just through the present of a grammatically (and metaphysically) self-determined subject, and through specific options for conjugating tense, but through an abiding and presumptive narratological frame that is inseparable from *ecological* or climatological conditions of worlding that *far* exceed the human. History is, as da Silva argues, about "comprehend[ing] the universality of differentiation" (2007, 64). Homogenization is paradoxically committed to differentiation, which is why I am trying to think it as a matter of grammar: homogenization does not flatten distinctions among things or entities but rather multiplies them by articulating them within *homogenizing* frames that purport to order those things into a known or knowable whole. Mark Rifkin's extension of work on queer temporalities to think about how this works in settler colonialism notes that worlds have their own specific temporalities, and the scene of colonial contact is in part

about the violent assertion of a single temporal, historical frame that includes Indigenous worlds precisely through disqualifying (and attempting to eliminate) their evental ontogenesis (where this is irreducibly spatiotemporal, a matter of land's durativity as a more-than-human sociality). He writes, "U.S. settler colonialism produces its own temporal formation, with its own particular ways of apprehending time, and the state's policies, mappings, and imperatives generate the frame of reference" (2). Riffing on Wynter, we might say that settler time overrepresents itself as if it were time itself, and this homogenizing "frame of reference" violently incorporates worlds into world. But we can tend otherwise, beyond settler temporality as Rifkin underscores: "What *was* does not provide a set pattern, like a mold, for what *will* or *could be*" (32).

Chapter One. "What is a Witch?" *Tituba*'s Subjunctive Challenge

1. Imani Perry writes that "recent critics generally believe that Tituba was not African, as she is generally represented, but either Indigenous or both Indigenous and African. In any case, she was of a people who were outside of or, at best, ancillary to recognition in the legal regime where they resided" (2018, 27).

2. While my claim is that the novel itself makes this move, my ability to notice that move and think about it as a crucial gesture in the "abolition of Man" (Weheliye 2014) has been made possible by Black feminist theorists like M. Jacqui Alexander (2005), Avery Gordon (1997), Hortense Spillers (2003), and Saidiya Hartman (1997; 2008) whose work has simultaneously analyzed anti-Black grammars of worlding (what I call the indicative) and experimented with "subjunctive" historical thinking in order to "paint as full a picture . . . as possible" of the lives coloniality has violently erased (Hartman 2008, 11).

3. Imani Perry, however, says that "Tituba was ultimately executed" (2018, 28). Rather than take a side in an argument about facts, I note this simply to underscore just how little certainty there is in the indicative archive around Tituba.

4. Martin Savransky writes: "In the wake of the tangled catastrophes of capitalism, colonialism, and extractivism, the mass disqualification of differences through which the modern world was born has radically devasted the conditions of livability of myriad human and more-than-human worlds in this world" (2021, 4).

5. My argument here is congruent with claims put forth in two books, both titled *Naming the Witch*. In James Siegel's book, he argues that "through the concept 'witchcraft,' there is an attempt to assimilate alien power to a cultural system . . . 'Witch,' rather than being an understood concept, then, in given historical circumstances points to a limit on an alterity which cannot be accepted" (2006, 221–22). Kimberly Stratton, exploring witchcraft accusations in ancient Greek, Roman, Christian, and Jewish worlds, notes that "magic functions as a discourse among competing discourses where it sometimes overlaps, supports, undermines, or subverts other discourses" (2007, 17). Moreover, she works by

asking "*who* defined magic, *which* practices were labeled magic, and *how* was power negotiated through the application of this label?" (18).

6. "Anthropocene" is the term used in most of the scientific literature to signal anthropogenic climate change's geological legibility (see Chakrabarty 2009). Since the primary question in that designation is how to figure the agent of such change, a range of critical questions arise about precisely who or what is causing the catastrophe. This, in turn, raises important questions about how to date the epoch. While many geologists have looked to nuclear events in the 1940s or capitalist extractive mechanics to propose the 1740s, Davis and Todd (2017) turn to the early seventeenth century, when colonial contact between Europeans and Indigenous Americans produced mass death. More generally, Wynter and McKittrick's (2015) conversation does a fantastic job of explaining the coloniality assumed in attributing to humans *as such* the responsibility instead of noting *which* humans (or which actions or systems) produced climate catastrophe. Others have proposed to see capitalism (Moore 2016), plantation economies (Yusoff 2018), or European homogenization (Grove 2019) as the primary agent. Haraway's (2016) "Cthulucene" is less invested in a locatable agent, preferring to see the mess as a kind of aggregate result of a whole mess of distributed "tenticular" relations.

7. Jane Bennett calls for opening space for "a *vital materiality*" to "take shape," before adding, "or, rather, it can take shape again, for a version of this idea already found expression in childhood experiences of a world populated by animate things rather than passive objects" (2010, vii). In Brian Massumi's analysis of zoos and animal sympathy, he writes: "The horror of the visible stifling of the animals' vitality is converted into fun—in large part the fun of recognizing oneself in the other. Of course, the operation does not always succeed. The children who are its main targets are often those least able to disregard the horror and unsee the singularity of the animal" (2014, 73). Between these two, we can discern a theory of enlightenment education as the destruction of childhood theories of vitality (across species and matters), which might invite speculative pedagogies that reject developmental logics of education as the progressive training in reason. Just as importantly, this opens onto the project of understanding how coloniality and its civilizing missions mapped developmental logics (derived from arguably racist and certainly racialized science) onto global politics: the Western "adult" countries had to govern the more "immature" countries (Kant's "What Is Enlightenment?" is clearly part of this project). The task of this book is to theorize animisms, vitalisms, fetishisms, and so forth not as "immature" knowledge practices that must develop into mature, enlightenment rationality, but as forms of relational ontology grounded in and grounding decolonial projects.

8. With Julietta Singh, I develop this "ecological" understanding of educational practices in a colonialist milieu in "Dehumanist Education and the Colonial University" (2021).

9. For Wilderson (2010), both anti-Black slavery and anti-Indigenous genocide are "gratuitous violence" that founds a social order (or world), and he distinguishes this from contingent violence that arises from particular political problems *within* a social order.

10. For thinkers like Spillers (2003), Weheliye (2014), Ferguson (2004), and Schuller (2017), sex and gender become, in this crucible, inextricable from racialization.

11. The concept of Negritude comes from Aimè Cèsaire's *Journal of Home-coming/Cahier d'un retour au pays natal* (2017). F. Abiola Irele, introducing this translation, argues that the concept indicates a kind of "justified self-consciousness" associated with the existentialism of Jean-Paul Sartre. Irele goes on, "Negritude implies in this perspective an effort to rehabilitate the black race, to reverse the ideological denigration it has had to endure and thus to vindicate the cause of the race" (Cèsaire 2017, 50).

12. See Levak, *The Witchcraft Sourcebook*, 286–89.

13. I'm especially struck by *Paradise Lost*: a poem that generates full characters with whom readers can identify, including Satan!, from the relatively meager narratives in the Hebrew book of Genesis. In terms of identification, see how the poem appears in Mary Shelley's *Frankenstein*, a novel that virtually hovers here precisely because of the "women don't write books" utterance, since early readers often tried to attribute the novel to her poet-husband Percy. I take up the identifcatory matrix in the monster's encounter with the poem in *Animate Literacies* (2019b).

14. Tinsley writes, of *Thiefing Sugar*, "In this project, I focus on how enslaved women and their descendants used *sex with each other* to effect a different kind of erotic autonomy, on how same-sex eroticism enters into the history of sexual labor in the Caribbean as a practice by which women take control of sexuality as a resource they share with each other" (2010, 20).

15. While Beliso-De Jesús is writing from within the practice of Santería to a certain extent, the book also works to conceal much of the esoteric practices in a gesture of what Audra Simpson (2015) might call ethnographic refusal. Beliso-De Jesús writes, "I have also remained committed to practitioners' investment in secretiveness as a constitutive element of access into ritual practice. Santería is a heavily guarded religious space that historically, for reasons of protection from persecution, has policed access to rituals through complex initiations that have served as a form of collective embodied security" (2015, 24).

Chapter Two. Feeling Subjunctive Worlds: Reading Second-Wave Feminist and Gay Liberationist Histories of Witchcraft

1. Unlike Reclaiming, whose organizing, as I explore below, seems committed to inclusion, W.I.T.C.H. was launched in part by Robin Morgan, who became one

of the most influential trans-exclusionary feminists of the 1970s. See Stryker, *Transgender History* (2017), especially 124–38.

2. I explain homogenization as a tendency of colonialist grammar in detail in the introduction. To summarize, I begin with Sylvia Wynter's argument that while the human is an evolutionarily open-ended *process* or praxis, in the post-1492 moment, coloniality intervenes precisely through homogenization: "The larger issue . . . is the incorporation of all forms of human being into a single homogenized descriptive statement that is based on the figure of the West's liberal monohumanist Man" (Wynter and McKittrick 2015, 23). Man, as the "overrepresentation of the human" (Wynter 2003, 260), proposes a single genre of the human that violently constructs itself through what Alexander Weheliye (2014) calls "racializing assemblages" that generate Man through the simultaneous production of its inhuman, nonhuman, and less-than-human constitutive outsides. The highly specific version of the self that emerges co-compositionally with colonialist modernity and its attendant humanisms is the subject through which the globalizing orders of coloniality are plotted. Jairus Grove, riffing in part on Wynter, has proposed that this homogenizing logic is precisely the source of the impending global climate collapse which sometimes gets called "the Anthropocene"—he rewrites it as "Eurocene"—but may just as easily be figured as the end of the world, or, to be precise, the end of world in the singular. He refers, in his account of the violences of the Eurocene, to "project[s] of homogenization at the expense of human animal and nonhuman animal forms of live that are aversive to the smooth transformations" of colonialist responses to climate change (2019, 7). This is also the violence Wynter foregrounds in her attention to the "dysselected" genres of the human—or what Jayna Brown (2021) calls genres of *existence*—where different praxes (always more-than-human) are violently overcoded through mutilating inclusion or are subjected to elimination.

3. Karen Barad writes: "To theorize is not to leave the material world behind and enter the domain of pure ideas where the lofty space of the mind makes objective reflection possible. *Theorizing, like experimenting, is a material practice*" (2007, 55). Concepts are material for Barad because they are apparatuses: "Open-ended practices involving specific intra-actions of humans and nonhumans, where the differential constitution of human and nonhuman designate particular phenomena that are themselves implicated in the dynamics of intra-activity, including their enfolding and reconstitution in the reconfiguring of apparatuses" (171–72). Matter and meaning are, then, entangled; meaning making practices are part of the world; worlds and meanings are co-constitutive, intra-active. Shifting concepts, then, is a praxis of worldmaking, but not one Barad believes we can refer to knowing human consciousness or agency: "Meaning is not a property of individual words or groups of words but an ongoing performance of the world in its differential dance of intelligibility and unintelligibility" (149).

4. Nor is Starhawk named on the last page of Isabelle Stengers's *Cosmopolitics II*, which states in the antepenultimate paragraph, "We need such syntax in order to 'dream the dark' and celebrate each event where heterogenesis is risked for itself and not as the result of some essential goodwill or the desire for peace" (2011, 416).

5. In an adjacent project, Hil Malatino writes, "To be transgender, on this account, is to be part of an ancient and sacred lineage of individuals who transcended both binary instantiations of gender as well as the naturalized linkage between biological sex and gender expression. This is the birth of the 'big tent' model of transgender identity, large enough to hold Jeanne d'Arc and Dennis Rodman, and it is conceived directly through an appeal to an ostensibly sacral, transhistoric, transcultural lineage of transgressors" (2022, 192). This has, as Malatino notes, everything to do with how contemporary trans worlding takes up the second-wave and gay-liberationist texts I read in this chapter.

6. Amin writes, "But how might effective genealogical analysis *actually* feel? While [Michel] Foucault uses dramatic metaphors reminiscent of the self-shattering, beyond pleasure and pain, that have been celebrated within much psychoanalytic queer theory, I would argue that the affects of genealogy are often more mundane. Genealogy often feels discomfiting or, to take up one of Foucault's favorite terms, *disturbing*. The ground seems to shift beneath our feet as the taken-for-granted bases of identification and political agency fracture and realign" (2017, 30).

7. Freeman writes, "Erotohistoriography is distinct from the desire for a fully present past, a restoration of bygone times. Erotohistoriography does not write the lost object into the present so much as encounter it already in the present, by treating the present itself as hybrid. And it uses the body as a tool to effect, figure, or perform that encounter" (2010, 95).

8. I also explore this interest with the concepts of "literacies against the state" (Snaza, 2019b) and "curriculum against the state" (Snaza 2019a).

9. My readings are informed by the work, mostly in the last twenty years, on questions of queer temporality, which has been extremely sensitive to problems of constructing what Carolyn Dinshaw calls "a different kind of past, . . . a history that is not straight" (2007, 185). See, especially, the "Queer Temporalities" special issue of *GLQ*, edited by Elizabeth Freeman (2007).

10. What's most surprising about this militaristic language to me is that *The Witch-Cult in Western Europe* is an extremely dry book, little more than a catalogue of quotations from largely Scottish (but also from elsewhere in Europe) historical records from witchcraft accusations and trials. Even its most scandalous thesis feels underemphasized. On the third page of the book, Murray writes: "The evidence proves that underlying the Christian religion was a cult practiced by many classes of the community, chiefly, however, by the more ignorant or those in the less thickly inhabited parts of the country. It can be traced back to pre-

Christian times, and it appears to be the ancient religion of Western Europe" (11). This is one of the only direct statements of the thesis in the entire book, although it is much more explicitly argued in 1931's *The God of the Witches*, which is both more rhetorically straightforward than *The Witch Cult*, and much more readable. Here, Murray links her argument to quantitative evidence: "The only explanation of the immense numbers of witches who were legally tried and put to death in western Europe is that we are dealing with a religion which was spread over the whole continent and had counted its members in every rank of society, from the highest to the lowest" (54). Murray's 1963 *The Genesis of Religion* is the most explicitly feminist version of the argument, with Murray linking the emergence of religion *as such* to "the superior mental capacity of the female animal" (1963, 27).

A 1994 article in *Folklore* by Jacqueline Simpson, entitled "Margaret Murray: Who Believed Her, and Why?," opens thus: "No British folklorist can remember Dr Margaret Murray without embarrassment and a sense of paradox. She is one of the few folklorists whose name became widely known to the public, but among scholars her reputation is deservedly low; her theory that witches were members of a huge secret society preserving a prehistoric fertility cult through the centuries is now seen to be based on deeply flawed methods and illogical arguments" (89). Simpson's article is an attempt to interpret the fact that Murray was elected to be President of the Folklore Society (the society that publishes *Folklore*) in 1953, at the age of ninety-one, despite her work being generally disputed or ignored within the society. Simpson, with no small amount of disdain pooling underneath every sentence, argues that Murray's election is best understood in terms of a highly specific intrafield debate about the status of witchcraft in the early years of the twentieth century, and the way her work captured a public interest seldom invested in folklore and the historical study of witchcraft. Within the field of folklore there had been

> a longstanding but sterile argument between the religious minded and the secularists as to what witches had been. At one extreme stood the eccentric and bigoted Catholic writer Montague Summers, maintaining that they really had worshipped Satan, and that by his help they had been able to fly, change shape, do magic and so forth. . . . In the other camp, and far more numerous at least among academics, were sceptics who said that all so-called witches were totally innocent victims of hysterical panics whipped up by the Churches for devious political or financial reasons. (Simpson 1994, 90)

Murray's earliest work—a 1917 article in *Folklore* and its elaboration into the 1921 book *The Witch-Cult in Western Europe*—"broke this deadlock" (90) offering a way of seeing witchcraft as real, but not supernatural: the covens described in antiwitchcraft discourse like the *Malleus Maleficarum* were esoteric, clandestine societies of believers in pagan religious practices that survived, in transformed ways, Christian imperialism. It is this argument that proves the most crucial for the later, explicitly feminist interpretations of "the witch" that I will soon take up, and it is this argument which has been the most roundly attacked by disciplinary historiographers.

The Witch Cult in Western Europe and her *Encyclopedia Britannica* entry on witchcraft that was published between 1929 and 1969 captured considerable public attention (and informed a great deal of the fiction written about witches during this period). See Marion Gibson's *Rediscovering Renaissance Witchcraft* (2018), especially 47–53 and 62–65. Gibson notes Murray's offering of "an image of lesbian sexuality" in *The Witch Cult* (51).

This popular, and presumably less skeptical, interpretation of witches clearly infuriates Simpson, who ends the essay with a subjunctive, conditional fantasy that Murray's influence could have been stopped had academics only attacked her theory more directly and energetically. At the time when academics were going about their business, instead of attacking Murray,

> unnoticed by academics, a tangled web of occult ideas and practices was spreading in popular culture, some of it directly or indirectly derived from Murray's works. Looking back, one can heartily wish that some prominent folklorist had tackled her errors openly in the 1930s or 1940s, instead of leaving the job to be done by historians in the 1970s and 1980s. If anyone had, it is hard to imagine that an encyclopedia and a leading university press would have continued to afford her a platform. (95–96)

While Simpson may wish the attack on Murray had come earlier, when it arrived it was sustained enough that in their 2010 preface to the new edition of *Witches, Midwives, and Nurses*, Ehrenreich and English felt compelled to write, of the 1973 version of the pamphlet:

> We made the assumption that witches may have met in "covens" or other organized groups, and we referred to Margaret Murray when we said that "some writers speculate that these may have been occasions for pagan religious worship." Murray's research has since been discredited, and today most scholars seem to agree that the beliefs of women who were executed as witches cannot be differentiated from those of the rest of the population, and most were avowedly Christian. Some pagan religions or remnants did survive in places but the connection between this and women accused of witchcraft remains unclear. (16)

11. This is a complex problem, one I take up in "Asexuality and Erotic Biopolitics" (2020b) and "Biopolitics without Bodies: Feminism and the Feeling of Life" (2020a; see bib cite p. 188).

12. See Britt Rusert's *Fugitive Science* (2017); Kyla Schuller's *The Biopolitics of Feeling* (2018); and Zakiyyah Iman Jackson's (2020) *Becoming Human*.

13. Silvia Federici's *Caliban and the Witch* (2004) makes an homologous case in explicitly biopolitical language, but with a much finer grained attention to

history, and a wider geopolitical scope (although it too only gestures toward the problem of coloniality).

14. While Ehrenreich and English don't position the shift in focus across the two chapters this way, I want to note Wynter's genealogy of colonialist humanism (1984; 2003) lets us say that the early modern European witch hunts were part of Man1's emergence, while the institutionalization of the American Medical Association (AMA) is intra-active with Man2.

15. Most importantly for the Women's Health Movement, I'm thinking about *Our Bodies, Ourselves*, written by the Boston Women's Health Book Collective and first published in 1970. The book continues to be published in updated editions. For an overview of biopolitics of the Women's Health Movement, see Michelle Murphy (2012), *Seizing the Means of Reproduction*.

16. This question animates recent attention in feminist, queer, abolitionist, and decolonial scholarship on eugenics, and on J. Marion Sims, whose pathbreaking work in gynecology was entirely entangled with highly racialized atrocities (performing surgeries on enslaved women without anesthesia, often with other doctors observing). See Jayna Brown, *Black Utopias* (2021); Zakiyyah Iman Jackson, *Becoming Human* (2020); Kyla Schuller, *The Biopolitics of Feeling* (2017); Kimberly TallBear, *Native American DNA* (2013); and Alys Eve Weinbaum, *The Afterlife of Reproductive Slavery* (2019).

17. This is precisely what's at stake in recent work on care like Leah Lakshmi Piepzna-Samarasinha's *Care Work: Dreaming Disability Justice* (2018) and Hil Malatino's *Trans Care* (2020).

18. We can see the vanishing Native trope in Evans's *Witchcraft and the Gay Counterculture* (1978). He acknowledges that "American civilization began in genocide" (118), and refers to Cotton Mather's sermons to argue that "Christian missionaries denounced the North American Indian approach to religion as witchcraft" (110). Yet Evans doesn't engage Indigenous thought as a problem that really bears on the present. Under the heading of accounting for the "costs" of the industrial system, he asks "What of the annihilation of the old cultures of Europe and the cultures of American Indians?," a formulation that risks flattening European folk religion with Indigenous practices, and grammatically relegates Indigenous thought to "annihilation." While the paragraph goes on to link this question, in a way we might call intersectional, with the struggle to abolish the ongoing anti-Black institutions that populate what Christina Sharpe (2016) calls the wake of slavery, the plight of Third World decolonial struggles, ecological activism, queer desire, and pacifism, Evans's rhetoric sees those present struggles as in need of a recuperative genealogy: "If we are to rise up from the dead and regain our rightful place in nature, we will have to do more than put our faith in the state, the party, or technology—all of which are mere props of industrialism. We will have to tap the saving energies that now lie buried in ourselves and nature. And that means we will have to summon forth powers that

have not been known since the days of the shamans" (135, emphasis mine). But what if some of those powers have been known, are known, and will be known? And what if Evans might have known this had he read something like George Manuel and Michael Posluns's *The Fourth World* (1974) or Vine Deloria Jr.'s *Custer Died for Your Sins* (1969) or *Behind the Trail of Broken Tears* (1974)? Evans's argument builds toward a politics that could be decolonial in alliance with *present* Indigenous groups, but instead his colonial grammar relegates Indigenous knowledge to a "buried" past.

19. Michelle Murphy defines protocol feminism as "a form of feminism concerned with the recrafting and distribution of technological practices by which the care and study of sexed living-being could be conducted. . . . Unlike medical protocols, offered as rational and apolitical technical achievements, feminists saturated protocols with politics" (2012, 28–29).

20. On scalability, see Anna Tsing, *The Mushroom at the End of the World* (2015, 37–43).

21. See Snaza and Singh, "Dehumanist Education and the Colonial University," the editors' introduction to "Educational Undergrowth," *Social Text* (2021).

22. There are reverberations of ideas like Evans's in gay theory from Guy Hocquenghem's *Homosexual Desire* ([1972] 1993) to Lee Edelman's *No Future* (2004).

23. I want to underscore that this move is where Evans most clearly modulates subjunctive potentiality into indicative fact. At the very end of "The Traffic in Women," Gayle Rubin writes, "There is even some data suggesting that marriage systems may be implicated in the evolution of social strata and perhaps the development of early states" (2012, 65). She notes that the "data are too sketchy" to make academic claims beyond the merely subjunctive ("may be"), and this speculative account of the emergent state's relationship to marriage throws into relief how Evans's claim that social formations were originally matriarchal or matrilineal and nonhierarchical, as well as based largely on polytheistic or goddess religions, tends toward the indicative. In Evans's account, as late as the Stone Age, women and female deities had a much more exalted status than they would come to have in later social formations. Paraphrasing Leonard Wooley, Evans writes: "The political and economic life of the human race was completely upset by these male invaders [imperialist warriors using bronze weapons]. In place of early tribal communalism, a new institution came into being: the state" (42). Generously, I read Evans as here offering a theory of the state as male supremacist institution that will, to play with Pierre Clastres's phrase, always operate against society (and its erotics, knowledges, and relations). This is a necessarily speculative matter, and one that anthropology ceaselessly confronts even as "empirical" evidence for the historical shift from matriarchal to patriarchal societies remains elusive. In his provocative analysis and reconfiguration of Clastres's argument, José Gil has sought "to show how a slight displacement in the structure of political power can bring about an

upheaval in social relations, in particular how the monopolizing by politics of the principle of the legitimate exercise of violence leads to a different regime of economic exchanges, and in consequence, to the possibility for the accumulation of goods for some to the detriment of others" (1998, 265). That is, Gil's proposition differs from Evans's in asserting the priority of *political* changes rather than economic ones in the emergence of state apparatuses. More important than this reversal, though, is a claim that rhymes with Evans's history: that the state arises only through the dismantling of political relations that, without needing to consciously thematize themselves worked to ward off not "the state" as such, but the modes of accumulation that are its material condition of possibility. Gil writes, "The mechanisms that impede the accumulation of wealth in societies without the State are of a political order. It is their destruction that allows the unleashing of the process of economic accumulation" (265). These "mechanisms" are magical rites—Gil's focus is on specifics ritual places that allow for bodily metamorphosis caught up in specific rites ensuring the circulation within the social body of "potencies"—that, when disrupted, create "a fundamental lack" that is then filled by the state, which comes to "occupy a place so important in the society that it soon appears indispensable" (264).

24. And, to me, the more plausible assumption that they might have been dismantled much earlier (at or in the emergence of [patriarchal] social formations organized around *war* more than by any social system that could be described as "industrial"). Jairus Grove's *Savage Ecology* sees war as the basic organization of colonial geopolitics for the last fifty years, drawing out the ways that what some call "the Anthropocene" is really a function of specifically European ways or organizing war as a planetary phenomenon. His argument is quite persuasive, but I think what Evans and (as we shall see) Starhawk offer puts the organization of social forms around warfare at the hinge between the Stone and Bronze Ages, in effect offering an even longer time frame for these politics. More specifically, Evans and Starhawk are interested in also creating a genealogy of the colonialist war geopolitics that sees it as inseparable from the emergence of patriarchal or male supremacist societies.

25. On "conditions of arrival," see Sara Ahmed, *Queer Phenomenology* (2006). For an extended, quasi-autoethnographic account of the Reclaiming covens, see Jone Salomonsen's *Enchanted Feminism: The Reclaiming Witches of San Francisco* (2002).

26. Jone Salomonsen offers a helpful overview of Reclaiming theologies and histories in *Enchanted Feminism* (2002). For discussion of Starhawk's relations to Gardner, see especially 6–8.

27. Even as she looks back on that history with pride, her retrospective introduction also writes, subjunctively, that: "I also hope that in the next years, we as a movement can become ever more inclusive, diverse, and accessible, that people of all backgrounds and ancestries will find a warm welcome in our communities and

a deep understanding of the complex issues of race and class in our socieities" (10). In some ways, what's most remarkable about this is that in the tenth anniversary introduction, she already wrote, "My major critique of this work now centers on questions of inclusiveness" (19). Salomonsen discusses the demographics of the Reclaiming circle (2002, 43–45), noting it "represented a diverse body" by many measures, but also noting that "except for one African American man, all of them were white" (44).

28. See Joshua Ramey, *The Hermetic Deleuze* (2012), for an extended discussion of the role of esoteric, hermetic traditions in Deleuze's philosophy, especially his use of "immanence" and "signs."

29. See Karen Barad's *Meeting the Universe Halfway* (2007) on "discourse" as a nonhuman phenomenon.

30. Starhawk's book just predates the appearance of many of the metaphors that come to ground feminist theories of what the Combahee River Statement ([1977] 2017) calls "interlocking oppressions": Marilyn Frye's (1983) "birdcage of oppressions," Kimberlé Crenshaw's (1989) "intersections," Patricia Hill Collins's (1990) "matrix." For a detailed account of the history of these metaphors in feminist theory, and their situation in feminist field imaginaries, see Jennifer Nash's *Black Feminism Reimagined* (2019).

31. On the more expansive notion of the erotic, see Ela Przybylo's *Asexual Erotics* (2019).

32. See Jone Salomonsen's *Enchanted Feminism* (2002) for an extended participatory ethnographic account of Reclaiming's practices of ceremonial initiation.

33. My understanding of Indigenous land politics is shaped by Glen Sean Coulthard's *Red Skin, White Masks* (2014), Leanne Betasamosake's Simpson's *As We Have Always Done* (2017), and Eve Tuck and Marcia McKenzie's *Place in Research* (2015).

34. See Tuck and Yang, "Decolonization Is Not a Metaphor" (2012), and Wynter, "The Ceremony Must Be Found" (1984).

35. This is, as Chad Shomura reminds us, a necessity because "biopower at the hinge between neoliberal capitalism and settler colonialism is predicated upon distributions of agency, aliveness, and inertia" (2016, 6), distributions that powerfully shape "settler attachments" but which often happen in ways settler subjects don't consciously register. Shomura writes, "An attachment is the complex working of psychic powers, settler fantasies, disciplinary mechanisms, and vibrant matter" (2016, 13), and "Attachments throw themselves together from an expanse of materialities in a process that is elusive and ongoing" (14).

36. Thinking of storytelling and other forms of ceremony as a material praxes of the world's continual becoming—a praxis that produces humans as subjects— Sylvia Wynter's theorization of "*genres of being human*" (Wynter and McKittrick 2015, 31) insists upon "the central role that our discursive *formations*, aesthetic fields, and systems of knowledge must play in the performative enactment of

all such genres of being hybridly human" (31). By "hybridly," Wynter means "that we are *simultaneously* storytelling *and* biological beings" (29). Borrowing Frantz Fanon's concept of sociogenesis from *Black Skin, White Masks*, Wynter's work could be said to take a nature-cultural approach to the entanglement of matter and meaning (such as we find in Haraway and Barad) that insists upon the constitutive role of coloniality in the biocultural evolution of genres of humanness, where colonial assemblages articulate the fully human person—she calls this "Man"—over and against "not-quite-humans and nonhumans" (Weheliye 2014, 3). While Wynter's genealogy of colonial modernity's production and modulation of Man as the overrepresentation of the human is complex (1984; 2001; 2003), this overrepresentation functions precisely through the circulation of stories authorizing conceptualizations of the human which are linked to the affective and "biological" modulation of the always-becoming body (we should speak rather, as Erin Manning often suggests, of bodying as a verb): "The larger issue, then, is the incorporation of all forms of human being into a single homogenized descriptive statement that is based on the figure of the West's liberal monohumanist *Man*" (Wynter and McKittrick, 2015, 23). Put simply, the global overrepresentation of various genres of being human by a "monohumanist *Man*" is inextricable from an economy of storytelling. What Wynter calls the "descriptive statement" is then something of a misnomer, since discourse "about" the human intra-actively produces that human: stories about the human always lean from the indicative to the performative, and humanist modernity may be conceptualized as a social system gathering the maximum saturation of violence around such performative acts and their (de)humanizing force.

37. My book *Animate Literacies* (2019b) offers extended meditations on the more-than-human materialities of literacies.

Chapter Three. Man's Ruin: Hearing Divide and Dissolve

1. See Julietta Singh, *Unthinking Mastery* (2018).

2. This sentence is inspired by Crawley (2017; 2020); Muñoz (2009); and Walcott (2021).

3. Timothy Morton refers to the sound of Sunn O)))—"gigantic oceans of sound"—as a "hyperobject" (2013, 192). Aliza Shvarts writes, "By making the amps the band, by blending into the fog, Anderson and O'Malley blur the distinction between the body and its surround, so what is mimetically represented and amplified is metal as a *distributed sense of form and feeling*" (2014, 6).

4. Allan Gardner, in the *Quietus* review, notes that "*Gas Lit*, which follows *Basic* and 2018's *Abomination* and is D&D's debut on UK label Invada, is billed as being 'for fans of' various Black writers, ceramicists, philosophical concepts, states of being, natural phenomena and precisely one musician (Adrienne Davies, from Earth)" (2021).

5. See Nelson Varas-Díaz's (2021) *Decolonial Metal Music in Latin America*. Varas-Díaz writes, "I posit that a significant sector of heavy metal music in Latin America is engaged in a process of social transgression that is decolonial. That sector explores the historical process of oppression through colonization linked to the fifteenth-century European expansionism, the devalued categories created in that historical process (e.g., race, ethnicity, geography, local history, local knowledge), and its ongoing manifestations today" (7). Thinking through a range of bands and scenes in different contexts, Varas-Díaz theorizes "*extreme decolonial dialogues*": "these are invitations made through metal music to engage in critical reflections about oppressive practices faced by Latin American communities in light of coloniality" (9).

6. Ian Cory, interviewing the band for Invisible Oranges asks directly about this: "Considering that metal, and rock 'n' roll broadly speaking, were originally derived from African American musical traditions, is there a political value to reclaiming it from the white male image it is currently associated with?" The band responds: "Absolutely. Rock 'n' roll is slowly being reclaimed and being properly accredited in tangible ways to African Americans. How incredible is it that Death were finally officially recognized by the Smithsonian Institution as the 'first punk band' after years upon years of death, pain, intensity, and heartbreak. From an ethnomusicology perspective, blackness has and forever will continue to invent, take us higher, lead to the evolution of, liberation of, and dominate music that's worth consuming. There is a massive problem. Why does Macklemore get an award and not Le1f? Why is Elvis eternal when Willie Mae Thornton is who we should be focusing on. Why has history incessantly tried to perpetuate genocide by forcibly removing blackness from the legacy of African musical traditions. 'Imitation is the whitest form of flattery'—Textaqueen" (2019).

7. Katherine McKittrick writes, "*Black sound is a way of being black and black being is an aurally aesthetic way of life*" (2021, 65). The Blackness of Divide and Dissolve's music is also legible in their song titles, for instance on their album *Basic* (2017): "Black is Beautiful," "Black Supremacy," "Black Power," "Black Resistance," "Black and Indigenous," "Black Vengeance," "Black Love," and "Crimes of the Future."

8. While I'm not quite systematic, and will occasionally use "hearing" and "listening" seemingly interchangeably, in general I tend to use "listening" to refer to particular acts of hearing—understood, as I said, as a more-than-human phenomenon—in which some kind of "subject" focuses, in some way, on that hearing. While my sense is that listening is a kind of epiphenomenon—just the tiniest fraction of what takes place in any more-than-human hearing—it offers a particular margin for play precisely via that subject's capacity to attend to that hearing.

9. I offer a much more extended account of the situation-event distinction in *Animate Literacies* (2019b).

10. Gilles Deleuze has underscored how resisting the division of "duration" (or action) into mathematizable segments (as digital versus analog recording does) drives the philosophy of Henri Bergson. In *Bergsonism*, Deleuze writes, "Pure duration offers us a succession that is purely internal, without exteriority. Space, an exteriority without succession. . . . The two combine, and into this combination space introduces the forms of its extrinsic distinctions or homogeneous *and* discontinuous 'sections,' while duration contributes to an internal succession that is both heterogeneous *and* continuous. We are thus able to 'preserve' the instantaneous states of space and to juxtapose them in a sort of 'auxiliary space': But we also introduce extrinsic distinctions into our duration; we decompose it into external parts and align it in a sort of homogeneous time" (1988, 37-38).

11. This endurance is in no way simply "good." One crucial form it takes is the explosion of "deadmedia" in landfills trafficked around the Earth. See Jussi Parikka, *The Anthrobscene* (2014).

12. Cecchetto writes, "Listening incommunicatively, we are reminded that worlds don't somehow stop worlding during their failures to communicate, even if worlding itself is in some sense the primal act of communication" (2022, 7).

13. Julie Beth Napolin links resonsnce with "hearing through": "What is at stake in this hearing through, this resonance?" (2020, 128).

14. See their bandcamp merch page: https://divideanddissolve.bandcamp .com/merch.

15. "Hungry listening" is, for Robinson, an English translation of two Halq'eméylem words: "shxwelítemelh" (an adjective indicating settler or white) and "xwélalà:m" (listening). This names "settler forms of perception," a way of listening as a settler that is unable to listen to Indigenous sounds except through processes of violent inclusion that require Indigenous sound to play by the rules— rhythmic, timbral, performative, aesthetic—of settler music and its logics.

16. Lethabo King writes that "the shoal creates a rupture and at the same time opens up analytical possibilities for thinking about Blackness as exceeding the metaphors and analytics of water and for thinking of Indigeneity as exceeding the symbol and analytics of land" (2019, 4).

17. See Owen Coggins's (2018) anthropological work on drone metal fans.

18. https://sunn.southernlord.com/store/o-ever-breathe-a-frequency -milo-t-shirt/.

19. One way to frame this would be to say that I'm interested in pushing what Marcus Boon calls "postcolonial slowness" (2022, 202) in the music of DJ Screw toward a *decolonial slowness*, where the difference is what I've been calling, after Antoine Faivre, concordance: Boon's "cosmopolitical" account of the politics of vibration is oriented toward a postcolonial world (singular), and I'm interest in a pluriveral politics of choreosonic patterning. I might say something similar about R. Murray Schafer's concept of the "soundscape," which asks, "Is the soundscape

of the world an indeterminate composition over which we have no control, or are *we* its composers and performers, responsible for giving it form and beauty?" (1977, 5). This chapter's questions modulate Schafer's by pluralizing worlds, and refusing to locate the agency of composition in a human agency that might speak in the form of a "we" (a matter I discuss in the introduction).

20. Sarah Jane Cervenak writes, of Gayl Jones's writing, that there is "a kind of aesthetic protection of some ungiven path, erotic or otherwise, that follows the elusive and out of place subject" (2021, 107), which underscores the way that decolonial tending can be care as protection of what Wynter might call a dys-selected sociality.

Chapter Four. Ceremony: Participation and Endarkenment Study

1. I would align this chapter, then, with decolonial and abolitionist approaches to "university studies." See Snaza and Singh, "Educational Undergrowth" (2021); Tuck and Yang, *Toward What Justice?* (2018); and Boggs, Meyerhoff, Mitchell, and Schwartz-Weinstein, "Abolitionist University Studies" (2019). On the present-ness of what Marxists call "primitive accumulation" see Couthard's *Red Skin, White Masks* (2014) and Federici's *Caliban and the Witch* (2004).

2. Thinking about those who don't belong, I'm evoking the introduction Julietta Singh and I wrote to the "Educational Undergrowth" issue of *Social Text* (2021, 3), and Roderick Ferguson's rule "Assume You Don't Belong" (2017, 92). I also want to note that I hear in Ferguson's evocation of "everyday people," Sly and the Family Stone's 1969 song "Everyday People."

3. See Roderick Ferguson's *The Reorder of Things* (2012).

4. This is the precise function of what Alexander Weheliye, in his reading of Wynter, calls "racializing assemblages" that "discipline humanity into full humans, not-quite-humans, and nonhumans" (2014, 3).

5. Wynter writes, for instance, of "a process unique to the human" (1984, 23), but in other places clearly sees the human as operating according to the same "laws" of biology and cybernetic systems that other living creatures are bound by.

6. We might note here Ashley Barnwell's argument in *Critical Affect* that what is at stake is not method but "genres of criticism": ways of thinking and writing that "best capture . . . the emotional complexity of social life" (2020, 1). Barnwell writes that "we might think about our methods as part of the very social flux that we seek to address" (15), which is, mutatis mutandis, the orientation I'm proposing here toward pedagogy.

7. Katherine McKittrick notes that "premature death is an algorithmic vari-able," spurring the question: "What happens to our understanding of black humanity when our analytical frames do not emerge from a broad swathe of numbing racial violence, but, instead, from multiple and untracked enunciations of black life?" (2021, 105).

8. As Kandice Chuh writes, in *The Difference Aesthetics Makes*, "one of the challenges confronting minoritized discourses now is precisely the need to generate ways of making sense beyond the paradigms of identity and representation, an effect of which as been to hold discrete what are in fact deeply imbricated histories, formations, and conditions" (2019, 77).

9. The other three phrases were: "I am who I am / Doing what I came to do" from Audre Lorde's *Sister Outsider* (2007); "The most effective way to do it is to do it" from Toni Cade Bambara's preface to *This Bridge Called My Back* (2015); and "Love Is lifeforce" from June Jordan's "The Creative Spirit," which was published for the first time in Gumbs's anthology *Revolutionary Mothering* (2016b). In *Breathing Aesthetics*, Jean-Thomas Trembley notes that "in her *Black Feminist Breathing Chorus* as well as in a trilogy of books developing a theoretical poetics, breath figures and physicalizes a feminist lineage that includes parental relations . . . but points to a broader set of inherited commitments: theoretical, political, and aesthetic" (2022, 112).

10. Gumbs (2014) recounts the story of visiting Butler's grave (and not finding it) in a blogpost: https://www.hoodedutilitarian.com/2014/07/when-goddesses-change/.

11. I am reminded here of Ashon Crawley's question, "Can breathing, then, be a collective memory and rememory?" (2017, 75).

12. The last paragraph of Cervenak's essay is this, which I share because it's always in the background of this chapter:

> I wonder then if the classroom can be a place for an ethical engagement with the explanatory as well as an ethical refusal to give it all the room. To not be entirely filled up with what needs to be talked about and dismantled, even if that might be part of the reason why we're there in the first place. So while the classroom moves within a teleological logic and bursts out of that telos to name, discuss, criticize, teach about, learn about, and undermine the institutional moorings of racial and sexual violence, it could do some other kind of nonteleological work. That is, it can also make room for sitting with silence, the refused-to-be-explained features of black, trans, and poor grief. The sedimented pains of getting to, sitting within, and leaving class. A time when dreams of social justice amble by plain old exhaustion, the weightedness and seeming weakness of the explanatory roaming along with passions and philosophies of the new—unspoken and otherwise. (2015, 225)

13. Gumbs comments:

> The major skill that I had to develop to be present for this work was to listen. Hearing different people read them, I can tell that it is what I heard when I hear people read the scenes at performances. That's important because the words are there or the punctuation that we have access to, and you know I'm doing weird stuff with punctuation, it's not a given that it would sound like

what I heard when somebody brings their own voice to it, but I still hear the rhythm that I heard. It means that rhythm holds the possibility for that ceremony. The shifts in the rhythm signify the shifts in the ceremony. I think that's how it shows up in the language. That's the language that gets you to get into the rhythm that makes this possible. (KMT 2018)

14. For Crawley, Black pneuma is "the capacity for plural movement and displacement of inhalation and exhalation to enunciate life, life that is exorbitant, capacious, and fundamentally, social, though it is also life that is structured through and engulfed by brutal violence" (2017, 38).

15. See Mel Y. Chen, "Agitation" (2018).

16. In "Anassignment Letters," Fred Moten writes, "Grading degrades intellectual practice and what we must consider, again immediately, is what the relation is between the degradation of intellectual practice and the maintenance of the already existing order of things. What I am trying to do, as emphatically and absolutely as I can, is refuse the administrative function" (2018, 229).

17. I hear in this formulation Sam Cooke's 1957 song "You Send Me."

Conclusion. On Deictic Participation in/as Tending

1. https://www.theguardian.com/global/2019/jun/16/are-crystals-the-new-blood-diamonds-the-truth-about-muky-business-of-healing-stones.

2. My thinking about hospitality as a modality of queer and decolonial tending is shaped by Jen Gilbert's *Sexuality in School* (2014) and Julietta Singh's "Future Hospitalities" (2017), both of which are, in different ways, queer riffs on Derrida and Doufourmantelle's *Of Hospitality* (2000). Gilbert is specifically interested in education, and school in particular, ultimately arguing that "if education is a relation of hospitality, then we will affect and be affected by each other" (2014, 93). Key here is a kind of openness to strangeness and estrangement: "When sexuality arrives as a foreigner, our challenge is to imagine how we could open the doors of education to this strangeness" (85). Julietta Singh (2017) imagines "future hospitalities" that "not only include those who are immediately engaged in the unfolding act of hospitality (guests and hosts) but also bring to the table a host of others—human, animal, vegetable, mineral—that are linked to the hospitable exchange" (212). She concludes that, "these future hospitalities are not only modes of expressing infinite openness toward those with whom we are directly entangled but also ways of being accountable to those absent beings whose lives, labors, and agencies have always made up the conditions of hospitality itself" (212).

3. It is, however, Donovan Schaefer's. In *Wild Experiment*, Schaefer theorizes "cogency theory":

To understand science, reason, secularism, and our everyday ways of think-ing about the world, we need to see them not as cloistered speculation but as rubbing elbows with the other passions of our embodied lives. Science as a felt process that registers the way things are in the world produces good knowl-edge, but it's also susceptible to contamination. It messes together with the other emotions that give form to our social, embodied lives. A racist society will **tend** to produce racist science not just because of bad data but because the coordinates of interpretation of that data—*of what feels true*—are dis-figured. Science also has a powerful engine of self-correction, though: our felt desire to *get things right*. The struggle—the agonism—between these **tendencies** is what an affective account of knowledge-making sets out to diagram. (2022, 8–9, bold emphasis added)

To the specific matter of something like vaccination, Schaefer suggests that "to understand why someone might be hostile to science, we need to locate them in a history of feeling. We need to know why their trust in science might be con-taminated. Then we need to extend bridges and rebuild that trust. This means rearranging the landscape of cogency" (233).

4. Amy Hollywood notes, thinking about this conundrum, "I can't begin to argue for the value of my own commitments without at least attempting to hear and understand those of my interlocutor—without assuming that she might have good grounds for her view even if it contradicts my own" (2016, 145). This provisional openness, for Hollywood, runs up against a kind of limit: "One pre-sumption I generally refuse to give up . . . is the necessity of skeptical question-ing and critical reflection" (145). While this might seem like another version of precisely the insistence on a homogenizing frame of critique that I just said I'm trying to call into question, when I read that sentence in the context of Hol-lywood's larger engagement with (feminine) medieval mystical experience and its affirmation of a specific interference in selfhood, what I come away from that passage feeling is that this "questioning and critical reflection" need not take a predetermined shape, nor need it be anchored in the agency of the "critical" post-enlightenment subject or self. This is to say, I am left here wondering if there is a wilder, more-than-human, more-than-living study which we access, in differential ways, based on precisely how we happen to take shape as patterns in the ongoingness of worlds.

References

Ahmed, Sara. 2006. *Queer Phenomenology: Orientations, Objects, Others*. Durham, NC: Duke University Press.

Ahmed, Sara. 2008. "Imaginary Prohibitions: Some Preliminary Remarks on the Founding Gestures of the 'New Materialism.'" *European Journal of Women's Studies* 15, no. 1: 23–39.

Ahmed, Sara. 2017. *Living a Feminist Life*. Durham, NC: Duke University Press.

Alexander, M. Jacqui. 1997. "Erotic Autonomy as a Politics of Decolonization: An Anatomy of Feminist and State Practice in the Bahamas Tourist Economy." *Feminist Genealogies, Colonial Legacies, Democratic Futures*, edited by M. Jacqui Alexander and Chandra Talpade Mohanty, 63–100. New York: Routledge.

Alexander, M. Jacqui. 2005. *Pedagogies of Crossing: Meditations on Feminism, Sexual Politics, Memory, and the Sacred*. Durham, NC: Duke University Press.

Amin, Kadji. 2017. *Disturbing Attachments: Genet, Modern Pederasty, and Queer History*. Durham, NC: Duke University Press.

Anderson, Benedict. 1983. *Imagined Communities: Reflections on the Origins and Spread of Nationalism*. London: Verso.

Anzaldúa, Gloria E. 2015. *Light in the Dark/Luz en Lo Oscuro: Rewriting Identity, Spirituality, Reality*, edited by AnaLouise Keating. Durham, NC: Duke University Press.

Asad, Talal. 2003. *Formations of the Secular: Christianity, Islam, and Modernity*. Stanford, CA: Stanford University Press.

Attali, Jacques. 1985. *Noise: The Political Economy of Music*. Translated by Brian Massumi. Minneapolis: University of Minnesota Press.

Bambara, Toni Cade. 2015. "Foreword to the First Edition, 1981." In *This Bridge Called my Back*, edited by Cherríe Moraga and Gloria Anzaldúa, xxix–xxxii. Albany: SUNY Press.

Barad, Karen. 2007. *Meeting the Universe Halfway: Quantum Physics and the Entanglement of Matter and Meaning*. Durham, NC: Duke University Press.

Barnwell, Ashley. 2020. *Critical Affect: The Politics of Method*. Edinburgh, UK: Edinburgh University Press.

Beliso-De Jesús, Aisha. M. 2015. *Electric Santería: Racial and Sexual Assemblages of Transnational Religion*. New York: Columbia University Press.

Bennett, Jane. 2001. *The Enchantment of Modern Life: Attachments, Crossings, and Ethics*. Princeton, NJ: Princeton University Press.

Bennett, Jane. 2010. *Vibrant Matter: A Political Ecology of Things*. Durham, NC: Duke University Press.

Berlant, Lauren. 2011. *Cruel Optimism*. Durham, NC: Duke University Press.

Best, Stephen, and Sharon Marcus. 2009. "The Way We Read Now." *Representations* 108, no. 1: 1–21.

Bey, Marquis. 2021. *The Problem of the Negro Is a Problem for Gender*. Minneapolis: University of Minnesota Press.

Bey, Marquis. 2022. *Black Trans Feminism*. Durham, NC: Duke University Press.

Boggs, Abigail, Eli Meyerhoff, Nick Mitchell, and Zach Schwartz-Weinstein. 2019. "Abolitionist University Studies: An Invitation." *Abolition Journal*, August 28, 2019. https://abolitionjournal.org/abolitionist-university -studies-an-invitation/.

Boon, Marcus, 2022. *The Politics of Vibration: Music as a Cosmopolitical Practice*. Durham, NC: Duke University Press.

Boyer, Paul S., and Stephen Nissenbaum. 1977. *The Salem Witchcraft Papers: Verbatim Transcripts of the Legal Documents of the Salem Witchcraft Outbreak of 1692*. New York: Da Capo.

Bradley, Rizvana, and Denise Ferreira da Silva. 2021. "Four Theses on Aesthetics." *e-flux* (120). https://www.e-flux.com/journal/120/416146/four-theses -on-aesthetics/.

Briggs-Cloud, Marcus. 2020. "Ugh! Maskoke People and Our Pervasive Anti-Black Racism . . . Let the Language Teach Us!" In *Otherwise Worlds*, edited by Tiffany Lethabo King, Jenell Navarro, and Andrea Smith, 273–90. Durham, NC: Duke University Press.

Brown, Jayna. 2021. *Black Utopias: Speculative Life and the Music of Other Worlds*. Durham, NC: Duke University Press.

Butler, Judith. 1990. *Gender Trouble: Feminism and the Subversion of Identity*. New York: Routledge.

Butler, Judith. 1993. *Bodies That Matter: On the Discursive Limits of "Sex."* New York: Routledge.

Butler, Judith. 2004. *Precarious Life: The Powers of Mourning and Violence*. London: Verso.

Butler, Octavia. (1993) 2000. *Parable of the Sower*. New York: Grand Central Publishing.

Byrd, Jodi. 2011. *The Transit of Empire: Indigenous Critiques of Colonialism*. Minneapolis: University of Minnesota Press.

Care Collective, the. 2020. *The Care Manifesto*. London: Verso.

Carter, J. Kameron. 2020. "Other Worlds, Nowhere (Or, the Sacred Otherwise)." In *Otherwise Worlds: Against Settler Colonialism and Anti-Blackness*, edited by Tiffany Lethabo King, Jenell Navarro, and Andrea Smith, 158–209. Durham, NC: Duke University Press.

Carter, J. Kameron. 2021. "The Excremental Sacred: A Paraliturgy." In *Beyond Man: Race, Coloniality, and Philosophy of Religion*, edited by An Yountae and Eleanor Craig, 151–203. Durham, NC: Duke University Press.

Cecchetto, David. 2022. *Listening in the Afterlife of Data: Aesthetics, Pragmatics, and Incommunication*. Durham, NC: Duke University Press.

Cervenak, Sarah Jane. 2015. "On Not Teaching about Violence: Being in the Classroom *After* Ferguson." *Feminist Studies* 41, no. 1: 222–25.

Cervenak, Sarah Jane. 2021. *Black Gathering: Art, Ecology, Ungiven Life*. Durham, NC: Duke University Press.

Césaire, Aimé. 2017. *Journal of Homecoming/Cahier d'un retour au pays natal: A Bilingual Edition*. Translated by N. Gregson Davis. Durham, NC: Duke University Press.

Chakrabarty, Dipesh. 2000. *Provincializing Europe: Postcolonial Thought and Historical Difference*. Princeton, NJ: Princeton University Press.

Chakrabarty, Dipesh. 2009. "The Climate of History." *Critical Inquiry* 35, no. 2 (Winter 2009): 197–222.

Chee, Alexander. 2018. "The Querent." In *How to Write an Autobiographical Novel*, 17–40. Boston: Mariner Books.

Chen, Mel Y. 2012. *Animacies: Biopolitics, Racial Mattering, and Queer Affect*. Durham, NC: Duke University Press.

Chen, Mel Y. 2018. "Agitation." *SAQ* 117, no. 3 (July 2018): 551–66.

Chen, Mel Y. 2023. "Emergent Agitation and Differential Being." In *Crip Genealogies*, edited by Mel Y. Chen, Alison Kafer, Eunjung Kim, and Julie Avril Minich, 297–318. Durham, NC: Duke University Press.

Chuh, Kandice. 2003. *Imagine Otherwise: On Asian Americanist Critique*. Durham, NC: Duke University Press.

Chuh, Kandice. 2019. *The Difference Aesthetics Makes*. Durham, NC: Duke University Press.

Clarke, Patrick. 2021. Divide and Dissolve Interview. *Quietus*, January 13, 2021. https://thequietus.com/articles/29418-divide-and-dissolve-interview-takiaya-reed-sylvie-nehill-gas-lit.

Clastres, Pierre. 1989. *Society Against the State*. Translated by Robert Hurley, in collaboration with Abe Stein. New York: Zone.

Coggins, Owen. 2018. *Mysticism, Ritual, and Religion in Drone Metal*. New York: Bloomsbury Academic.

Combahee River Collective Statement. 2017. *How We Get Free: Black Feminism and the Combahee River Collective*, edited by Keeanga-Yamahtta Taylor, 15–27. Chicago: Haymarket.

Condé, Maryse. (1986) 1992. *I, Tituba, Black Witch of Salem* [*Moi, Tituba, sorcière . . . Noire de Salem*]. Translated by Richard Philcox. New York: Ballentine.

Condé, Maryse. (1979) 2000. *La parole des femmes: Essai sur des romancières des Antilles de la langue française*. Paris: Harmattan

Coole, Diana, and Samantha Frost, eds. 2010. *New Materialisms: Ontology, Agency, and Politics*. Durham, NC: Duke University Press.

Cory, Ian. 2018. "The Language of 'Abomination': An Interview with Divide and Dissolve." *Invisible Oranges*, January 30, 2018. https://www.invisibleoranges .com/language-of-abomination-an-interview-with-divide-and-dissolve/.

Coulthard, Glen Sean. 2014. *Red Skin, White Masks: Rejecting the Colonial Politics of Recognition*. Minneapolis: University of Minnesota Press.

Craig, Eleanor, Amy Hollywood, and Kris Trujillo. 2021. "Introduction: The Poetics of Prayer and Devotion to Literature." *Representations* 153, no. 1 (Winter 2021): 1–10.

Crawley, Ashon T. 2017. *Blackpentecostal Breath: The Aesthetics of Possibility*. New York: Fordham University Press.

Crawley, Ashon T. 2020. "Freedom | Stayed | Hallelujah." In *Otherwise Worlds: Against Settler Colonialism and Anti-Blackness*, edited by Tiffany Lethabo King, Jenell Navarro, and Andrea Smith, 27–37. Durham, NC: Duke University Press.

Cvetkovich, Ann. 2012. *Depression: A Public Feeling*. Durham, NC: Duke University Press.

Cvetkovich, Ann. 2019. "Processing Killjoy's Kastle: A Deep Lez Performance." In *Inside Killjoy's Kastle: Dikey Ghosts, Feminist Monsters, and Other Lesbian Hauntings*, edited by Allyson Mitchell and Cait McKinney, 123–136. Vancouver, CA: University of British Columbia Press.

Daggett, Cara New. 2019. *The Birth of Energy: Fossil Fuels, Thermodynamics, and the Politics of Work*. Durham, NC: Duke University Press.

da Silva, Denise Ferreira. 2007. *Toward a Global Idea of Race*. Minneapolis: University of Minnesota Press.

da Silva, Denise Ferreira. 2014. "Toward a Black Feminist Poethics: The Quest(ion) of Blackness Toward the End of the World." *Black Scholar* 44, no. 2: 81–97.

da Silva, Denise Ferreira. 2020. "Reading the Dead: A Black Feminist Poethical Reading of Global Capital." In *Otherwise Worlds: Against Settler Colonialism and Anti-Blackness*, edited by Tiffany Lethabo King, Jenell Navarro, and Andrea Smith, 38–51. Durham, NC: Duke University Press.

Davis, Angela Y. 2003. *Are Prisons Obsolete?* New York: Seven Stories Press.

Davis, Angela Y. 2016. *Freedom Is a Constant Struggle: Ferguson, Palestine, and the Foundations of a Movement*. Chicago: Haymarket.

Davis, Heather, and Zoe Todd. 2017. "On the Importance of a Date, or Decolonizing the Anthropocene." *Acme* 16, no. 4: 761–80.

Debaise, Didier. 2017. *Nature and Event*. Durham, NC: Duke University Press.

de la Cadena, Marisol. 2015. *Earth Beings: Ecologies of Practice across Andean
Worlds*. Durham, NC: Duke University Press.

de la Cadena, Marisol, and Mario Blaser, eds. 2018. *A World of Many Worlds*.
Durham, NC: Duke University Press.

Deleuze, Gilles. 1988. *Bergsonism*. Translated by Hugh Tomlinson and Barbara
Habberjam. New York: Zone.

Deleuze, Gilles, and Félix Guattari. 1983. *Anti-Oedipus*. Translated by Robert
Hurley, Mark Seem, and Helen R. Lane. Minneapolis: University of Minnesota Press.

Deleuze, Gilles, and Félix Guattari. 2002. *A Thousand Plateaus*. Translated by
Brian Massumi. Minneapolis: University of Minnesota Press.

De Line, Sebastian. 2016. "All My/Our Relations: Can Posthumanism Be
Decolonized?" Open Coop Academy Series *Between and Beyond*. https://
onlineopen.org/all-my-our-relations.

Delpit, Lisa. 1995. *Other People's Children: Cultural Conflict in the Classroom*.
New York: W. W. Norton.

Derrida, Jacques, and Anne Dufourmantelle. 2000. *Of Hospitality*. Translated by
Rachel Bowlby. Stanford, CA: Stanford University Press.

Dewey, John. 1916. *Democracy and Education*. New York: Basic Books.

Dillard, Cynthia B. 2006. *On Spiritual Strivings: Transforming an African
American Woman's Academic Life*. Albany, NY: SUNY Press.

Dimock, Wai Chee. 2009. "Subjunctive Time: Henry James's Possible Wars."
Narrative 17, no. 3: 242–54.

Dinshaw, Carolyn, Lee Edelman, Roderick Ferguson, Carla Freccero, Elizabeth
Freeman, Jack Halberstam, Annamarie Jagose, Christopher Nealon, and
Nguyen Tan Hoang. 2007. "Theorizing Queer Temporalities: A Roundtable
Discussion." *GLQ: A Journal of Lesbian and Gay Studies* 13, nos. 2–3: 177–95.

Divide and Dissolve. 2017. *Basic*. DERO Arcade Records.

Divide and Dissolve. 2018. *Abomination*. DERO Arcade Records.

Divide and Dissolve. 2021. *Gas Lit*. INVADA Records.

Edelman, Lee. 2004. *No Future: Queer Theory and the Death Drive*. Durham,
NC: Duke University Press.

Ehrenreich, Barbara, and Deirdre English. (1973) 2010. *Witches, Midwives, and
Nurses: A History of Women Healers*. 2nd ed. New York: Feminist Press.

Escobar, Arturo. 2018. *Designs for the Pluriverse: Radical Interdependence,
Autonomy, and the Making of Worlds*. Durham, NC: Duke University
Press.

Escobar, Arturo. 2020. *Pluriversal Politics: The Real and the Possible*. Durham,
NC: Duke University Press.

Evans, Aden. 2005. *Sound Ideas: Music, Machines, and Experience*. Minneapolis: University of Minnesota Press.

Evans, Arthur. (1978) 2013. *Witchcraft and the Gay Counterculture: A Radical View of Western Civilization and Some of the People It Has Tried to Destroy*. Seattle and San Francisco: Contagion.

Faivre, Antoine. 1994. *Access to Western Esotericism*. New York: SUNY Press.

Fanon, Frantz. 1963. *The Wretched of the Earth*. Translated by Constance Farrington. New York: Grove.

Fanon, Frantz. 1967. *Black Skin, White Masks*. Translated by Charles Lam Markmann. New York: Grove.

Federici, Silvia. 2004. *Caliban and the Witch: Women, the Body, and Primitive Accumulation*. New York: Autonomedia.

Federici, Silvia. 2018. *Witches, Witch-Hunting, and Women*. New York: PM Press.

Federici, Silvia. 2019. *Re-Enchanting the World: Feminism and the Politics of the Commons*. Binghampton, New York: PM Books.

Ferguson, Roderick. 2004. *Aberrations in Black: Toward a Queer of Color Critique*. Minneapolis: University of Minnesota Press.

Ferguson, Roderick. 2012. *The Reorder of Things: The University and Its Pedagogies of Minority Difference*. Minneapolis: University of Minnesota Press.

Ferguson, Roderick. 2017. *We Demand: The University and Student Protests*. Berkeley: University of California Press.

Foucault, Michel. 1978. *The History of Sexuality Volume 1: An Introduction*. Translated by Robert Hurley. New York: Vintage.

Foucault, Michel. 1994. *The Order of Things: An Archaeology of the Human Sciences*. Translated by Alan Sheridan. New York: Vintage.

Foucault, Michel. 1984. "What Is Enlightenment?" Translated by Catherine Porter. In *The Foucault Reader*, edited by Paul Rabinow, 34–50). New York: Panthenon.

Freeman, Elizabeth, ed. 2007. "Queer Temporalities." Special issue, *GLQ* 13 (2–3).

Freeman, Elizabeth. 2010. *Time Binds: Queer Temporalities, Queer Histories*. Durham, NC: Duke University Press.

Freeman, Elizabeth. 2019. *Beside You in Time: Sense Methods and Queer Sociabilities in the American 19th Century*. Durham, NC: Duke University Press.

Frost, Samantha. 2016. *Biocultural Creatures: Toward a New Theory of the Human*. Durham, NC: Duke University Press.

Gardner, Allan. 2021. "Gas Lit Review." *Quietus*, January 25, 2021. https://thequietus.com/articles/29468-divide-and-dissolve-gas-lit-review.

Gaskill, Malcolm. 2010. *Witchcraft: A Very Short Introduction*. New York: Routledge.

Gibson, Marion. 2018. *Rediscovering Renaissance Witchcraft*. New York: Routledge.

Gil, José. 1998. *Metamorphoses of the Body*. Translated by Stephen Muecke. Minneapolis: University of Minnesota Press.

Gilbert, Jen. 2014. *Sexuality in School: The Limits of Education*. Minneapolis: University of Minnesota Press.

Glover, Kaiama. 2012. "Confronting the Communal: Maryse Condé's Challenge to New World Orders in *Moi, Tituba. . . .*" *French Forum* 37, no. 3: 181–99.

Glover, Kaiama. 2021. *A Regarded Self: Caribbean Womanhood and the Ethics of Disorderly Being*. Durham, NC: Duke University Press.

Gordon, Avery F. 1997. *Ghostly Matters: Haunting and the Sociological Imagination*. Minneapolis: University of Minnesota Press.

Gore, Ariel. 2017. *We Were Witches*. New York: Feminist Press.

Gore, Ariel. 2019. *Hexing the Patriarchy: 26 Potions, Spells, and Magical Elixirs to Embolden the Resistance*. New York: Seal.

Grande, Sandy. 2018. "Refusing the University." In *Toward What Justice? Describing Diverse Dreams of Justice in Education*, edited by Eve Tuck and K. Wayne Yang, 47–65. New York: Routledge.

Grove, Jairus Victor. 2019. *Savage Ecology: War and Geopolitics at the End of the World*. Durham, NC: Duke University Press.

Gumbs, Alexis Pauline. 2016a. *Spill: Scenes of Black Feminist Fugitivity*. Durham, NC: Duke University Press.

Gumbs, Alexis Pauline, ed. 2016b. *Revolutionary Mothering: Love on the Front-lines*. New York: PM Press.

Gumbs, Alexis Pauline. 2018. *M. Archive: After the End of the World*. Durham, NC: Duke University Press.

Gumbs, Alexis Pauline. 2020. *Dub: Finding Ceremony*. Durham, NC: Duke University Press.

Haraway, Donna. 1989. *Primate Visions: Gender, Race, and Nature in the World of Modern Science*. New York: Routledge.

Haraway, Donna. 1991. *Simians, Cyborgs, and Women: The Reinvention of Nature*. New York: Routledge.

Haraway, Donna. 2008. *When Species Meet*. Minneapolis: University of Minnesota Press.

Haraway, Donna. 2016. *Staying with the Trouble: Making Kin in the Chthulucene*. Durham, NC: Duke University Press.

Harding, Sandra. 2008. *Sciences from Below: Feminisms, Postcolonialities, and Modernities*. Durham, NC: Duke University Press.

Harney, Stefano, and Fred Moten. 2013. *The Undercommons: Fugitive Planning and Black Study*. Brooklyn, NY: Minor Compositions.

Hartman, Saidiya V. 1997. *Scenes of Subjection: Terror, Slavery, and Self-Making in Nineteenth-Century America*. Oxford: Oxford University Press.

Hartman, Saidiya. 2008. "Venus in Two Acts." *Small Axe 26* 12, no. 2: 1–14.

Hartman, Saidiya. 2019. *Wayward Lives, Beautiful Experiments: Intimate Histories of Social Upheaval*. New York: W. W. Norton.

Hocquenghem, Guy. [1972] 1993. *Homosexual Desire*. Translated by Daniella Dangoor. Durham, NC: Duke University Press.

Hollywood, Amy. 2016. *Acute Melancholia, and Other Essays: Mysticism, History, and the Study of Religion*. New York: Columbia University Press.

Ingold, Tim. 2011. *Being Alive: Essays on Movement, Knowledge, and Description*. New York: Routledge.

Jackson, Zakiyyah Iman. 2020. *Becoming Human: Matter and Meaning in an Antiblack World*. New York: New York University Press.

Jones, LeRoi [Amiri Baraka]. 1963. *Blues People: The Negro Experience in White America and the Music That Developed from It*. New York: William Morrow.

Jordan, June. 2016. "The Creative Spirit and Children's Literature." In *Revolutionary Mothering: Love on the Front Lines*, edited by Alexis Pauline Gumbs, China Martens, and Mai'a Williams, 11–18. New York: PM Press.

Kant, Immanuel. 1970. "An Answer to the Question: 'What Is Enlightenment?'" Translated by H. B. Nisbet. In *Kant's Political Writings*, edited by Hans Reiss, 54–60. Cambridge: Cambridge University Press.

King, Tiffany Lethabo. 2019. *The Black Shoals: Offshore Formations of Black and Native Studies*. Durham, NC: Duke University Press.

King, Tiffany Lethabo. 2020. "Dub: Finding Ceremony Book Review." *Antipode Online*, September 14, 2020. https://antipodeonline.org/2020/09/14/dub-finding-ceremony/.

King, Tiffany Lethabo, Jenell Navarro, and Andrea Smith, eds. 2020. *Otherwise Worlds: Against Settler Colonialism and Anti-Blackness*. Durham, NC: Duke University Press.

Kirby, Vicky. 2011. *Quantum Anthropologies: Life at Large*. Durham, NC: Duke University Press.

KMT, Joy. 2018. "We Stay in Love with Our Freedom: A Conversation with Alexis Pauline Gumbs." *LA Review of Books*, February 4, 2018. https://lareviewofbooks.org/article/we-stay-in-love-with-our-freedom-a-conversation-with-alexis-pauline-gumbs/.

Latour, Bruno. 1993. *We Have Never Been Modern*. Translated by Catherine Porter. Cambridge, MA: Harvard University Press.

Latour, Bruno. 2004. *Politics of Nature*. Translated by Catherine Porter. Cambridge, MA: Harvard University Press.

Levack, Brian, ed. 2015. *The Witchcraft Sourcebook*. New York: Routledge.

Lewis, A. J., n.d. Unpublished manuscript.

Little Bear, Leroy. 2001. "Native and Western Science: Possibilities for a Dynamic Collaboration." Simon Ortiz and Labriola Lecture on Indigenous Land, Culture, and Community, Arizona State University. YouTube: https://www.youtube.com/watch?v=ycQtQZ9y3lc.

Lorde, Audre. (1984) 2007. *Sister Outsider: Essays and Speeches*. Berkeley, CA: Crossing Press.

Lott, Eric. 1995. *Love and Theft*. Oxford: Oxford University Press.

Luciano, Dana, and Mel Y. Chen. 2015. "Has the Queer Ever Been Human?" *GLQ* 21, nos. 2–3 (June 2015): 183–207.

MacCormack, Patricia. 2020. *The Ahuman Manifesto: Activism for the End of the Anthropocene*. New York: Bloomsbury Academic.

Malatino, Hil. 2020. *Trans Care*. Minneapolis: University of Minnesota Press.

Malatino, Hil. 2022. *Side Affects: On Being Trans and Feeling Bad*. Minneapolis: University of Minnesota Press.

Manning, Erin. 2006. *Politics of Touch: Sense, Movement, Sovereignty*. Minneapolis: University of Minnesota Press.

Manning, Erin. 2013. *Always More than One: Individuation's Dance*. Durham, NC: Duke University Press.

Manning, Erin. 2016. *The Minor Gesture*. Durham, NC: Duke University Press.

Manning, Erin. 2020. *For a Pragmatics of the Useless*. Durham, NC: Duke University Press.

Marshall, Paule. (1970) 2005. "Reena." In *The Black Woman*, edited by Toni Cade Bambara, 19–40. New York: Washington Square Press.

Marx, Karl. 1990. *Capital Volume 1*. Translated by Ernest Mandel. New York: Penguin Classics.

Massumi, Brian. 2014. *What Animals Teach Us about Politics*. Durham, NC: Duke University Press.

Massumi, Brian. 2019. *99 Theses on the Revaluation of Value*. Minneapolis: University of Minnesota Press.

Massumi, Brian, and Erin Manning. 2015. "Immediation." In *Politics of Affect*, by Brian Massumi, 146–76. Malden, MA: Polity.

McKinney, Cait. 2020. *Information Activism: A Queer History of Lesbian Media Technologies*. Durham, NC: Duke University Press.

McKittrick, Katherine. 2021. *Dear Science, and Other Stories*. Durham, NC: Duke University Press.

Mitchell, Allyson, and Dierdre Logue. 2019. *Inside KillJoy's Kastle: Dykey Ghosts, Feminist Monsters, and Other Lesbian Hauntings*. Chicago: University of Chicago Press.

Moi, Toril. 2017. "'Nothing Is Hidden': From Confusion to Clarity; or, Wittgenstein on Critique." In *Critique and Postcritique*, edited by Elizabeth S. Anker and Rita Felski, 31–49. Durham, NC: Duke University Press.

Moore, Henrietta, and Todd Sanders, eds. 2001. *Magical Interpretations, Material Realities: Modernity, Witchcraft, and the Occult in Postcolonial Africa*. New York: Routledge.

Moore, Jason, ed. 2016. *Anthropocene or Capitalocene? Nature, History, and the Crisis of Capitalism*. Oakland, CA: PM Press.

Morton, Timothy. 2013. *Hyperobjects: Philosophy and Ecology after the End of the World*. Minneapolis: University of Minnesota Press.

Moten, Fred. 2003. *In the Break: The Aesthetics of the Black Radical Tradition*. Minneapolis: University of Minnesota Press.

Moten, Fred. 2017. *Black and Blur*. Durham, NC: Duke University Press.

Moten, Fred. 2018. *Stolen Life*. Durham, NC: Duke University Press.

Muñoz, José Esteban. 2010. *Cruising Utopia*. New York: New York University Press.

Muñoz, José Esteban. 2020. *The Sense of Brown*. Edited and with an introduction by Joshua Chambers-Letson and Tavia Nyong'o. Durham, NC: Duke University Press.

Murphy, Michelle. 2012. *Seizing the Means of Reproduction: Entanglements of Feminism, Health, and Technoscience*. Durham, NC: Duke University Press.

Murphy, Michelle. 2017. *The Economization of Life*. Durham, NC: Duke University Press.

Murray, Margaret. [1921] 2019. *The Witch Cult in Western Europe*. London: Aziloth Books.

Murray, Margaret. 1931. *The God of the Witches*. London: Oxford University Press.

Murray, Margaret. 1963. *The Genesis of Religion*. New York: Philosophical Library.

Napolin, Julie Beth. 2020. *The Fact of Resonance: Modernist Acoustics and Narrative Form*. New York: Fordham University Press.

Nash, Jennifer Christine. 2019. *Black Feminism Reimagined: After Intersectionality*. Durham, NC: Duke University Press.

Nelson, Melissa. 2017. "Getting Dirty: The Eco-Eroticism of Women in Indigenous Oral Literatures." In *Critical Sovereign*, edited by Joanne Barker, 229–60. Durham, NC: Duke University Press.

Noble, Vicki. [1983] 1994. *Motherpeace: A Way to the Goddess through Myth, Art, and Tarot*. New York: HarperOne.

Nyong'o, Tavia. 2019. *Afro-Fabulations: The Queer Drama of Black Life*. New York: NYU Press.

Palmié, Stephan. 2002. *Wizards and Scientists: Explorations in Afro-Cuban Modernity and Tradition*. Durham, NC: Duke University Press.

paperson, la. 2017. *A Third University Is Possible*. Minneapolis: University of Minnesota Press.

Parés, Luis Nicolau, and Roger Sansi, eds. 2011. *Sorcery in the Black Atlantic*. Chicago: University of Chicago Press.

Parrika, Jussi. 2014. *The Anthrobscene*. Minneapolis: University of Minnesota Press.

Perry, Imani. 2018. *Vexy Thing: On Gender and Liberation*. Durham, NC: Duke University Press.

Piepzna-Samarasinha, Leah Lakshmi. 2018. *Care Work: Dreaming Disability Justice*. Vancouver: Arsenal Pulp.

Pitts-Taylor, Victoria. 2016. *The Brain's Body: Neuroscience and Corporeal Politics*. Durham, NC: Duke University Press.

Povinelli, Elizabeth. 2011. *Economies of Abandonment: Social Belonging and Endurance in Late Liberalism*. Durham, NC: Duke University Press.

Przybylo, Ela. 2019. *Asexual Erotics: Intimate Readings of Compulsory Sexuality*. Columbus: Ohio State University Press.

Puig de la Bellacasa, María. 2017. *Matters of Care: Speculative Ethics in More Than Human Worlds*. Minneapolis: University of Minnesota Press.

Quashie, Kevin. 2021. *Black Aliveness, or a Poetics of Being*. Durham, NC: Duke University Press.

Ramey, Joshua. 2012. *The Hermetic Deleuze: Philosophy and Spiritual Ordeal*. Durham, NC: Duke University Press.

Reis, João José. 2011. "Candomblé and Slave Resistance in Nineteenth-Century Bahia." In *Sorcery in the Black Atlantic*, edited by Luis Nicolau Parés and Roger Sansi, 55–74. Chicago: University of Chicago Press.

Rich, Adrienne. 2003. "Compulsory Heterosexuality and Lesbian Existence (1980)." *Signs: Journal of Women in Culture and Society* 15, no. 3 (Autumn): 11–48.

Rifkin, Mark. 2017. *Beyond Settler Time: Temporal Sovereignty and Indigenous Self-Determination*. Durham, NC: Duke University Press.

Rifkin, Mark. 2019. *Fictions of Land and Flesh*. Durham, NC: Duke University Press.

Rivera, Myra. 2021. "Embodied Counterpoetics: Sylvia Wynter on Religion and Race." In *Beyond Man: Race, Coloniality, and Philosophy of Religion*, edited by An Yountae and Eleanor Craig, 57–85. Durham, NC: Duke University Press.

Roberts, Tyler. 2013. *Encountering Religion: Responsibility and Criticism after Secularism*. New York: Columbia University Press.

Robinson, Dylan. 2020. *Hungry Listening*. Minneapolis: University of Minnesota Press.

Rosenberg, Jordy. 2014. "The Molecularization of Sexuality." Special issue, *Theory and Event* 17, no. 2.

Rubin, Gayle S. 2012a. "Thinking Sex: Compulsory Heterosexuality and Lesbian Existence (1980)." In *Deviations: A Gayle Rubin Reader*, 137–81. Durham, NC: Duke University Press.

Rubin, Gayle S. [1975] 2012b. "The Traffic in Women." In *Deviations: A Gayle Rubin Reader*, 33–65. Durham, NC: Duke University Press.

Rusert, Britt. 2017. *Fugitive Science: Empiricism and Freedom in Early African-American Culture*. New York: NYU Press.

Salomonsen, Jone. 2002. *Enchanted Feminism: The Reclaiming Witches of San Francisco*. New York: Routledge.

Sandoval, Chela. 2000. *Methodology of the Oppressed*. Minneapolis: University of Minnesota Press.

Savransky, Martin. 2021. *Around the Day in Eighty Worlds: Politics of the Pluriverse*. Durham, NC: Duke University Press.

Schaefer, Donovan. 2022. *Wild Experiment: Feeling Science and Secularism after Darwin*. Durham, NC: Duke University Press.

Schafer, R. Murray. 1977. *The Soundscape: Our Sonic Environment and the Tuning of the World*. Rochester, VT: Destiny Books.

Schuller, Kyla. 2017. *The Biopolitics of Feeling: Race, Sex, and Science in the Nineteenth Century*. Durham, NC: Duke University Press.

Scott, James C. (1998) 2020. *Seeing Like a State: How Certain Schemes to Improve the Human Condition Have Failed*. New Haven, CT: Yale University Press.

Scott, Joan. 1992. "Experience." In *Feminists Theorize the Political*, edited by Judith Butler and Joan W. Scott, 22–40. New York: Routledge.

Sedgwick, Eve Kosofsky. 2003. *Touching Feeling: Affect, Pedagogy, Performativity*. Durham, NC: Duke University Press.

Serres, Michel. 2007. *The Parasite*. Translated by Lawrence R. Schehr. Minneapolis: University of Minnesota Press.

Sharpe, Christina. 2016. *In the Wake: On Blackness and Being*. Durham, NC: Duke University Press.

Shaviro, Steven. 2009. *Without Criteria: Kant, Whitehead, Deleuze, and Aesthetics*. Cambridge, MA: MIT Press.

Sheldon, Rebekah. 2016. "Dark Correlationism: Mysticism, Magic, and the New Realisms." *Symploke* 24, nos. 1–2: 137–53.

Sheldon, Rebekah. 2019. "Accelerationism's Queer Occulture: 'Or, Thinking According to the Alien Ovum of Nature.'" *Angelaki* 14, no. 1: 118–29.

Shomura, Chad. 2016. "Decolonizing Home: Settler Attachments and the Matter of Hawai'i." The Study of Women, Gender, and Sexuality Summer Fellows Workshop. Gilman Hall. Johns Hopkins University. Baltimore, MD. February 25, 2016.

Shvarts, Aliza. 2014. "Troubled Air: The Drone and Doom of Reproduction in Sunn O)))'s Metal Maieutic." *Women and Performance* 24, nos. 2–3: 203–19.

Siegel, James. 2006. *Naming the Witch*. Stanford, CA: Stanford University Press.

Simpson, Audra. 2014. *Mohawk Interruptus: Political Life across the Borders of Settler States*. Durham, NC: Duke University Press.

Simpson, Leanne Betasamosake. 2017. *As We Have Always Done: Indigenous Freedom Through Radical Resistance*. Minneapolis: University of Minnesota Press.

Singh, Julietta. 2017. "Future Hospitalities." *Cultural Critique*, 95: 197–216.

Singh, Julietta. 2018. *Unthinking Mastery: Dehumanism and Decolonial Entanglements*. Durham, NC: Duke University Press.

Snaza, Nathan. 2019a. "Curriculum Against the State: Sylvia Wynter, the Human, and Futures of Curriculum Studies." *Curriculum Inquiry* 49, no. 1: 129–48.

Snaza, Nathan. 2019b. *Animate Literacies: Literature, Affect, and the Politics of Humanism*. Durham, NC: Duke University Press.

Snaza, Nathan. 2020a. "Biopolitics without Bodies: Feminism and the Feeling of Life." *Feminist Studies* 46, no. 1: 178–203.

Snaza, Nathan. 2020b. "Asexuality and Erotic Biopolitics." *Feminist Formations* 32, no. 3: 121–44.

Snaza, Nathan. 2023. "Why This? Affective Pedagogy in the Wake." In *The Affect Theory Reader 2: Worldings, Tensions, Futures*, edited by Gregory J. Seigworth and Carolyn Pedwell, 255–72. Durham, NC: Duke University Press.

Snaza, Nathan, and Julietta Singh. 2021. "Dehumanist Education and the Colonial University." Editorial introduction to *Social Text* 39, no. 1: 1–19.

Snorton, C. Riley. 2017. *Black on Both Sides: A Racial History of Trans Identity*. Minneapolis: University of Minnesota Press.

Snow, Cassandra. 2019. *Queering the Tarot*. New York: Weiser Books.

Sollée, Kristen J. 2017. *Witches, Sluts, Feminists: Conjuring the Sex Positive*. New York: ThreeL Media.

Sparkly Kat, Alice. 2021. *Post-Colonial Astrology: Reading the Planets through Capital, Power, and Labor*. Berkeley, CA: North Atlantic Books.

Spillers, Hortense. 2003. *Black, White and In Color*. Chicago: University of Chicago Press.

Starhawk. (1979) 1999. *The Spiral Dance*. Special 20th anniversary edition. New York: HarperOne.

Starhawk. 1982. *Dreaming the Dark*. Boston: Beacon.

Stengers, Isabelle. 2011. *Cosmopolitics II*. Translated by Robert Bononno. Minneapolis: University of Minnesota Press.

Stratton, Kimberly. 2007. *Naming the Witch: Magic, Ideology, and Stereotype in the Ancient World*. New York: Columbia University Press.

Stryker, Susan. 2017. *Transgender History: The Roots of Today's Revolution*. Revised edition. New York: Seal.

TallBear, Kim. 2013. *Native American DNA*. Minneapolis: University of Minnesota Press.

Tea, Michelle. 2017. *Modern Tarot: Connecting with Your Higher Self through the Wisdom of the Cards*. New York: HarperElixer.

Tinsley, Omise'eke Natasha. 2010. *Thiefing Sugar: Eroticism between Women in Caribbean Literature*. Durham, NC: Duke University Press.

Todd, Zoe. 2016. "An Indigenous Feminist's Take on the Ontological Turn: 'Ontology' is Just Another World for Colonialism." *Journal of Historical Sociology* 29, no. 1: 4–22.

Trembley, Jean-Thomas. 2022. *Breathing Aesthetics*. Durham, NC: Duke University Press.

Treppel, Jeff. 2018. "Divide and Dissolve Use Drone to Combat Oppression and Intolerance." *Bandcamp Daily*, March 2, 2018. https://daily.bandcamp.com /features/divide-and-dissolve-abomination-interview.

Tronto, Joan. 1993. *Moral Boundaries: A Political Argument for an Ethic of Care*. New York: Routledge.

Tsing, Anna Lowenhaupt. 2005. *Friction: An Ethnography of Global Connection*. Princeton, NJ: Princeton University Press.

Tsing, Anna Lowenhaupt. 2015. *The Mushroom at the End of the World: On the Possibility of Life in Capitalist Ruins*. Princeton, NJ: Princeton University Press.

Tuck, Eve, and Marcia McKenzie. 2015. *Place in Research: Theory, Methodology, and Methods*. New York: Routledge.

Tuck, Eve, and K. Wayne Yang. 2012. "Decolonization Is Not a Metaphor." *Decolonization: Indigeneity, Education and Society* 1, no. 1: 1–40.

Tuck, Eve, and K. Wayne Yang. 2018. "Introduction: Born Under the Rising Sign of Social Justice." In *Toward What Justice? Describing Diverse Dreams of Justice in Education*, edited by Eve Tuck and K. Wayne Yang, 1–17. New York: Routledge.

Varas-Díaz, Nelson. 2021. *Decolonial Metal Music in Latin America*. Bristol, UK: Intellect Books.

Walcott, Rinaldo. 2021. *The Long Emancipation: Toward Black Freedom*. Durham, NC: Duke University Press.

Wallen, Doug. 2021. "Divide and Dissolve Wield Sonic Extremes Against White Supremacy." *NME*, January 25, 2021. https://www.nme.com/features/divide-and-dissolve-gas-lit-album-2021-interview-radar-2864131.

Warren, Calvin. 2018. *Ontological Terror: Blackness, Nihilism, and Emancipation*. Durham, NC: Duke University Press.

Washuta, Elissa. 2021. *White Magic*. New York: Tin House.

Watts, Vanessa. 2013. "Indigenous Place-Thought among Humans and Non-Humans (First Woman and Sky Woman Go on a World Tour!)." *Decolonization: Indigeneity, Education and Society* 2, no. 1: 20–34.

Weheliye, Alexander G. 2005. *Phonographies: Grooves in Afro-Sonic Modernity*. Durham, NC: Duke University Press.

Weheliye, Alexander G. 2014. *Habeas Viscus: Racializing Assemblages, Biopolitics, and Black Feminist Theories of the Human*. Durham, NC: Duke University Press.

Weinbaum, Alys Eve. 2019. *The Afterlife of Reproductive Slavery: Biocapitalism and Black Feminism's Philosophy of History*. Durham, NC: Duke University Press.

Wiegman, Robyn. 2012. *Object Lessons*. Durham, NC: Duke University Press.

Wilderson, Frank B., III. 2010. *Red, White and Black: Cinema and the Structure of US Antagonisms*. Durham, NC: Duke University Press.

Willey, Angela. 2016. *Undoing Monogamy: The Politics of Science and the Possibilities of Biology*. Durham, NC: Duke University Press.

Winters, Joseph. 2021. "The Sacred Gone Astray: Eliade, Fanon, Wynter, and the Terror of Colonial Settlement." In *Beyond Man: Race, Coloniality, and Philosophy of Religion*, edited by An Yountae and Eleanor Craig, 245–68. Durham, NC: Duke University Press.

Wolfe, Patrick. 2006. "Settler Colonialism and the Elimination of the Native." *Journal of Genocide Research* 8, no. 4: 387–409.

Wynter, Sylvia. 1984. "The Ceremony Must Be Found: After Humanism." *boundary 2* nos. 12/13 (1984): 19–70.

Wynter, Sylvia. 1995. "1942: A New World View." In *Race, Discourse, and the Origin of the Americas: A New World View*, edited by Vera Lawrence Hyatt and Rex Nettleford, 5–57. Washington, DC: Smithsonian Institution Press.

Wynter, Sylvia. 2001. "Towards the Sociogenic Principle: Fanon, Identity, the Puzzle of Conscious Experience, and What It Is Like to Be 'Black.'" In *National Identities and Sociopolitical Changes in Latin America*, edited by Mercedes F. Durán-Cogan and Antonio Gómez-Mariana, 30–66. New York: Routledge, 2001.

Wynter, Sylvia. 2003. "Unsettling the Coloniality of Being/Power/Truth/Freedom: Towards the Human, After Man, Its Overrepresentation—an Argument." *CR: The New Centennial Review* 3, no. 3: 257–337.

Wynter, Sylvia. 2007. "Human Being as Noun? Or Being Human as Praxis? Towards the Autopoetic Turn/Overturn: A Manifesto." https://www.scribd.com/doc/237809437/Sylvia-Wynter-The-Autopoetic-Turn#scribd.

Wynter, Sylvia, and Katherine McKittrick. 2015. "Unparalleled Catastrophe for Our Species? Or, to Give Humanness a Different Future: A Conversation." In *Sylvia Wynter: On Being Human as Praxis*, edited by Katherine McKittrick, 9–89. Durham, NC: Duke University Press.

Yates, Francis. 2001. *The Occult Philosophy in the Elizabethan Age*. New York: Routledge.

Young, Hershini Bhana. 2006. *Haunting Capital: Memory, Text, and the Black Disasporic Body*. Hanover, NH: Dartmouth University Press.

Yusoff, Kathryn. 2018. *A Billion Black Anthropocenes or None*. Minneapolis: University of Minnesota Press.

Zolf, Syd. 2021. *No One's Witness: A Monstrous Poetics*. Durham, NC: Duke University Press.

Index